WITHDRAWN

Personal Recollections
of Wagner

A DA CAPO PRESS REPRINT SERIES

The Lyric Stage

GENERAL EDITOR: DALE HARRIS
SARAH LAWRENCE COLLEGE

Personal Recollections
of Wagner

BY

ANGELO NEUMANN

Translated from the Fourth German Edition

BY

EDITH LIVERMORE

DA CAPO PRESS • NEW YORK • 1976

Library of Congress Cataloging in Publication Data

Neumann, Angelo, 1838-1910.
  Personal recollections of Wagner.

  (The Lyric stage)
  Reprint of the 1908 ed. published by Holt, New
York.
  1. Wagner, Richard, 1813-1883.
ML410.W1N42 1976 782.1'092'4 [B]   76-16506
ISBN 0-306-70843-4

Published by Da Capo Press, Inc.
A Subsidiary of Plenum Publishing Corporation
227 West 17th Street, New York, N. Y. 10011

RICHARD WAGNER
GEBOREN LEIPZIG 22. MAI 1813
GESTORBEN VENEDIG 13. FBR. 1883

Bust by Anton zur Strassen
in the foyer of the Leipsic Stadttheater.

Personal Recollections of Wagner

BY

ANGELO NEUMANN

Translated from the Fourth German Edition
BY
EDITH LIVERMORE

NEW YORK
HENRY HOLT AND COMPANY
1908

THE QUINN & BODEN CO. PRESS
RAHWAY, N. J.

CONTENTS

PART I

ABROAD

PART II

THE RING IN LEIPSIC

PART III

BERLIN

iii

CONTENTS

Part IV

HOPES AND PLANS

Part V

THE RICHARD WAGNER THEATRE

ILLUSTRATIONS

PART I

ABROAD

PERSONAL RECOLLECTIONS
OF WAGNER

CHAPTER I

VIENNA

IT was the celebrated singing teacher of those days,
Therese Stilke-Sessi of Vienna, who gave me my first
introduction to the genius of Richard Wagner and fired
me with an early enthusiasm for his new and wonderful
style. This remarkable woman was training me for the
stage and taught me among other things the part of Wolfram von Eschenbach in " Tannhäuser." I mention this
particularly as in those years—the early forties—it was
rare indeed to find a singer with this rôle in his repertoire, and managers then found it most difficult to cast
this important part.

Being young and impressionable, I soon became an
ardent disciple of the Master, yet even I at this time, in
spite of my devotion to the cause, found it utterly impossible one night to sit through an entire performance of
" The Flying Dutchman " given at the Royal Opera in
Vienna under exceptionally favourable circumstances. I
frankly confess that I left, thoroughly bored with that
long duet, at the close of the second act. I was then a
mere boy of nineteen, however, and my judgment could
hardly have been considered quite sound.

The cast that evening was a memorable one and
worthy to be recorded: Senta, Louise Dustmann; Mary,

Caroline Bettelheim; Daland, Karl Mayerhofer; Erik,
Gustav Walter.   John Nepomuk Beck sang the Flying
Dutchman, and the conductor was Heinrich Esser.

In the year 1862, after engagements in Pressburg and
Dantzic, I myself became a member of the Royal Opera
Company in Vienna, and this very year Richard Wagner
began his career in that city. He was presenting his
" Tristan," which after forty-seven preliminary rehearsals
was finally set aside as utterly impracticable for the
stage!

At the same time, however, he was striving to interest
the Viennese in his works by giving those wonderful concerts in their great theatre. He then lived at the Hotel
Kaiserin Elizabeth, and as my rooms were in that same
quarter, it often chanced that I met him on the street
going to and from rehearsals,—generally talking to himself, and usually flourishing his great red bandanna. The
Master's hair was brown in those days, and he invariably
wore a high silk hat and a long frock coat—never by any
chance buttoned up.

His presence brought life and swing into the artist
world of Vienna, and the question of the hour was, " Do
we, or do we *not*, approve of these innovations? "   I myself—together with most of the younger musicians—was
a most enthusiastic partisan of the Master, and took a
gleeful share in his triumphs at those concerts. The
greatest of these, perhaps, was the Tausig Concert, which
took place in the huge " Redouten Saal,"—Wagner himself conducting. It opened with the Overture to " Freischütz," and before its finish the audience broke out in
uncontrollable enthusiasm. Even the Master himself
seemed satisfied with this performance and at its close
called up Richard Levy, the leader of the horns, with
whom he had worked untiringly at the rehearsals and
whom he now publicly embraced for his magnificent
playing. I can see him yet as he stood there on the plat-

form—always with that unfailing red handkerchief in his hand—mumbling, " There, there! That will do now! There! That will do!"—in vain attempt to stop the frantic cheering.

One night Wagner was present at a performance of " Lohengrin " in the old Kärnthnerthor Theatre. He sat in the director's box, and between the acts came behind the scenes with the manager, Matteo Salvi. We soloists were introduced and he said a few slight words of praise,— which we afterwards heard were polite fictions, for he wrote to a friend that he was anything but pleased with the performance! Our cast was as follows:—Lohengrin, Alois Ander; Telramund, John Nepomuk Beck; The King, Dr. Karl Schmidt; Herald, Angelo Neumann; Elsa, Louise Dustmann; Ortrud, Marie von Destinn; Conductor, Heinrich Esser.

Naturally with so many innovations it was no easy task in those early days to satisfy his requirements; and at best the work was thankless, for it was an accepted fact that music-lovers who could sit out the " Huguenots " or the " Prophet " (each fully as long as " Lohengrin ") would leave the theatre thoroughly exhausted after two acts of this new and intricate Wagner music. " What! you sat through the *whole* of ' Lohengrin '? " they would ask if I happened to join my friends late at some café after the opera; for in those days I rarely missed a Wagner performance!

In the spring of 1864 Karl Eckert (late conductor of the Vienna opera) called me to Stuttgart to play a short engagement. When I returned to my hotel after our first rehearsal of " Don Giovanni " I was greatly annoyed by a man in the next room, who seemed to be pacing up and down in the most horribly squeaky boots. It continued so incessantly and the noise was so irritating that I finally rang for the porter and asked what sort of a caged lion it was they kept next door! To my great surprise the man answered that my restless neighbour was Richard Wagner!

Later my host, a great music-lover and a friend of all artists, confided to me that Wagner was in great financial straits and had been forced to abandon the table-d'hôte (it was then customary to pay at the table), as he was utterly without funds. Marquart, our genial host, then asked me to go to Wagner and offer him the two best rooms in the house and a standing invitation to their table-d'hôte in the name of the hotel management, saying that he wanted no pay, but was only glad and proud to have so great an artist as his guest! I had to decline this delicate commission, having no personal acquaintance with the Master, but I explained the circumstances to my friend Eckert, who seemed to be the only man in Stuttgart knowing Wagner well enough to act in the matter. Eckert himself relieved Wagner's financial embarrassment, for he dared not tell the Master of Marquart's well-meant proposition. Mme. Eckert had sent to Vienna for a small deposit of seven hundred Gulden she had there in the bank. " And Wagner must wait till that comes," they said, " before he can leave for Switzerland! "

That night was my first performance of Don Giovanni. Wagner sat in the parquet and seemed quite contented with our rendering. If, as Weissheimer says in his book of recollections, " Neumann's abnormally long legs stuffed into those interminable white tights . . . appeared to amuse the Master," I shall not contradict him here! Possibly that costume may have made me look longer than usual! But my friends say this is a libel!

On my way home I stopped to see Eckert, who had not been at the theatre owing to a family bereavement; and after congratulating me on my success, of which he had already heard, he said, " Did you know that the King has called Wagner to Munich? He left to-day." So I have always felt that fate brought us together at one of the most important turning-points of his life. I was his neighbour in those days, and through my friend Eckert and his charming wife shared his anxieties and his joys.

The next day the Eckerts told me the details of the royal summons to Munich, but in all this time I never met the Master personally. This I mention here to refute the statements of Weissheimer as to the episode of our meeting in Stuttgart May, 1865.

Now comes the occasion of the first performance of the " Meistersinger " at the Royal Opera House in Vienna, undertaken by John Herbeck in spite of the opposition of his directors and his entire staff. They could not understand the zeal he showed in this cause, and court officials even went so far as to attend rehearsals to corroborate their pet theory that Wagner was " impossible." I myself belonged to the few who had fallen under the spell of the music, and my small rôle of the Night-watchman allowed me to take a critical part at the rehearsals and to see most of the performance from the front.

On that first night, as is well known, the storm of opposition and criticism was tremendous. Usually it was the Wagnerites who made themselves conspicuous at these early performances by their enthusiasm; but here it was his opponents who made a stormy scene. Toward the close of the second act, at the moment of Beckmesser's drubbing and just before the Night-watchman's second entrance, such a hullabaloo arose in the audience that I could scarcely sing my final lines. For fully ten minutes after the fall of the curtain they had it back and forth among the audience, repeating the scene on the stage between the enemies and adherents of the Meistersinger.

A strange coincidence now furnished the anti-Wagnerites with new ground for their dislike. The tenore-buffo of the Royal Opera Company, Julius Campe, who had created the rôle of Beckmesser in Vienna with great effect,

fell ill some six months later and died soon after in Reich-
enhall.   Thereupon all the cavillers solemnly declared that
he had fallen a victim of the strenuosity of that rôle—
a verdict that seems simply absurd in these enlightened
days.

In May, 1872, Richard Wagner was present at a performance of "Rienzi" in the newly opened Royal Opera
House. John Herbeck, who had succeeded Dingelstedt
as its manager, had given the utmost care to the stage
setting and the general detail, and conducted the opera
himself that night. At the fall of the curtain he eagerly
rushed to Wagner's box, expecting naturally some slight
word of praise for his efforts. Imagine his dismay at
being greeted by the Master with the following—"That
fellow you hired to sing Rienzi! Why, I wouldn't even
hire him to carry out a fiddle case!"

I shall now tell another story connected with that visit
of Wagner to Vienna. On the 12th of May the Master
conducted a concert in our new music hall, and on this
occasion the hornist, Richard Levy, had the misfortune
to make a slip on a high note—a "Gicks," as they call it
in the orchestra. If I remember rightly, it was in one of
the most difficult and intricate passages of the Scherzo in
the Symphony Eroïca. Edward Mauthner, a well-known
wit and writer of comedies, took this occasion to jeer at
his friend the soloist from his place in the front row. In
the intermission, when all those qualified (or who considered themselves qualified) as artists had assembled in
the green-room, Wagner took the occasion to reprimand
any who had seen fit to laugh at such a slip. Those who
understood the mechanism of the horn and its technical
difficulties, he said, would surely realise that the greatest
artist could come to grief, since the least drop of moisture
in the instrument was fatal. With that he embraced our
hornist warmly to console him for his misadventure.

Presently Levy, who was a wag of the first order,

stepped up to Mauthner, saying, "My dear fellow, that was not nice of you at all to laugh at my little 'Gicks.'" Mauthner tried glibly to explain, but Levy continued solemnly, "No, really it was not nice of you at all,— and most ungrateful. Truly, I wouldn't do such a thing to you. I've never yet laughed at one of your comedies in all my life!" The cheers and uproar that followed this sally may be imagined, and Wagner led all the rest in his gleeful shouts at the discomfiture of the luckless playwright.

Late in the fall of 1875 I had the good fortune still to be a member of this company when Wagner conducted his rehearsals for the new setting of "Lohengrin" and "Tannhäuser" at the Royal Opera in Vienna. I was especially interested, as I then contemplated taking the superintendence of a theatre myself.

What an inspiring director he was! How well he understood the art of spurring on his men, of getting his best work out of each one, of making every gesture, each expression tell! These rehearsals convinced me that Richard Wagner was not only the greatest dramatist of all time, but also the greatest of managers, and a marvellous character actor as well. Now at the end of these long thirty years I can still distinctly recall certain incidents of his wonderful mimetic powers. I never hear a performance of "Tannhäuser" or of "Lohengrin" without his image rising before me in certain scenes.

How wonderfully he took the part of Tannhäuser finding himself at the crossways in the forest after his release from the enchantments of Venusberg. Riveted to the spot, he stood like a graven image, with arms upraised; then gradually, at the entrance of the pilgrims, came to life with a tremendous shuddering start, and finally, overcome with emotion, sank to the ground as the chorus proceeded; to break out at the end in his great cry—"Ach, schwer drückt mich der Sünden Last!"

What stately dignity and what knightly fire he put into this rôle as Tannhäuser listens to the song of Wolfram. Then in the great final scene of the first act how he dominated, moved, and inspired his company—assigning places, prescribing gestures, and arranging expressions, till the tableau was perfect and the whole cortège, Landgrave, knights, chorus, horses, and dogs took their places with utmost artistic precision. These were moments to make an indelible impression on my mind.

His plan for the entrance of the guests has been the model for all later performances. It was his idea that the Landgrave and Elizabeth should stand with their backs to the audience, receiving their guests as the pages ushered them in. Previously to this they had taken their places upon the throne, and the pages had simply preceded the guests and announced them *en masse*. The incident of the widow bringing her two daughters was customary, to be sure; but it was Wagner who first showed us how, after the official greeting, Elizabeth should sweep forward, take the young girls by the hand, present them graciously to all her court, and lead them back to their mother before she went to take her place beside the Landgrave on the daïs.

In the Minnesingers' contest where Tannhäuser's usual proceeding had been to advance to Wolfram, and, flourishing his fist in the latter's face, to sing, " O Wolfram, der du also sangest! " Wagner forbade this crude gesture entirely. In the closing scene, as he showed Tannhäuser his position at the cry, " Weh mir, Unglücksel'gen! " his acting was a triumph of art. Then turning abruptly, he took the part of Elizabeth, and mounting the steps of the throne with an expression of lofty exaltation, he stood till the fall of the curtain, his hands clasped and eyes raised in fervid appeal—carrying us along with him and inspiring us all with an indescribable awe for the scene.

But he reached his greatest heights in Tannhäuser's

account of his pilgrimage. His first words to Wolfram,
" Hör an, Wolfram, hör an!" began with touching eagerness, but he rose to heart-rending intensity where he
describes the curse, " Hast du so böse Lust geteilt," etc.
In each one of these scenes it was a great dramatic genius
who stood before us.

In rehearsing " Lohengrin " he took each part in turn,
not only the title-rôle, but Telramund and the King as
well, showing each player his every attitude and motion.
No words can describe the deep feeling he put into the
part of Lohengrin.

The Elsa of our cast was making her début, so he
went through that whole long act with the King, showing
her each expression, each movement of the hand. But
when Wagner finally in the scene of the combat—dressed
as he was in every-day clothes—put on Lohengrin's helmet and grasped his sword and shield to plunge into the
battle with Telramund, a ripple of amusement made itself
heard among the by-standers. Yet we soon forgot this
in our wonder and amazement at his dexterity and skill
in handling his weapons. It seemed as though he had
been trained to the sword from youth, and that combat
was the breath of his nostrils. Telramund indeed was
hard pressed to fight him off. Then, at the appropriate
bar, he fell on his adversary and finished him. Kneeling
now beside the prostrate foe and lightly touching him
with the point of his sword, he sang his great triumphant
phrase like some wonderful avenging angel—" Durch
Gottes Sieg ist nun dein Leben mein."

How well he simulated Elsa's rapture as she throws
herself into Lohengrin's arms, and how he arranged for
the eager interest and acclamation of the chorus. As the
curtain fell on this great scene—orchestra, chorus, soloists and the director crowded wildly about the Master,
clamouring in their enthusiasm to shoulder him and bear
him off in triumph. But Wagner, though evidently

touched by this spontaneous ovation, waved them back, saying earnestly, "That'll do, that'll do, children; that'll do." Then we went on to the second act, where he showed us, in the great scene between Telramund and Ortrud, how the latter rises snake-like from her prostrate pose on the Minster steps as she finds she has won Telramund for her purpose. Now came the scene between Ortrud and Elsa, and I must say here that the Elsa of this cast was Mila Kupfer-Berger, one of the most beautiful creatures who ever took that rôle.

Wagner then sang the part of Elsa, as Ortrud tries to lure her to her ruin. Nothing more wonderful could be imagined than the way he acted her first deferential hearing, then gradually her feeling of having been entrapped, and finally her repulse of Ortrud, as with ecstatic eyes upraised she breaks out with the great cry—

> "Du Ärmste kannst wohl nie ermessen,
> Wie zweifellos mein Herze liebt."

No one who had not seen Wagner play the rôle could believe how marvellously it was done. Then I remember in this scene he insisted that the great closing phrase of Elsa's duet with Ortrud, " Es gibt ein Glück, das ohne Reu'," should be sung in one breath, without a pause. This unfortunately is not followed out in the present day, as few singers seem to be capable of it.

The Master laid the greatest stress on the careful and detailed arrangement of the wedding procession. In the last twenty years I've had no opportunity to see a performance of " Lohengrin " at the Royal Opera in Vienna, so cannot say whether Wagner's scenic arrangements are still carried out. He directed that the procession should move from the gallery on the left to the Minster on the right. After the pages' phrase, " Make way! " the men's chorus had twenty-seven bars of pantomime to the music, their gestures directed to the gallery above, and at the

twenty-seventh bar appeared the bride's cortège, slowly
making its way from the threshold to the great stairs that
filled the centre of the background.   The pages and ladies-
in-waiting were to spread out in broad arrangement on
the steps, and at the theme

Elsa was to arrive at the topmost step.
At this point Wagner took up her rôle.   And now the
procession went on.   With arms outstretched, the palms
turned toward the audience, with uplifted countenance
and radiant eyes—and never a glance at the steps he
was to traverse—Wagner moved serenely down in stately
progress, followed (at the interval prescribed by the flowing train and the pages who bore it) by four noble ladies
in waiting, and finally by Ortrud.   So he proceeded, advancing nearly to the footlights; then turning a wide
circle, swept on to the left toward the Minster steps.
Up to the instant when Elsa is about to mount the first
stair and Ortrud rushes to bar her way, Wagner main-
tained that wonderful look of radiant exaltation, his
whole progress a triumph of histrionic art.
Omitting many wonderful details, I must mention now
his great final scene in the second act.   When King Henry
leads Elsa and Lohengrin for the second time to the Minster steps and they are about to mount, Wagner ordered
the King to proceed alone up the stairs and to enter the
church in advance without turning again to the others.
Then the Master took Lohengrin's place, and turning to
Elsa, who stood on the step below, with radiant face
turned up to him, he drew her tenderly to his level, till
they stood together in fervent clasp—united before the
Minster door.   Then Elsa, still hanging on Lohengrin's
look, turns her head for an instant to those below as if to

testify to her people of her perfect ecstasy. At this moment resounds the "Warning" motif, and Ortrud—withdrawn from the train and standing on the left opposite the Minster—raises her arm in sinister threat. Elsa in wildest panic hides her head on Lohengrin's breast, while he, drawing her backward, still wrapped in his close embrace, slowly mounts the stairs and approaches the portal of the church with face turned sternly toward the crowd below. The curtain falls as they slowly progress backwards up the stairs.

The most remarkable effect, however, was in the third act, where Wagner played nearly the whole scene in the bridal chamber. I shall never forget the unutterable expression of grief on his face as Lohengrin perceives that Elsa is about to break her vow, and his unearthly look of tender eagerness as he draws her to the window. With a sweeping gesture of his free arm (his right arm still folds his bride in close embrace) he sings, "Atmest du nicht mit mir die süssen Düfte." His clear-cut, forceful and spiritual face grew incredibly beautiful at such a moment. And when we pressed about him afterwards, wildly shouting our enthusiasm and our praise, he quite failed to understand what had moved us. So thoroughly had he been taken up with the impersonation of his character and the exigencies of his rôle.

Many more instances I might give of his important innovations in the art of scenic effects, but I fear this book would then be merely a compendium of dramatic technicalities. If I have given my enthusiasms too free a rein on this subject, it is because of the overwhelming impression made on me by the scenes of those days—impressions that have lasted quite throughout my long life.

CHAPTER II

LEIPSIC

ON the 21st of May, 1876, I went from Vienna to Leipsic to take the place of Friedrich Haase in the Leipsic Theatre, collaborating there with Dr. August Förster, former manager of the Hofburg Theatre in Vienna.

Called from my modest place in the ranks of the Vienna Opera Company, I naturally found many difficulties in my new position as head of one of the leading stages of Germany, and had many a battle to fight at first. When the people of Leipsic heard I meant to open my career with a performance of " Lohengrin," they even went so far as to warn Förster against my youthful rashness. Our staff of singers, they said, was utterly inadequate (though they knew nothing at all about them), and as for the scenic arrangements, they were impossible with the means at our command. Besides—this new conductor. Who was he? They were firmly convinced that any opera in Leipsic would be a complete fiasco without their old favourite Gustav Schmidt.

And who *was* this young conductor whose name at that time was quite unknown, and whom I had called to Leipsic immediately upon the announcement of my own appointment? I was confident that Josef Sucher, whom I had known and heard in Vienna, could hardly fail to be well received, and would soon be famous not only in Leipsic but throughout the musical world.

Our rehearsals proceeded against almost insurmountable difficulties. An absurd and trifling personal misunderstanding between Förster and Haase (my predeces-

15

sor) made it impossible for us to have the use of either of the larger stages in Leipsic, and all our preliminary rehearsals had to be held in the small and inadequate Carola Theatre. Its stage was cramped enough for the actors alone, but when it came to the tremendous scenic effects and a mechanical apparatus such as we needed for " Lohengrin," the difficulties were almost overwhelming and our disheartening critics felt that we must surely fail.

When finally, however, we took over the new theatre and held our first general rehearsal (on July 3d, only the day before our performance) it proved we were thoroughly equipped for our struggle and could look forward to the opening night with comparative calm. Certainly all indications pointed to the fact that a struggle it was to be. Anonymous and open threats poured in to the office. Two hundred " siffleurs," they said, had been engaged to down us!

August Förster and his charming wife entered their box that night in great trepidation, and all eyes were fixed upon us, watching for the effect of the fiasco. Leipsic at that time was celebrated for its coterie of bigoted conservatives, and many a first night had been the scene of a tremendous uproar. So those who enjoyed a spicy scandal were looking forward to this evening as a special treat in that line. A feverish hush of expectancy settled over the audience, from the orchestra chairs to the topmost gallery, and a wave of rebellion, that we theatrical people are always keen to scent, assured us that things were about to happen. We began to smell blood. The very names of the victims were murmured here and there. The artists—even their hitherto infallible orchestra— were bound to come to grief under this new régime. But most of the obloquy naturally was directed toward the young and untried manager who had dared to foist his new ideas—*and* his new conductor—upon the staid public of Leipsic, and who was to be incontinently slaughtered that night and held up to the world in derision. With breathless attention, then, they watched the young conductor as he entered and took his chair. He looked up at us in the manager's box, smiling genially over his great gold-rimmed glasses, then gave the signal for " Attention!" At this, a storm of muttering broke out in the house and a wave of protest, before which Sucher was clever enough to give way; and not till it had died down did he attack his opening bars.

In that critical hush, then, began the Overture to " Lohengrin." But when the last lingering note had sounded —arose such a clamour, such a tumult of applause from every nook and corner of the house, that our opponents felt they had lost the day and their sport was over for that evening. Now the curtain rose, and the first wonderful tableau made such an impression that a ripple of delighted enthusiasm ran through the audience.

I shall say no more of this first performance; but the next day the verdict was that Leipsic had never before heard " Lohengrin " as it really should be given. Both Josef Sucher and I felt, however, that the triumph accorded us was due solely to the influence of the Master in those Vienna days, for we had merely carried out as far as in us lay the lessons we had learned under his wonderful tuition. Our success, though, was all the more remarkable from the fact that the Lohengrin of that evening was not really adequate to his rôle.

The lucky star that rose that night stayed with us during our entire engagement, and each time the critics counted on our dismal failure it was they themselves who were discomfited. So with our first performance of " Don Giovanni." " An utter shipwreck " was the prophecy. They even went so far as to send a deputation (friends of Förster's, they said they were) to beg us in our own interests to give up the performance. It was set for the following night, so I assured Förster the thing would be a perfect success, and received the deputation with absolute calm, saying, " ' Don Giovanni ' will *certainly* be given to-morrow night, gentlemen. Anything you may have to say on the subject I shall be most charmed to hear —*after* the performance." Then I coolly went back to the stage and proceeded with my rehearsals. That night of " Don Giovanni " was a new triumph. Our tempo, and particularly our " secco-recitatif," classically interpreted in the traditional style of Mozart and the Vienna school, delighted the connoisseurs. For Leipsic audiences were great Mozart devotees, and our success as interpreters of this composer established us beyond peradventure in the affections of our public.

And Glück, too, whose operas had hitherto not been popular in Leipsic, would have been delighted to see the streams of applicants at the box office when we gave his " Armida," which had never before been given here. At the advance sale for the second performance, special policemen were called to keep order in the line, and the demand was so great that the box office could not be closed until five, instead of at two as usual. It was this success that encouraged us to give the works of Glück in a complete cycle; and we may say that from this time on our opera was on an unshakable footing.

If I go too much into the details of these days it is because these events are steps in the progress of our theatrical career.

The introduction of other masterpieces, " The Flying Dutchman," " Rienzi," " Meistersinger," " Tannhäuser," later " Euranthe " and " Oberon "—and finally that " daring novelty," Verdi's " Aïda "—all followed in due course, and are milestones and red-letter days in the history of the opera in Germany.

CHAPTER III

BAYREUTH, 1876

NATURALLY the affairs of the opera in Leipsic absorbed all my energies and allowed me no time for excursions except on occasions of the utmost importance; and such an occasion was the season of musical festival that opened at Bayreuth August 13, 1876, when the Nibelungen Ring was first presented to the public. It was clearly our duty to be present; and we had arranged that Förster was to attend the first cycle and I the second, a week later, as we could not both be absent at the same time.

The storm of conflicting opinion aroused by the work is too well known to need repetition, and Förster listened to the cycle under the influence of the most rabidly intolerant clique of critics. That seems the only excuse for so cultivated and thorough a musician to have taken the stand he did when he announced on his return: " My dear fellow, the thing is not presentable. ' The Valkyre,' yes, perhaps—but even that is only barely possible. As for the other three—utterly out of the question. It won't be worth your while to take the trip."

Such an opinion expressed by such a man, whose verdicts had hitherto seemed infallible, decided me to give up the second cycle; especially as important rehearsals demanded my presence in Leipsic at the time.

Presently something occurred that goes to show what trifles will sometimes direct the most important actions of our lives. I might even truthfully say that my whole later relation to the Master of Bayreuth hung on this trivial incident. A mutual friend from Vienna—

19

Julius Nilius—had returned with Förster from Bayreuth, and one evening, quite contrary to my habit, I went with them to a restaurant for supper after the performance. There the conversation naturally turned on their impressions of the " Ring." When I admitted that I'd given up going on the strength of Förster's account, Nilius exclaimed, " I want to tell you something, my dear fellow. Of course I can't judge whether or not the staging is possible; but of one thing I'm quite sure; and that is, that in your capacity as director of the opera in Leipsic it's nothing short of your duty to see this performance, no matter what it conflicts with." As he said this, he drew from his pocket a ticket for the second cycle and handed it to me.

It was then about eleven o'clock, and the last train for Bayreuth left at twelve; the last possible chance of my getting there the next day in time for the opening of the second cycle. I turned to Förster, saying, " Do you know, I believe Nilius is right." Then I rushed home, just across the street, ordered my things packed, drove to the station, which was some distance off, and having barely time to catch my train, I arrived in Bayreuth the following morning. The second cycle was to begin with " Rhinegold " that afternoon, August 20, 1876, at five o'clock.

I shall not attempt to describe the excitement that prevailed in Bayreuth in those days. I shall simply say that if impressions could be weighed, the preponderating element of public opinion would have proven strongly adverse to the performance.

Under these circumstances I first entered the Bayreuth Theatre. My seat was in the centre of the front row and commanded an uninterrupted view of the stage. From the moment of the introduction with that long-drawn chord of E major, when the green gauze curtains rolled gradually away to reveal the swimming Rhine maidens, I

was under a spell that lasted till the final note—a spell of
dissolving pictures on the stage, and the incomparable
magic of the harmonies in the orchestra. I was particularly entranced by the trio of the Rhine daughters, and
heaved a sigh of devout satisfaction when at the close,
while Wotan and the other gods are striding towards the
rainbow bridge, their beautiful song is repeated from the
distance.

I still fail to understand why it was just that portion
of the opera that provoked the most savage criticism.

At the close of that performance of " Rhinegold " I
was incapable of speaking to a soul, so deeply sunk was
I in all that I had seen and heard. To be sure, I had
known Richard Wagner as a stage manager in Vienna,
and admired his methods; but in this performance I realised that a new field had been opened by the greatest of
the world's stage directors; that it was an epoch-making
performance, and from now on our work lay along alto-
gether different lines.

I went back to my hotel and looked for a quiet corner
to eat my lonely supper, then directly to bed—to lie
half waking and half dreaming, wrapped in the delicious melodies of " Rhinegold." Early next morning
I awoke refreshed, and waited impatiently through the
day for four o'clock—the time set for the opening of
" The Valkyre."

While all the elect, and most of the non-elect, felt it
their duty to cavil and jeer at the artistic impossibilities
of " Rhinegold," " The Valkyre " on the contrary seemed
to be more suited to their comprehension. It is unnecessary to record the deep effect that this first performance
had upon me. I shall simply say that, great though my
enthusiasm was for all these splendid artists, Heinrich
Vogl as Loge; Schlosser as Mime; Ferdinand Hill as
Alberich; and especially Franz Betz as Wotan—Albert
Niemann's performance of Siegfried transcended them

all, and I was moved to the very depths of my being. Also I think no one who had the good fortune to hear Franz Betz as Wotan and Amalia Materna as Brunhilda will ever forget their great scene together in the third act.

As far as mere scenic effects go I must admit that the great tableau of the fire-magic was absolutely unconvincing; but on the other hand I shall never again see a more beautiful setting than the scene in Hunding's hut as it was given that summer of 1876 in Bayreuth.

One can readily understand how eagerly I looked forward to the last two days. Siegfried seemed like a clear fresh spring on a parching summer day. Though George Unger (of whom I shall speak more, later) was not to my mind an ideal Siegfried, yet he was not enough of a disturbing element to mar the beauty of the whole. Technically, the fire scene in the third act of this performance was a marvellous achievement.

In these Bayreuth days I chanced to meet Ludwig Bösendorfer, the well-known amateur and head of that celebrated firm, whom I had known formerly in Vienna. Naturally we exchanged impressions on the performance. He was a great friend of Franz Liszt and a passionate lover of music, but my unbounded enthusiasm for this work seemed to astonish him considerably. A thought had struck me, and was taking shape in my mind, and I could see it seemed to please him too. I conceived the idea of transplanting this whole colossal undertaking to Leipsic and giving it there next year in a complete cycle!

All my arguments seemed in favour of the proposition, and my intense personal enthusiasm made my companion feel their force. First we had that wonderful Gewandhaus Orchestra at our command; then I planned to add to our thoroughly capable cast such voices as the Master should recommend. Moreover the geographical position of Leipsic was greatly to our advantage, and finally it was the birthplace of the Master himself. My excitement must have made me eloquent, for the next day he went to Liszt with my plan. The latter promised to lay the matter before Richard Wagner, and as a result Bösendorfer ordered me to appear at Wahnfried next morning at nine o'clock, to see Liszt and the Master personally about my undertaking.

Promptly at the given hour I appeared at Wahnfried. Liszt received me with his well-known gentleness and talked with me awhile, discussing the plan in a tone that fell in exactly with my views. Then he wrote a few hasty words on a scrap of paper, folded it in note form, and sent it up to Wagner, who was still in his bedroom. Presently the servant came down with the answer. Liszt looked at it a moment, smiled, then frowned and seemed to hesitate, but finally decided to let me see what Wagner had written. On one side I read in Liszt's handwriting, " Incomprehensible man. Neumann is here. Come down and talk it over with him," and Richard Wagner had written on the reverse, " Still more incomprehensible one. I've nothing on but my shirt—hence can't come down. Have considered Neumann's proposition, but still cling to the hope of repeating the Ring at Bayreuth next season."

So my great plan had failed for the time. Liszt and Bösendorfer, however, agreed with me that a repetition of the festival in Bayreuth the following year would be impossible, as was eventually the case. For Bayreuth, as we all know, was closed from 1876 until 1882.

CHAPTER IV

AN ATTEMPT AND A FAILURE

My enthusiasm for what I had heard in Bayreuth may be measured by the fact that Förster, who had been so firmly convinced of the impracticability of the Trilogy, was converted by my account and resolved on the 27th of August to send the following letter to the master:

Honoured Sir:

My friend and colleague Angelo Neumann has been assured by M. the Abbé Liszt that I might hope for a favourable answer as to a request I am about to make. It is this:

That great Germanic work of art—recently produced at Bayreuth in the presence of the assembled world of culture, amid the applause of your fellow-citizens, and to the delight and amazement of our musical fraternity —it is now my eager wish to present this noble work to the city of Leipsic; and it is these rights of production that I now humbly crave from its great author.

In Leipsic!—It is your native town, honoured Master. A city that has triumphantly disproved the saying, "Nemo propheta in patria." For no other place can boast such swarms of your disciples and ardent admirers. Wagner is the idol of our Leipsic audiences.

Lying as it does in the very heart of Germany, Leipsic is excellently calculated to become a Mecca for the converts to the new art. We shall present these works in a spirit of reverence, and receive the pilgrims at its shrine with cordial hospitality, winning strangers to the cause by our own eager enthusiasm.

Grant me the honour, then, of producing your matchless works here in your native town. Other considerations may possibly influence you in our favour. I, the director, Angelo Neumann, the leader of our musical department, Josef Sucher, our conductor, all three are most ardent admirers of your genius. Our staff is capable, and in case it should prove inadequate we will gladly enrol new artists for the more trying parts. We are ready to comply with all your demands as to requisitions, scenic effects, etc., and our highest efforts shall be directed to a worthy presentation of your great works.

If it should be your decision not to repeat the Festival at Bayreuth immediately, I should be willing to take over your stage mechanism, decorations, etc., and should hold myself in readiness to return the same at your instant demand.

As regards the financial question, which as theatrical manager I shall have to touch upon, I beg to offer you a full ten per cent. of the daily box office receipts, and directly upon the signing of the contract would place at your disposal a deposit such as you may decide upon as security for your percentage of these profits.

Though young in the direction of a theatre, I am an experienced stage manager, and long to test my abilities in this most formidable of tasks. It would be my pride and my most earnest endeavour thus fittingly to present to my Fatherland this greatest triumph of our national art.

So let me hope, honoured Master, for a favourable answer to my anxious question. . . .

To this letter Wagner answered in friendly refusal:

Honoured Sir:
My work is not complete. I have learned much of its lack of finish from this first presentation. Give me time then to work it over carefully in these next few years

and to present it again at Bayreuth in a more perfect form. Accept my heartiest thanks, however, for your cordial expressions of interest; and believe me with the warmest assurance of regard,

Richard Wagner.

Bayreuth, September 6, 1876.

From that time until the 31st of January, 1877, we had no further intercourse with Bayreuth until Wagner himself took up the thread, and wrote the following to Josef Sucher:

To the Conductor of the Leipsic Orchestra.
Honoured Sir:

I wish you could arrange for me that the directors of the Leipsic theatre may definitely engage the tenor George Unger for their future productions of my operas.

Acting on my advice this young man—who has exceptional qualities, placing him far above the average singer, but who had some few faults which teaching could eradicate—cancelled an excellent engagement in Frankfort and placed himself under the tuition of Prof. Hey in Munich that he might better sing my rôle of Siegfried, which he created with such signal success. But the time has now come to find him a permanent engagement.

It would gratify me exceedingly to feel he was in a company where he would not waste too much time in acquiring an unimportant repertoire, but where he could bend all his energies to the study of my rôles—to which I hope he can soon entirely devote himself. I am now looking for such a company, and in casting about I recall the charming letter I received last fall from your director, Dr. Förster, with regard to the rights for the " Nibelungen " in Leipsic.

I hold the theatre of my native town, under Dr. Förster's guidance, to be better for my purpose than any

other in Germany—with the exception of the Royal Opera
houses. So if Dr. Förster will agree to engage Unger
for these rôles I am quite ready to enter into negotiations with him as to copyrights—in case (as I very much
hope) he still wishes to present them.

You will see from my anxiety for Unger how highly I
esteem him. I consider him absolutely invaluable to any
company, if he is intelligently cast and allowed to sing
the rôles that suit him best.

My respects to Dr. Förster.

Yours,
Richard Wagner.

A second letter, of which I have no copy, followed this
first, and as a result Förster sent the following, energetically taking up the matter of the Nibelungen.

Leipsic, February 24, 1877.

Honoured Sir:

It is only to-day that I am able finally to answer the
two kind letters Josef Sucher has handed me, for I have
been travelling lately and since my return have been quite
ill.

First let me thank you for the hearty interest you have
shown in me, and in the institution which stands under
my guidance. As to the business details in your letters,
Sucher has already told you how gladly I shall agree
to Unger's engagement.

But first I must ask—not only in my own interests,
but in those of the singer himself—how far we can depend upon him for the interpretation of your rôles.

One passage in your letter wakens high hopes in me
—though causing you, I know, a keen disappointment.
The Bayreuth festival you say will not take place this
year. May I then go back to my old question of August 27th and take up this matter again? I am still fired
with the desire to give your great work in all its entirety

here in Leipsic; and it strikes me now as still more feasible
even than before. May I repeat also my tentative question
as to the transfer of the mechanical apparatus, decorations, properties and all the technical appurtenances of
your works?

I wish to emphasise also my former offer of the percentage, and the deposit for the payment of the same.

The perspective which opens now to my fancy is most
seductive. With pride and pleasure I see your native
town Leipsic honoured next to " Bethlehem-Bayreuth "
as the Nazareth of your musical dramas.

In George Unger we should then have a Loge and a
Siegmund, as well as a Siegfried, whose interpretations
satisfy even the critical genius of their creator. And
then there may be Tristan yet to follow.

I hope soon to have a line in your valued hand, my dear
Master, giving us the glad assurance that Unger is thoroughly fitted for these more important rôles,—or is he
only capable of singing Tannhäuser, Lohengrin and
Walter Stolzing? . . .

The following was Wagner's reply:

Honoured Sir:

It is my earnest wish that you shall agree to the engagement of Unger, for the reasons I have stated in my
letters to Sucher. In all my previous efforts I have
found no tenor in whose hands I could place my rôle of
Siegfried with more perfect confidence than in those of
George Unger. His one drawback was a fault in enuncia-
tion which he was still studying to correct; though the
exigencies of his work in Bayreuth and the strenuosity of
his rôles necessarily interrupted his work in that direction. At my advice he again refused a favourable engagement (as he had the year before) and applied himself once' more to his studies—with the most perfect
results, as I can bear witness. The question now was to

place him where he would not forget all I had taught
him, amid the dreary wastes of a modern opera repertoire.
These then are my reasons for establishing him in a
company whose directors agree with me on certain higher
questions of our art.

In case you fit Unger, my dear director, with the rôles
that I consider him capable of interpreting, I shall certainly feel myself pledged to a close and personal interest and supervision of your future programmes.

Before he goes to you I shall see that Unger is prepared to sing not only my older operas but also Tristan,
Siegmund, and finally even Loge to my perfect satisfaction.

As to your rights for the " Nibelungen Ring " I can no
longer refuse, this time, on the score of hoping to give it
myself this year. Difficulties at home and abroad make
it impracticable, if not impossible, for me to carry out
my former plans. It would be too much of a strain for
me to undergo this year. This decision—to which I now
find myself forced—changes many of my plans.

The King of Bavaria, who has hitherto had the sole
rights of presenting my " Ring," but who has not chosen
to avail himself of the privilege, may now soon direct
their presentation. This naturally would alter my arrangements, and my earlier resolve to reserve these
dramas absolutely for the Bayreuth stage for the space
of three years, would then be waived.

Let me assure you now, that if I rearrange my plans,
you at the head of the Leipsic theatre shall be the first
one to whom I shall entrust my work. I ask only a
brief, a *very* brief time to work out my new plan of
action; for naturally all my arrangements must now be
changed, as I can hardly hope for a repetition of the
Bayreuth festival even for next year. Yet I do not wish
to be hasty in this matter, consequently a transfer of the
scenic effects and apparatus is not to be contemplated

for a moment. But when I consider that the longer I
delay my performances at Bayreuth the greater will be
my difficulties in re-assembling my scattered cast, and
that I shall have to select a new set of artists, the complicated difficulties of my problem stagger me for a moment and seem to lead to a modification of my original
ideas to meet the existing circumstances.

I should prefer to talk this over with you, my dear
sir; so I take the liberty (somewhat brusquely, I fear)
of asking you to come and spend the day with me in
Bayreuth. If this were convenient I should like to say
that I shall be at home until the end of April, excepting
the days from the 9th to the 12th of March.

Pardon my many digressions in this letter, and believe
me,

Yours very truly,

Richard Wagner.

Bayreuth, February 28, 1877.

To this invitation Wagner added, after Förster had
sent his acceptance, the following telegram setting a
definite time:

Dr. Förster, Director Leipsic Theatre.

Bayreuth, March 23, 1877.

You are bidden to Sunday dinner at two o'clock.
Heartiest welcome.   Wagner.

So Förster went to see Wagner. They concluded a
treaty whereby the Leipsic theatre received for two years
the sole German rights of presenting the Ring outside
of the Royal Operas in Munich and Vienna. As to the
further details of their plan the following telegrams will
be explanatory.

Bayreuth, April 22, 1877.

Can't understand Unger's report that you're waiting
my definite decision before engaging him; when as I wrote

I am awaiting your action in the matter to decide. Can't give you exclusive rights, for Munich has had them for years. Can give you sole rights for northern Germany, as Munich has for southern and Vienna for Austria. For later model presentation in Bayreuth should only wish your friendly co-operation. Let me know at once before I can decide, especially as to Unger, whom I can no longer put off.

                                        Richard Wagner.

                             Bayreuth, April 24, 1877.
Settlement of Unger's affairs urgent for family reasons —can't understand delay. Reiterate acceptance of your former contract without further conditions. Expect immediate answer as to Unger's engagement. If not satisfactory will apply elsewhere both for him and for my works to-morrow.

                                        Richard Wagner.

This was our answer:

                              Leipsic, April 25, 1877.
Regard your telegram unconditionally accepting our terms of August 27th as final. Will send contract for Unger to-morrow. Let me know when to expect him. With high hopes for a successful season and great triumphs for our German art, I am with grateful recognition and deepest respect,
                         Yours,
                                     August Förster.

To which Wagner's next explicit letter gives a desirable commentary:

Honoured Sir:
I was extremely sorry that our pleasant personal relation (I am still deeply indebted to you for your journey to Bayreuth) has been reduced to this curt telegraphic style. In the few friendly lines you left with me on your

departure you promised to send me a written contract
—(sit venia verbo)—which I am eagerly awaiting, less
on my own account than for the sake of poor Unger.

Our tenor finally could wait no longer. He starts for
London on a concert tour and leaves without knowing
whether he is to have the Leipsic engagement or not,
whether he shall send his frail young wife to wait for
him there, . . . etc., etc.

You cannot have failed to see that I not only like
Unger and wish to help him, but that I regard him as
the only tenor I have ever heard who fully carries out my
conception of the part; and for this reason I have spared
no effort to perfect him in my rôles and would wish
to see him placed where he can best advance the cause of
my art.

So, all other things being equal, I should prefer to
give the rights for my "Nibelungen Ring" to a theatre
that would engage Unger, and thus give me the assurance
that the weightiest rôles would be interpreted to my perfect satisfaction and in the spirit of their conception—
as far as human circumstances will allow. But I have
told you all this before.

To return to the main clause of our contract and to
clear this up thoroughly: I shall release you and your
staff (and this has probably been your stumbling-block)
from any further obligations, financial or otherwise, as
to my coming festivals at Bayreuth.

Since our last talk there has been a meeting of the
Wagner Society of Leipsic, who have pledged themselves
to support my undertakings and help me carry out my
programme here. How far their good intentions will
carry them remains to be seen; however, they are a factor
and must be reckoned with, and I shall have to acknowledge them before the public as my backers and my moral
support. To my mind, however, it would be better if they
concerned themselves rather with furnishing me an au-

dience than with financing the details of my performances. This experiment will take some time and I am pledged to see that these performances shall be satisfactory and on the plane of my highest ideals. In case then of the realisation of these hopes I should be unable to keep all the leading strings in my hands at once, and should find it necessary to depute the direction of my affairs as best I may.

As I have already wired you, I have given the Munich theatre (which had the initial rights), as well as the Royal Opera of Vienna, and your theatre in Leipsic, the exclusive privilege of presenting my " Nibelungen " in Germany. These three theatres (and Leipsic of course only as long as it stands under your direction) are severally pledged to contribute their best forces for my festival performances at Bayreuth when I shall call for them; as well as to put at my disposal any members of their technical staff to form what I might call my executive board. These performances are to take place as soon as the Wagner Society feels itself financially strong enough to bear the cost, and the three aforesaid theatres will then be requested (probably through me) at the beginning of that theatrical season to announce a suspension of all their Wagner performances for the period of our festival at Bayreuth. As I shall have all three theatres to draw from I can easily arrange to divide my conscriptions so that ordinary operatic performances need not be interrupted, and the season in the aforesaid cities could easily proceed. This is the outline of my plan.

Now as to the special stipulations. I believe the following agrees with our contract of a year ago:

I

. . . You are to have the absolute rights of presentation for my four-part musical drama, " The Nibelungen Ring," for the period of your personal direction of the

Leipsic theatre (or for the term of three, four or five years, not exceeding six).

No other theatre (with the exception of the Royal Operas in Munich and Vienna) shall have the privilege of making such a contract with me until the expiration of your term. As to the performances of " Siegfried " and " Götterdämmerung," the director of the Royal Opera in Munich (who has my pledge for their initial performances and who has long since given the other two, but hesitates about these last) will be pressed to an immediate performance, in order that the Leipsic theatre may acquire the rights of presentation within the coming year—1878. In Vienna it will still be some time before they venture the performance.

II

. . . For this exceptional favour, whereby I give the direction of the Leipsic theatre the precedence of all the towns of northern Germany for a term of years, the director of said theatre will pay me, on the signing of our contract, an indemnity of ten thousand Marks (twenty-five hundred dollars).

III

. . . The author's share for the whole term is to be ten per cent. of the gross receipts of the box office (subscription seats included).

This contract will be null and void on the day of the retirement of Dr. Förster from the management of the Leipsic theatre (or at the expiration of the given term of years) ; and the aforesaid rights will then revert to the author or to his heirs.

As concerns the matter of the scenic effects, decorations, costumes, etc., I have the following to propose:

I find I am still two hundred thousand Marks in debt to the treasury of Bavaria and there is a clause in my contract to the effect that they may hold my properties for that debt. I have now suggested that I turn over these effects to them for their own performance of the " Ring." If, however, they would prefer the money (which is quite probable, as they already have the technical apparatus for " Rhinegold " and " The Valkyre ") I have intimated that you might be glad to take these things off their hands. In case they agree, the necessary business details can be arranged directly with them. I have not yet had their answer.

I take up all these questions to-day, for I wish to have them definitely settled before my departure for London, which will involve a tremendous pressure of other af- fairs. I leave on Saturday, and should be very glad if the matter could be so settled that you would undertake the payment for me of a debt in Leipsic of four thousand Marks which is due at the end of this month—this would save me a vast amount of trouble.

Now let me hear from you immediately, my valued friend and associate in the " Nibelungen " affairs, and be- lieve me, with the assurance of my constant appreciation and respect,

Yours,

Richard Wagner.

Bayreuth, April 25, 1877.

This letter, which, like the subsequent ones, proved Wagner's clear head and business-like disposition, was answered by Förster as follows:

Leipsic, April 27, 1877.

Honoured Master,

Through my telegram of day before yesterday you know already that I consider our contract of last year as definite and binding by your wired agreement of that same day.

I still hold to that decision, though your yesterday's letter has altered several points in the situation.   Accord-

ing to this letter I cannot hope to present the Ring until
the end of the year 1878, as the Royal Opera of Munich
has the privilege of the first performance. Nevertheless
as I have said I shall hold fast to my items of the contract and shall repeat them in detail as regards the
points you raise in your letter of April 25th.

I

You give me, for the period of my engagement at
Leipsic, absolute rights of production for your four-part
musical drama—"The Nibelungen Ring." No other
theatre beside the Royal Operas in Vienna and Munich
shall have the least claim to the work until a full year
after our first complete representation.

The Opera in Munich has the first rights for " Siegfried " and " Götterdämmerung "; yet at the end of the
year 1878 the Leipsic theatre shall have a perfect right to
present these two operas whether they have yet been given
or not.

II

In consideration of this concession I agree to pay as
security for your percentage of the profits, a premium of
ten thousand Marks, of which I am ready to deposit four
thousand Marks at your order here in Leipsic on the 30th
of April. A further deposit of three thousand Marks will
be made on the 1st of July, 1877; and the final three thousand Marks are to be paid at the close of the first performance of the first half of the Trilogy.

III

This contract is to be null and void on the day of my
dismissal from the management of the Leipsic theatre,
and the rights are then to revert to the author or to his
heirs.

I agree to your proposal of our mutual concession and co-partnership in case of a possible repetition of your Bayreuth festival.

We wait the result of your steps with regard to the scenic arrangements and the appurtenances of your Bayreuth theatre, and stand ready to meet you half-way. But I should urge an immediate decision, as in case this negotiation falls through I should have to make other arrangements directly.

How gladly, my dear and honoured Master, I would keep all business out of this arrangement, dwelling only upon its artistic side and the glory of such a compact! Any one knowing me well could assure you of that. Unfortunately, however, my connection with the stage and my public position necessitate my conducting this affair on strictly business lines.

The resources of my theatre are limited in comparison with those of my predecessors, as the greater part of our gains are swallowed up in paying for the new franchise we have just been granted by the city. When I freely offered you a royalty of ten per cent., induced thereto by the tremendous impression your work had made on me, my condition here was different—yet even so I was going far beyond the usual honorarium in offering you that percentage. Yet I did offer it, for I hold you to be by far the greatest among the poets and composers of our day and nation,—high above all other dramatists with whom one has to deal.

When, however, I consider how tremendous must be my outlay in order to carry out your scenic requirements with due regard to your artistic ideals, I can scarcely hope that the " Nibelungen Ring " will be in any sense a business success for us. Yet these performances and the confidence you have shown in ceding me these rights— a high honour indeed—will undoubtedly place my theatre in the front ranks of the artistic world; and hence my

eagerness to obtain this concession for the presentation
of your great works.

You are dealing now, my dear Master, with a man of
an artistic temperament—one to whom bargaining is
distinctly distasteful, and one who would gladly and
freely offer an artist of your calibre the best that lay
within his power!

I hope you may be utterly convinced of this, and in
proof of such conviction telegraph at once, telling me
where to send the first payment on your account.

With sincerest admiration,

Believe me,

Yours in grateful reverence,

Dr. August Förster.

Between the lines one cannot fail to read a certain
tendency in Dr. Förster to withdraw from the plan on
which he had looked at first so reluctantly, and then—
fired by my enthusiasm—had taken up so eagerly. My
personal enemies, already quite a goodly number, rallied
to the standards of Wagner's foes, and I watched with
doubt and anxiety the effect of their attacks upon this
high-souled and gifted man. Would he stand firm? I
thought it rather doubtful, with his vacillating temperament! In the meantime came another message from
Wagner.

Bayreuth, April 28, 1877.

Agree throughout,—with exception of minor point to
your disadvantage. Not *after the expiration* of the year
1878, but *at the end* of the year—that is, " Siegfried "
and " Götterdämmerung " in the course of the second half
of the year. Wish to emphasise also, for your business
success, the length of your exclusive rights for northern
Germany—which concession is somewhat of a sacrifice
for me as well, since Hanover and Hamburg have made
application for the same within the year, and will

have to be denied in favour of Leipsic. Kindly pay the deposit to Gustav Steckner, purveyor to the king, and take his receipted bill.

Greetings,

Richard Wagner.

This telegram was followed on the same day by a weighty letter from the Master:

Honoured Sir and Friend:

In re-reading your good letter I am struck with your § II., "The Premium, as a first instalment of my percentage of the proceeds." I take it you mean—"as an advance." A "Premium," however, is a fixed stipend! That reminds me there was a clause in our former contract concerning a raise of my dividend from the usual seven per cent. to ten per cent., on which basis you were willing to give me an instalment;—i. e., an *advance,* amounting to seven per cent. of the gross receipts from the day of the first performance, the remaining three per cent. to follow when the advance payment had been cancelled.

Following the precedent of my Vienna contract I took an unusual step in deciding upon a premium as well as the ten per cent. royalty, in view of the acknowledged superiority of your theatre. According to your clause II., however, you seem to intend to pay my premium out of the profits; which would necessitate my waiting quite a time for the beginning of my royalties.

Will you be so good now as to explain your meaning more fully. I think this difference need not affect our transaction, for my reasons for preferring the Leipsic theatre—under your direction—have nothing to do with material advantages; these would readily have been secured by connection with Hamburg, Hanover, Cologne or Frankfort, all of which have applied for the rights. These theatres, however, all wished to present " The Valkyre," or any one of my cycle, *singly*. Naturally in giving you the precedence of these other cities for a term of years I should submit to a pecuniary loss which you would be called upon to make good. I consider the ten thousand Marks as an indemnity for my waiving these other contracts, a step naturally very much to your advantage, as your audiences would then not be confined to Leipsic alone, but would be drawn from the adjacent cities as well.

I beg you to consider this matter, and you will see that this is no idle talk, but a statement of facts: and I hope you will find my proposition fair. If you are willing I should give Hamburg, Hanover, etc., equal rights, the matter would be different and I could then give them to you more cheaply.

I have already wired a correction of your error as to the time of your production—not *after* the end of the year as you understood it, but *in the course* of the year.

I leave for London early on Monday. My address there will be

12, Orme Square, Bayswater, W.

I expect to hear at any moment from the treasury in Munich, and shall let you know without delay.

With warmest greetings,

Yours very devotedly,

Richard Wagner.

Bayreuth, April 28, 1877.

This was Förster's answer:

Leipsic, May 3, 1877.

Honoured Master,

I am delighted to see in your last letter the stress you lay upon the difference in our interpretations in the matter of the ten thousand Marks.

We shall end, I am sure, by a perfect agreement. Certainly in my offer of a definite sum on August 27, 1876—I believe we settled it at ten thousand Marks—I meant that this should simply be a security for payment of royalties due you. Far from intending to pay you seven per cent. above this deposit, and then adding three per cent. to the usual profits, I believe I never mentioned such a thing either in my letters or in my conversation.

I will gladly meet you, however, on this point, if the ten per cent. basis is irksome to you, since you would then be forced to wait for your profits.

I make you the counter-proposition of six per cent. from the start,—instead of ten per cent.,—to be covered by an advance deposit of ten thousand Marks; and the remaining four per cent. to be paid at the conclusion of each performance.

I trust this will settle the disputed point quite to your satisfaction.

I shall merely add that I have paid the four thousand Marks to the firm of Steckner as per order; and wishing you every success in your English venture, and the best of health,—hoping you will return to your native land recuperated spiritually as well as financially,—I am,

Yours very truly,

August Förster.

Wagner's answer followed immediately.

London, W.   12, Orme Square, Bayswater.

My dear Dr. Förster:

I regret exceedingly that our affair has been so long drawn out by evasive answers on your part, and that we have not yet reached the conclusion I had hoped for, before beginning my arduous London task.

Now I must tell you—for at last I find the time to-day—that we are very *far* from an agreement as to our point of difference. As I said,—after a hasty reading of your last letter to Bayreuth, I was so delighted to find Unger's affairs settled that I wired at once agreeing to your proposition. Directly, however, on re-reading your

letter I noticed the difference in your acceptation of
the word, with regard to which I wrote you at once.

Your letter of May 3d—which unfortunately I have
not been able to answer until now—indicates, however,
that if, as you say, the proceeds of the Leipsic theatre—
which until recently were so considerable—have fallen
off so tremendously, I cannot consider your offer of a
mere percentage as sufficient safeguard for my undertaking. For if you mean to buy the *exclusive* rights—
always with the exception of the two Operas in southern
Germany—and your theatre in Leipsic intends to ex-
clude all competitors in the performance of my " Nibelungen Ring," the world may well ask what huge com-
pensation I have demanded for such a concession!

Can I entrust my works to a theatre, and feel that they
will present them with a due regard for my artistic satisfaction—to say nothing of my material satisfaction—
if they have so little respect for the author that they
cannot indemnify him for ceding them his entire rights
during a period of at least three years!

You have also introduced into our former contract a
clause stipulating that your exclusive rights shall extend
throughout the year following your final performance.

Then finally as to the disputed point of the " Premium." This is to be deposited to my account in advance, and to be paid off as rapidly as possible throughout your three years of monopoly on a ten per cent. basis
—which is precisely what other theatres, *eo ipso,* are now
offering me!

I think you have entered into this agreement with too
much doubt as to your risk, and I must now make my own
final conditions.

. . . Either; ten thousand Marks of Premium—or fixed
stipend—for my concession of the exclusive rights you
demand for these performances: as well as ten per cent.
of the gross receipts of the box office—the ten thousand

Marks to be paid between the 1st of July and the 1st of September of this year in deposits of three thousand Marks each:

. . . Or; a royalty of ten per cent. with an advance of four thousand Marks—prepaid—and a continuous dividend of five per cent. until the expiration of the contract; with no further conditions as to *exclusive* rights for any definite time, but a clause binding the Leipsic theatre to produce " Siegfried " and " Götterdämmerung " within a given period.

. . . *Or else;*—the Leipsic theatre withdraws its contract entirely! In case you adopt this latter course I have only to return you the four thousand Marks already paid to my order.

As to your contract with Unger (in accepting the final alternative)—you may consider yourself released. He has been most successful here and can easily find another engagement:—whereas on the other hand he might find his contract with you rather difficult. It is a question in my mind whether a tenor can afford, for the sake of the salary, to engage to sing my difficult rôles one hundred and twenty nights in the year;—I think it would be more humane to offer half the salary and a percentage for each night's performance, limiting these to one hundred. Yet that is a matter to be settled at another time.

I thank you heartily for your good wishes for my health and prosperity. I need them, and hope they will be effectual; for my life is anything but easy at present!

With kindest greetings,

I am yours very faithfully,

Richard Wagner.

May 10, 1877.

This uncongenial trip to London was undertaken by the Master to raise money for covering the deficit of his first production of the " Ring " at Bayreuth. While this

letter was on the way, Förster sent another saying among
other things:

. . . Would it not be possible for you to give two or
three great Wagner concerts in our new Leipsic theatre
on your return from London with the artists you have
with you?   It would be a brilliant precursor of our first
performance of " Rhinegold "—in the fall, I hope—and a
point of importance in Unger's career here. . . .

The fears I had felt were only too soon justified.   I
found myself almost alone now, against the host of
Wagner's enemies, Josef Sucher and a friend of Förster
(Ludwig Staackmann the publisher) being my only allies.

In the meantime came the above letter from Wagner
giving Förster an opportunity to break off negotiations.
The grounds for this lay deeper far than I had thought.
An undeniable authority in dramatic matters, Förster's
musical judgment was unsound! He lacked the courage
of his own convictions, and was alarmed by the least
sign of opposition.   The mob had declared that Wagner
was not fit to be played in the " Gewandhaus " ! This
could not fail to sway Förster. He longed for some
pretext for evading the contract, and my influence,
usually of weight in such matters, was powerless now
against the popular verdict.   So, in spite of my efforts,
Förster sent the following:

                                        Leipsic, May 15, 1877.
Honoured Master:
    Your London letter of May 10th puts our matter on
quite another footing.
    I had understood our contract to have been ratified by
your telegraphic acceptance of April 27. . . . That another contract should be necessary regarding the exclusive rights for the " Ring " seems rather remarkable.
    Under no circumstances can I consider your first re-
vision of April 28th, or your later addition to our original

agreement, of May 10th. My offer to you was clear and unmistakable. Your answer to the same was an unqualified acceptance.

My sense of justice forces me to be thus plain, and to stand now for my simple dues.

The matter takes another aspect when I ask myself whether it would be expedient to press my indubitable rights and insist upon the carrying out of our original contract.

My answer to this question is, no; it would not be expedient. If you could give a definite answer to my definite offer, and then—under cover of a different interpretation of a phrase—break that compact, the question rises in my mind whether you might not at some future day change your views again. This uncertainty would give rise to such uneasiness that,—while it might not dim our appreciation of your great works,—it would certainly cloud all our pleasant personal relations;—raising difficulties in our preparations and endangering the success of our production.

As a matter of principle then, I herewith declare our contract null and void, and ask for the immediate return of the four thousand Marks,—as well as my release from the contract with Unger.

With highest regards, and very respectfully,

Dr. August Förster.

In spite of the brusqueness of this letter Wagner sent a telegram which touched me deeply in its evident effort to smooth matters:

London, May 17, 1877.
Wait for letter before looking at papers.   Wagner.

On the arrival of this wire and the letter which followed, whose contents cut me to the heart, I made one more determined effort to convert Förster to my views.

But the host of opponents still continued to harp on the idea of a deficit in view of the enormous sums I demanded for the scenic arrangements (about twenty-five thousand dollars).

Wagner's letter, a model of clearest logic and noblest altruism, reads as follows:

My dear Sir:

The exalted opinion that I have of you, and the high hopes that we might have collaborated pleasantly, demand that I defend myself at once against your charges.

It is a new thing for me to be regarded as difficult and intriguing in the matter of my contracts; when my lack of care and usual indifference to business have hitherto caused me so much annoyance, and have been the constant reproach of all my friends.

Another thing quite new to me is your use of the word "Premium" in the sense of "Advance," and hence my telegraphic acceptance of your proposition. I thought I understood your point absolutely,—though you will remember I questioned that very point in my letter which followed.

And finally it is news to me that you could have considered the matter definitely settled by my telegram of acquiescence, wherein I distinctly stated I was waiting for the contract; which as usual in all theatrical matters needed *both* our signatures to be binding.

The question now is what to do; as you are evidently so delighted to be rid of the whole affair that you have decided to drop it. In considering the matter, I find, in spite of my temporary discouragement, that I have sufficent tranquillity of mind to wish to avoid any further such complications,—disagreeable as they always are to me!

My concession to you of the exclusive rights has made a great sensation in the press—presumably not without some instigation.   The breaking now of our contract would cause even more clamour, and would probably force me to a general declaration of my reasons.   It is needless to say how distasteful this would be to me.   Let us avoid all that and carry out this matter quietly and in order.

If you have no further grounds then for refusing, I beg you will immediately send your contract for my signature in due form, and I will agree to the terms of your final offer.

With highest esteem,
Yours,
Richard Wagner.

London, W.   12, Orme Square, Bayswater.   May 17, 1877.

The opposition now had won over Förster so completely that he was blind to my pain at his action.   And even that wonderful letter, and Wagner's magnanimous yielding to his conditions, made no impression upon him.   So he wrote again on the 22d of May (Wagner's birthday in fact) :

Honoured Master:

It was not only our difference with regard to the ten thousand Marks which led me to write you as I did, it was rather the impression of your previous letter which decided me to withdraw from the presentation of your great works.

This impression has not been corrected by your last. My cordial enthusiasm, and the friendliness with which I stood ready to meet you, have been obliterated by these unfortunate circumstances which have arisen between us.

As Clavigo has it—" Break the heart from out a plant, —it may yet wax and grow!   Countless shoots may spring:—it may even become a sturdy bush!   But the pride and kingly carriage of the original tree are gone forever ! "

When you wrote me from London on the 10th of May that " You hardly considered the means at our disposal sufficient guarantee for the carrying out of our undertaking " you broke the heart from out the plant!

One such word of yours, if ever published, would be sufficient to kill our enterprise, and to benumb both the artists and the audience.

I cannot resist the impression that whatever may have been your original enthusiasm for this compact, you have lost all interest in it now; and this lack it is which interferes with all our preliminary arrangements. Your commercial interests have triumphed over the artistic, and reflection has followed hard upon inspiration!

Honoured Master, I am still a devoted admirer of your genius. I can follow the tortuous windings and the psychological evolutions of your thoughts and inventions, and far be it from me to criticise them—I wish to say here that your defence in your last letter imputes things to me which I have never said—but for all this I cannot avoid the impression that I am dealing not only with an artist of the first rank, but with a business expert of the most finished type,—and that my position is unsafe.

That being the case, would it not be better quietly and simply to drop our original plan? You seem to think I am delighted to be rid of it—on the contrary I resign it with a heavy heart. Yet notwithstanding, I consider it far better to drop it quietly now, than to come to a crash later on.

As far as the newspapers are concerned the matter is quite within our own control. Neither side need be injured by the announcement of our change of plans. The sensation caused by the publication of our contract was not due to *my* indiscretion, and I shall take pains to have its dissolution announced in a calm impersonal manner. If you handle it in the same spirit we need expect no disagreeable consequences whatsoever.

If I were more sure of your sincere good wishes, your sympathy for our success, and your trust in my good intentions and unselfish devotion to the cause,—I should never feel the necessity of advising you in such a matter.

I cannot disguise my deep distress, nor the pain with which I relinquish this plan,—which has become a vital matter to me.

With unalterable respect,

Yours,

Dr. Förster.

So the connection was broken again between Bayreuth and Leipsic—this time through our own fault. It is needless to say how I suffered under this misunderstanding which all my influence with Förster had seemed powerless to prevent.

At a breakfast given in honour of the singer Marie Wilt, a personal friend of Förster and a man of influence in the musical world—whose name, however, I shall withhold—carried away by the trend of public sentiment, raised his glass and drank to the successful breaking off of the Nibelungen undertaking. They wanted me to drink with them, but when they tried to touch my glass I threw it over my shoulder in a rage and strode from the room as it fell crashing to the floor.

Marie Wilt tried afterwards to comfort me by saying— "Don't mind them! You'll carry it out yet. Did you see how anxious and worried Dr. Förster looked as you threw that glass away?"

And truly, within six months I carried out her prophecy in the most brilliant fashion.

PART II

THE RING IN LEIPSIC

CHAPTER V

A NEW CONNECTION

Two circumstances now combined to make Förster regret his cancelled contract with Richard Wagner. In the first place, eagerly as we looked for novelties, we found nothing really worth our while; and furthermore, our negotiation for the " Nibelungen " had not been without its effect in the theatrical world. Shortly after the publication of our failure came the news that Hamburg, Schwerin, and other cities had acquired the rights of producing the " Ring," and were to open with a performance of " The Valkyre "—a proceeding I had always felt to be inartistic since my first hearing of the cycle in Bayreuth.

Rumour even had it that Wagner had consented to sell the rights for " The Valkyre " singly to the Berlin Opera—the opinion of the " masses " in those days being that this was the only one of the " Ring " that was " possible."

And should Leipsic now stand aside, instead of leading the van as I had so fondly hoped?

I took heart and wrote the following letter to the Master:

Leipsic, November 12, 1877.

Honoured Sir and Master:

Allow me as director of the theatre in Leipsic to ask you a simple but urgent question.

During the negotiations early in the spring, my

honoured Master, our contract was to include the rights for all northern Germany. An unpleasant misunderstanding caused the shipwreck of these plans,—to my intense disappointment; for since my opportunity of hearing your gigantic works in Bayreuth I have had but one single ambition—to present them here in Leipsic,— your native town,—where "Wagner" is better understood and more appreciated than elsewhere.

It cannot be your intention to withhold them any longer from a stage of such importance as this of Leipsic; and as I hear you have already concluded a compact with Berlin for " The Valkyre," so that the exclusive rights for northern Germany have lapsed,—I urgently beg you to let us know on what terms you can give us the rights for the entire work—which I personally should prefer—or for any part of the same.

Let me know at your earliest convenience
      And greatly oblige,
                  Yours in respectful devotion,
                        Angelo Neumann.

To which Wagner answered:

My dear Sir:

I have not given Berlin the rights for " The Valkyre," since I do not intend ever to give up parts of my " Nibelungen " *singly*. Director Pollini of the Hamburg Opera has arranged for the production of the entire Trilogy— with no further conditions, however, as to exclusive rights.

As under these circumstances no theatre could have the monopoly now, I am ready to take up the matter with the honourable directors of the Leipsic theatre, sinking the consideration of the " Premium,"—the exact meaning of which was our difference,—and accepting for the performances of the aforesaid Trilogy simply a royalty of ten per cent., with an advance payment of ten thousand

Wer das fährt nach großem Ziel,
Lern am Steuer ruhig sitzen.
Unbekümert, ob am Kiel
Lob und Tadel hochauf spritzen.   (Geibel)

April 1883   Angelo Neumann

From a picture in the Künstlerzimmer of the Leipsic Stadttheater.

Marks (to be paid as we had formerly agreed) and
to be refunded through the royalty on the five per cent.
basis.

Very sincerely yours,

Richard Wagner.

Bayreuth, November 19, 1877.

In these modern days it will seem incredible that after
this conciliatory letter it took fully two months to arrange matters for a further proceeding. This delay is
explained by the fact that Förster was still subject to his
old attacks of distrust as to the success of the Ring, and
furthermore that we had to work out an estimate of its
cost. Finally, however, our doubts were settled, and another circumstance now came to my aid. Our theatrical
season of 1877 closed with a deficit of one hundred and
twenty-one thousand Marks. With this argument I went
to Förster on January 20, 1878, saying, " My dear fellow,
this can't go on. As far as I can see,—try as I will,—I
find nothing new in the operatic world, bearing the least
comparison to the ' Ring ' in importance, or in drawing
power. Our accounts just now look rather sorry, even
without the additional outlay for the ' Nibelungen ' you
were so afraid of! If you are willing, we will now set
aside one hundred thousand Marks for the production of
the Trilogy and go energetically to work, arranging for
the performance of the complete cycle as no other theatre
outside of Bayreuth has dared to do.

" Say yes, and I'll telegraph at once to Richard Wagner
asking for an interview. For now, nothing but a personal
interview will put the thing through on time."

To which Förster replied (and I can never be sufficiently grateful to him for this answer, as the trend of
public opinion was still strong against me), " My dear
fellow, secretly I have long since been convinced that you
were right! I give you ' carte blanche ' now; but I fear

it's too late. He won't want to have anything to do with us!"

Not stopping for any further discussion, I rushed to telegraph:

Richard Wagner—Bayreuth.

Kindly let me know if I may have the honour of an interview with you to-morrow.

Director Neumann of the Leipsic Opera.

That night as I went to the theatre they handed me the Master's answer:

Director Neumann, Leipsic.

Bayreuth, January 20, 1878.

Gladly. To-morrow at four or at eight P. M.

Wagner.

and not until the answer reached me did I tell Förster of my wire.

I started that same night for Bayreuth, but owing to the wretched connections—it was in the dead of winter— did not arrive till the following afternoon at two. At four o'clock I presented myself at Wahnfried and was ushered directly into the Master's well-known study, where the first things that caught my eye were two remarkable portraits, one of his wife, Mme. Cosima, and the other a likeness of Schopenhauer. Presently Mme. Wagner appeared and greeted me cordially, saying, " My husband is still asleep. Will you put up with my company for a while?—I don't want to wake him." So we had a charming talk of about half an hour and I took the occasion to explain my errand to this delightful and interesting woman. Finally the Master appeared, and for the first time I met him face to face—for I can hardly count the fleeting occasions of our previous meetings. He wore his famous skull-cap, a short dark house jacket, and grey trousers. Coming directly toward

me with his most gracious manner, he said, " I'm glad
you've taken up the old plan again. I was keenly disappointed when that fell through. I can see that you're
thoroughly in earnest too—you don't look like a man
who would take that trip from Leipsic to Bayreuth
in the dead of winter simply for amusement." Then he
picked up his little son Siegfried (then a child of seven),
took him on his knee, and turned to me, saying, " Well,
what have you to say to me? "

Then I began and laid my project before him. First
of all I said: " I propose to give the whole cycle in two
series within the space of five months—thus: ' Rhinegold '
and ' The Valkyre ' on two consecutive evenings, the
28th and 29th of April. Then on the 21st of September
will follow the first performance of ' Siegfried,' and ' Götterdämmerung ' on the 22d."

My enthusiasm for his work lent conviction to my
words, and I could see I had made a favourable impression. His eyes sparkled with satisfaction when I declared
I should never consent to give ' The Valkyre ' first and follow it with ' Rhinegold,' as other managers had invariably
done. At this assurance he interrupted me with an
excited gesture and, turning to his wife, said: " Listen,
Cosima, to what Neumann is saying. He means to give
the cycle complete, and in sequence, and has even set the
days for each performance. But I'm afraid he'll break
his word as all the rest have done." Then turning again
to me, he continued: " If you were really to do that,
you'd be the first sensible theatrical manager I ever met."
At this I simply reiterated my first statement: " Master,
I assure you I shall carry out this plan: the first performance of ' Rhinegold,' April 28th, the first performance of
' The Valkyre,' the 29th. Then, in September, ' Siegfried '
on the 21st and ' Götterdämmerung ' on the 22d."

After my declaration there was a momentous pause, in
which Wagner eyed me searchingly for some time; then

suddenly he exclaimed: " Tell me, how did you happen to
set those particular days for your performances? "

" It's very simple," I answered. " In Leipsic we have
the Easter Passion music on the 28th of April and the
St. Michael's Mass on the 21st of September. I hardly
think there could be better occasions than these for the
first presentation of the ' Ring.' "

A Leipsiger himself, Wagner was visibly impressed
by my reasoning. He scanned me keenly again for a
while, then turning to his wife, asked: " What would you
say about it? Shall I trust this man? " After her affirmative answer and the few sympathetic words she
spoke in my favour, the Master turned again to me and
began a series of questions with regard to our facilities
for staging, the orchestra, and our singers. Then he went
on to describe the enormous difficulties of his scenic effects, giving me minute details that proved later of the
utmost value. He seemed pleased with my absorbed attention, and was especially delighted at my frank criticism of certain technical defects in the Bayreuth performances that I hoped eventually to improve under his
guidance. Among these were the scene of the Rhine
maidens, the progress to Walhalla, and particularly the
Magic fire scene. This latter we afterwards staged at
Leipsic so adroitly that it became a model for all later
performances. The Rhine-maiden scene, however, was not
perfected till 1896, when it was given at Bayreuth with
an absolutely ideal finish of detail.

After we had settled a number of artistic and business
particulars to the satisfaction of both sides, Wagner,
beaming with benignity, waved me to his seat at the
desk and asked me to draw up the articles of our contract. Whereupon I remarked: " I should rather you
sat at the desk, Master, and let me dictate to you! " He
looked at me in blank surprise, yet did not seem offended.
" What! " he said. " *You* mean to do the dictating and

I'm to take your orders down?" "Yes, Master, exactly. For in the first place I shall dictate such terms as will be to the best advantage of both sides, and furthermore I shall then have a document from your hand which will always be of inestimable value to me."

Richard Wagner was charmed with this answer and smiled complacently at his wife. Leaning his right arm on the desk he finally turned to me, saying: "Very well then, you may dictate." Then he sat down and wrote out the following articles as I suggested them, making only a few nominal alterations in the terms I proposed.

CONTRACT.

I have this day made over to Dr. August Förster, director of the Leipsic theatre, the privilege of producing my "Nibelungen Ring" under the following conditions, and for the term of his connection with said theatre (or for that of director Angelo Neumann).

The directors of the above theatre acquire the right of giving the aforesaid work immediately, on payment to me of a royalty of ten per cent. of the daily receipts of the box office and five per cent. of the subscription receipts (these last not to exceed eight hundred and seventy-four Marks twenty pfennigs).

As security for this royalty the author is to receive an advance deposit of ten thousand Marks, to be paid in the following instalments: two thousand five hundred Marks down at the signing of the contract, two thousand five hundred Marks on the 1st of April, 1878, and the final sum on April 1, 1879.

This deposit is to be paid back on a basis of five per cent. of the royalties until the entire amount * is cancelled.   Richard Wagner.

Bayreuth, January 21, 1878.

* Wagner here makes a mistake in the spelling which Neumann copies and comments upon. N.B.—These letters are given with absolutely literal fidelity.

After he had finished his writing and we had shaken hands on the success of our undertaking, I was asked to the family supper at Wahnfried. This, unfortunately, I had to decline, for it was growing late, and if I meant to take the evening train back to Leipsic, it was high time I took my leave. I had not a day to lose if I meant to be on time with my preparations.

They understood my haste, and after the most cordial farewells, the kindest of wishes, and a blessing on my work, I left Wahnfried and *flew* rather than walked to my hotel, then from there to the station. And when I walked into my partner's office the following morning, and handed him the contract signed and written in Wagner's own hand, his delight this time was genuine and deep. He put his arm about my shoulder and kissed me with tears in his eyes as he said: " Neumann, you've done it! Why didn't I follow your advice last year! I realised that you were very sore about it at the time."

Our entire staff, particularly Josef Sucher, received the news with eager enthusiasm. That *we* should have the good fortune of giving these colossal works! They besieged me with questions. " Did I really think we could possibly be ready to bring out ' Rhinegold ' and ' The Valkyre ' on the 28th and 29th of April? " " Two such tremendous works with their unutterable technical difficulties to follow each other on two successive days! " I answered so definitely in the affirmative that no one dared to contradict me. Förster—I am glad to express my gratitude to him here—gave me absolute " carte blanche," and agreed from the start on any outlay that I saw fit to make.

Only one body was against us—the Gewandhaus orchestra—and this was a matter of the gravest importance! As in Leipsic, more than in any other town, their orchestra is highly prized, has a tremendous influence in all musical affairs, is received everywhere, and in fact constitutes an assemblage of the first artists of the city, one can readily see that this was an almost insurmountable obstacle.

I shall refer to this matter later.

That very day of my return I sent a wire to the studio of Lütkemayer in Coburg, asking him to come immediately to Leipsic, as I meant to entrust the entire decoration to him in case he were willing to contract for its delivery within the given time.

Then I telegraphed to Wagner, asking him to place his Bayreuth orchestral scores at our disposal that we might have quick copies made; and finally I sent off the following letter:

Leipsic, January 23, 1878.

Honoured Master:

According to our agreement I have the pleasure of sending you the stipulated first instalment of two thousand five hundred marks, and beg you to favour me with your receipt, and return enclosed contract duly signed. I hope soon to have an answer to my request by wire. It goes without saying that we will engage to return the borrowed scores in perfect condition.

The matter that will most interest you, my dear Master, is that I am now firmly convinced I shall be able to keep my word and bring out "Rhinegold" and "The Valkyre" on two consecutive nights. However, I do not pledge myself absolutely until after my interview tomorrow with the scene-painter.

Dr. Förster, who sends his most respectful greetings, seemed extraordinarily pleased at the reopening of our connection, so unfortunately broken off last year.

I gave him your message, telling him to "dry his tears." He says he can't remember having shed any, though I can assure you he nearly did when he got the news (quite out of pure joy, however)!

With deepest respect and devotion,

Angelo Neumann.

Richard Wagner answered by return post:

My dear Sir:

Enclosed please find the contract duly signed. I have ordered my agent to send you at once the scores for orchestra and chorus of the " Rhinegold " and " The Valkyre." They are to be placed at your disposal for purpose of copying—for six months; and I wish to remark that these scores (owing to the deficit after my Bayreuth festival) are no longer my property, but must be obtained through the Royal Opera of Munich.

I can't remember having said anything about Dr. Förster's " tears"—but if he's pleased now, (I) am pleased myself.

Hoping great things of our undertaking,
                    Believe me,
                              Most sincerely yours,
                                        Richard Wagner.
Bayreuth, January 25, 1878.

(Enclosure)

I herewith acknowledge the receipt of two thousand five hundred marks, on this day January 25, 1878.
                                        Richard Wagner.

I now posted off to Berlin to ask Prof. Döpler for his models (at that time still unpublished) and for the benefit of his personal supervision in the costuming of the cast. Through him I then secured the head of the wardrobe department at Bayreuth, a woman of great experience, who had supervised the carrying out of his designs in the performances of 1876. Thanks to Prof. Döpler's recommendation and the keen interest he himself took in our affairs, the work was finished on time. He showed his interest in our success by coming down from Berlin twice to see how the work was going. Our armour, weapons, shields and other properties were made at the same time in the Görsch workshops in Berlin after his designs.

When our cast was published, the Leipsic papers made a great to-do about our having entrusted the rôle of Siegmund to a new and untried member of our staff. Their violent opposition made it seem best to have his name appear, not as one of our company, but as a guest (he having recently been called there to sing a trial engagement). This seemed to pacify the public and called forth nothing further from the critics. Yet I was firmly convinced he was the very one who would soon be the prime favourite with our Leipsic audiences, and so it proved indeed. This was George Lederer, our heroic tenor—a most wonderful artist—and such a triumphant success in the rôle of Siegmund that he became the idol of the public from that day on, and kept his place as one of our principal stars for fully thirteen years.

One shock was still to come that upset my calculations for the moment and nearly made me doubt the possibility of carrying out our programme on time. I had given the rôle of Brunhilda to Olga Parsch, one of our most finished artists, an excellent Ortrud, Eglantine, Leonore, etc. She had been married within the year, and now at this date she came to announce that she herself was expecting a little "Siegfried" and could not possibly sing! There I was—everything ready—but no Brunhilda!

The next day found me on the way to Salzburg, where I had heard of a young woman who was highly recommended. I could not hear her on the stage, as she was not billed to sing for some days. I begged her, however, to sing for me in her own rooms. Result:—a charming voice, a thorough artist, but *not* the Brunhilda I was looking for! In the first place she was far too young. However, I engaged her on the spot as one of the Valkyre. It was Paula Schöller, later of the Royal Opera of Munich.

From Salzburg I went to Vienna, where I heard Marie Widl as Elsa in " Lohengrin." Then I knew that this was my Brunhilda! But how to get her away from Vienna? The next day I had an interview with her at the house of her teacher, Prof. Gänsbacher. She was young, not very well known, and not often asked to sing important rôles, so I found her all eagerness for my plan when I told her she was to sing the Brunhilda.

Next I went to the director of the Royal Opera, Franz Jauner, saying what a great card it would be for his company, as well as for the young artist herself, if he let me have her for a short engagement and she should score a triumph in Leipsic as Brunhilda. After many days of effort and much talk, I finally succeeded in convincing Jauner. He gave the young singer a furlough, in return for which I was pledged to let him have my other soprano, Marie Wilt, to take her place meanwhile.

And presently Marie Widl was in Leipsic, eagerly going over the score, with Josef Sucher at the piano.

While these arrangements were pending with one of his scholars, Prof. Gänsbacher asked me to hear another pupil sing. His extreme youth and ungainly figure were not in the least prepossessing. Not to be rude, however (though I was really pressed for time), I sat down while Prof. Gänsbacher went to the piano and the young man began to sing. Marie Widl, who had noticed my impatience and had guessed the unfavourable impression he had made on me, whispered, "Oh, please, Herr Director, do listen to him—he really sings beautifully!" And on my word I've never regretted it! He sang Rigoletto, Luna, and Wolfram, and I was struck with his marvellous interpretation. As I shall have much to say of him later, I shall simply mention here that I engaged him on the spot. His name was Julius Lieban.

And now another star was to be added to our firmament; so that my trip to Vienna was of vast importance, not only for these special Nibelungen productions but also for the management of the Leipsic opera in general.

Otto Dessoff, formerly conductor of the royal orchestra, director of the Philharmonic concerts, and head of the Vienna Conservatory, and now director of the Frankfort opera, had written me at Leipsic, saying: " My dear friend, I wish to recommend a young musician formerly one of the pupils in my conservatory. At the present moment he is the second violin in the Royal Opera of Vienna. I want you to take notice of him, for he has ambition and, in spite of his youth, a musical knowledge that occasionally strikes me as marvellous." Dessoff was a connoisseur in such matters whose judgment one could not doubt. As I not only prized his opinion as an artist, but valued him as a man and a brother, I took note of the name he mentioned and let the young fellow know of my arrival in Vienna. He came to call, and within the hour I had secured him for our company. The only place vacant was the position of chorus master, which Victor Messler had left on the success of his opera " The Pied Piper of Hamelin."

This position our new candidate kept for only three months, however. From the very first rehearsals I took occasion to write to Dessoff how invaluable I had found his young friend and how deeply grateful I was for his recommendation. The assistance this young musician gave us in our gigantic task (presenting two such complicated works at once) called forth our amazement and delight. It often happened that an orchestra rehearsal was going on in the main hall with Sucher conducting, while we were rehearsing some part of the chorus or the ensemble on the stage at the same time—or *vice versa*. Then it was that our new chorus leader, who took Sucher's place at the piano—and often without opening the score—prompted the singers in each of their rôles word for word, keeping them all up to time. When Sucher finally had so much to do he could no longer conduct the solo or ensemble work, it was a pleasure to see how eagerly all the artists demanded that this young fellow should take his place at the piano.

It is my candid opinion that we owe the triumphant success of our tremendous task as much to the unbending energy of Arthur Nikisch (for that was the young fellow's name) as to the faithful rehearsals of Sucher himself.

The first piece of work that I ever entrusted to his sole direction was the operetta " Jeanne, Jeannette and Jeanneton "—a charming thing, but very little known in Germany. It was given in the old Leipsic theatre, not with our regular orchestra but with the so-called Büchner orchestra. His conducting of the score made a great sensation and I soon gave him other work— Halévy's " Lightning," also in the old theatre and with a strange orchestra—for he was not considered ready for the Gewandhaus orchestra as yet. The success of this latter score was greater even than the first. And now came a momentous event in the career of this young genius, which to the readers of these later days will probably seem utterly incredible.

I had taken my vacation at Aigen near Salzburg, where I have spent many a delightful summer since, and where I am even now writing these memoirs. Before going I had worked out our programme in every detail, leaving a plan as to all rehearsals, etc., with my partner. According to this arrangement Arthur Nikisch was to conduct the performance of " Tannhäuser "—as Josef Sucher, our Wagner conductor, was absent on leave at the same time.

Presently comes a telegram from Dr. Förster, which seems to mean that my vacation must be cut short and I must go back to Leipsic. It was brief but pregnant. " Orchestra refuses to play under Nikisch. Too young! What shall I do? "

Just as I was about to leave for Leipsic an idea struck me and I telegraphed Förster—" Don't postpone ' Tann-

häuser' on any account. Keep to programme, Nikisch
conducting rehearsal to-morrow. Call meeting of orchestra to-day, or to-morrow *before* rehearsal, and show
them clearly they are exceeding their rights in this matter.
If they insist, the result will be on their own heads! After
having explained their rights and their limitations tell
them, if they are still of the same mind, they may hand
in their resignations at the 'Tannhäuser' rehearsal to-
morrow; and at the end of the overture may say whether
they will hold to their decision or not. In case the orchestra should then resign I shall come directly back to
Leipsic."

I now not only had the gratification of knowing that
the orchestra had agreed to my proposition and attended
the rehearsal—though firmly determined to resign after
the overture—but I had the still greater satisfaction of
learning that my confidence had not been misplaced and
that the young artist had scored a triumph! A triumph
indeed that was double, for not only did the conductor
prove his mettle, but the men again proved their dis-
cernment and the matchless spirit of musical enthusiasm
that animated them.

The success of this young leader in that overture was
so unqualified that the musicians themselves begged him
with a storm of cheers and congratulations to continue
the rehearsal at once; and with this performance of
"Tannhäuser" Arthur Nikisch entered the ranks of the
foremost conductors of Germany.

CHAPTER VI

" RHINEGOLD " AND " THE VALKYRE "

WE will go back now to our preparations for the great work. There were many, naturally, who doubted our success. The city was divided into two camps, one noisily belligerent—*against* Wagner and our project; and the other serenely confident—believing in the Master and our triumph. These factions even had their effect upon the singers. I shall never forget how Otto Schelper stopped on the way to his dressing-room at the final rehearsal of " Rhinegold " and said, " Herr Director, are you really in earnest—*are* you going to give ' Rhinegold '? " He could not overcome his impression of a coming defeat. And this was the man who within two days was to celebrate the most glittering triumph in his artistic career and whose Alberich was to be famous from that time on! In spite of these doubts all felt they must do their best. And seldom has so much enthusiasm and heartiness been put into the preparation for a performance. I can never be grateful enough to those whose keen interest and unselfish devotion made it possible for us to achieve our triumph within the given time. First and foremost of these was Otto Schelper, who threw himself soul and body into the two great rôles he gave on two consecutive nights—Alberich and Wotan.

Possibly our very readiness within the fixed time-limit may have tinged the wonder of the bystanders with a slight shade of mistrust. An indescribable tension settled over Leipsic when it was finally announced—" We are ready!

To-morrow, April 25th, the final rehearsal of ' Rhinegold '
—day after to-morrow, the 26th, final rehearsal of ' The
Valkyre '; on the 27th a holiday for all the singers, to be
devoted to the last technical, scenic and mechanical
arrangements."

Such a tension and eager waiting for artistic develop-
ments is only possible where, as is the case in Leipsic, a
cultivated and critical public is called upon to give its
verdict—a public that comprises the parties for and
against, each competent to judge, and each most enthusiastic. When therefore it became known that the final
rehearsals were to take place before a select audience, all
Leipsic was anxious to be there—friend and foe alike;
and although the house was packed to the rafters at
these rehearsals, only a smaller part of those who applied
for cards could be admitted.

And fancy now—in the midst of all this excitement,
word is brought that Hans Richter and Anton Seidl have
arrived! They had surprised me the day before with
the news that the Master had sent them down to Leipsic
to attend our rehearsals, to let him know their opinions
and to make any alterations they might see fit—even to
suspend the performances entirely if necessary.

My famous calm of manner was indeed put to the test
on this occasion. But it survived, and I bore it philo-
sophically.

I welcomed them both with genuine heartiness (Hans
Richter especially, whom I had known in Vienna as a
young fellow of nineteen playing the horn in the orchestra). I took them both on to the stage, showed them our
scenic and mechanical arrangements, and talked things
over generally. Anton Seidl particularly demanded num-
berless alterations in the scenic effects and held to his
points most tenaciously. As it was time for the final
rehearsal I said, " Gentlemen, you see we are about to
hold our dress rehearsal, and we can hardly change now

without endangering the whole performance. I'll make you a proposition: You shall have a box in the centre of the house from which you can watch all our operations. You shall have a table and writing materials placed at your disposal. As we cannot have the rehearsals interrupted, since we have invited a special audience for the occasion, will you be so kind as to jot down everything that strikes you as needing correction, and after the rehearsal we will go over this, point by point, and decide whether your alterations are feasible or not. If my arrangement should be quite inadequate, we have one day of reprieve, and you will have time to send word to the Master; we can then decide upon our course."

The success of these two general rehearsals was so tremendous and the enthusiasm so great that even our friends were surprised. At the close of the second act of " The Valkyre " I had to respond to a storm of calls and appear with Sucher and all our staff of artists, to thank the assembled multitude for their appreciation of the great work. When Richter and Seidl met me afterwards in the office to make their criticisms, it was again Seidl who had a number of alterations to propose and assured me he would have to insist upon them. Thereupon I said, " Gentlemen, if I mean to carry out my contract as to time, the performances will have to take place exactly as you have seen them these two days." Then Hans Richter broke in, saying, " My dear Seidl, what we have seen and heard in these last two days is so superb that the only thing for us is to go directly to the telegraph office and announce to the Master—' Magnificent! Neumann has done wonders!' "

Seidl now agreed to the dictum of his older and more experienced colleague. I mention Hans Richter's manly and positive stand with particular appreciation and thankfulness, as I well knew that both had come to Leipsic in a spirit of distrust; consequently his short but memorable expression of feeling made a deep impression upon me.

A suspension of the performance would have been almost impossible, owing to the tremendous excitement and expectation roused not only in Leipsic but throughout the country. Orders were received from all parts of Germany—Berlin, Breslau, Frankfort, Weimar, Halle, Schwerin, etc. It is sufficient to say that the advance sales for the first series aggregated over forty thousand Marks (ten thousand dollars).

On the 28th and 29th of April, amid the wildest enthusiasm, took place the first two performances of the Trilogy. I had kept my word, given that day in Wahnfried just three months before.

Our cast was as follows:

April 28, 1878

Rhinegold

Wotan......................Hermann Kratze
Donner......................Franz Hyneck
Froh.........................Walter Pielke
Loge...........................Ludwig Bär
Alberich......................Otto Schelper
Mime.....................Frederick Rebling
Fasolt...........................Karl Resz
Fafner.........................Karl Ulbrich
Fricka......................Rosa Bernstein
Freia........................Anna Stürmer
Erda..........................Emma Obrist
Woglinda..................Clara Mohnhaupt
Wellgunda.................Julie von Axelson
Flosshilda....................Paula Löwy

April 29, 1878

The Valkyre

Siegmund	George Lederer
Hunding	Karl Resz
Wotan	Otto Schelper
Sieglinda	Rosa Sucher-Hasselbeck
Brunhilda	Marie Widl
Fricka	Rosa Bernstein
Gerhilda	Julie von Axelson
Ortlinda	Anna Stürmer
Valtraute	Katharina Klafsky
Schwertleite	Paula Löwy
Helmwige	Clara Mohnhaupt
Sigrune	Paula Schöller
Grimgerda	Rosa Caspari
Rossweisse	Emma Christ

The following day we had the pleasure of receiving a congratulatory telegram from the Master:

" All hail the town of Leipsic, belovèd native place,
And hail its great conductor—the bravest of his race! "
Richard Wagner.

At the news of our success Liszt even came over from Weimar and expressed his flattering comments on our performance; and this not only in Leipsic, but he went so far as to write to Wagner himself, from which letter I quote this remarkable passage—" Neumann has managed the affair in *some* respects better even than you did in Bayreuth! "

Following the chronological order, I shall insert here a letter from the Master in answer to a question:

(Hastily,—and with a carbuncle on my leg!)
My dear Director:
But—if I give my power of attorney I surely must

know what I am about?—Naturally Herr Eben has been empowered by my banker, Feustel, to act in this matter in my name.

I congratulate you again most heartily—I've already expressed to you my delight at your whole interpretation of the dramas. I shall write to Schelper soon.

Best of wishes for you and Dr. Förster.

Yours,

Bayreuth, May 9, '78.   Richard Wagner.

Soon after the remarkable success of the two first portions of the " Ring," the idea came to me of giving the work in Berlin. And Wagner too seemed inclined to the plan, as is shown in the following letter from Mme. Cosima:

My dear Herr Neumann:

With the greatest of pleasure I am letting you know of my husband's consent to the Berlin performances. It would please him, however, if you could change a few of the details of your management. Would you consent to employ ballet-master Frickau of Dessau and Anton Seidl, both of whom are fully conversant with my husband's views and would facilitate a better adjustment of the action to the music?

Your performance in Leipsic is said to have been so beautiful that my husband feels he would like to see the few minor alterations made that would perfect it absolutely; whereby the Berlin production would become a model for other stages.

With heartiest congratulations, my dear Herr Neumann, on the success of your plucky venture and the friendliest greetings from my husband, I wish to sign myself yours with deepest respect,

May 14, 1878.   C. Wagner (née Liszt).

P. S. My father has written us of your performance in the most gratifying manner.

Two days later Wagner confirmed his wife's letter with the following:

My dear Director:

By the way, it probably goes without saying I can count—with no further business preliminaries—on my ten per cent. of the gross receipts for the two Berlin performances (even possibly on more, including the subscription seats in the Berlin Opera).

Until the cancelling of the advance deposit of five thousand Marks, however, you are to have half of this (five per cent.) to pay off said account.

Kindly send me word of agreement.

Yours truly,

Richard Wagner.

Bayreuth, May 16, 1878.

This Berlin project was now the subject of our frequent letters, as many difficulties blocked the path. Meanwhile we went on in Leipsic with our preparations for " Siegfried " and " Götterdämmerung," from the beginning of which Wagner tried to induce us to engage Seidl.

Bayreuth, June 21, 1878.

My dear Director:

You will readily understand that I am most keenly interested in the production of my " Nibelungen " dramas in Leipsic, which you are pushing with such vigor. Consequently my dearest wish is to see them absolutely perfect. Believe me when I tell you that no one (be he never so gifted and painstaking) who has not learned all these things thoroughly *here under me* in Bayreuth, can carry out my plans with absolute fidelity.

The news I get from Munich of the last performance of " Siegfried " (and coming from such a source I am forced to believe it) makes me very anxious as to this production.

I must beg you to follow my scenic arrangements in

Bayreuth as closely as possible; with the exception of certain minor details (comparatively trifling errors).

Do not fail to employ Brückner Bros. in Coburg for the decorations and Brandt for the mechanical effects.

Take my advice and engage my young musical director Seidel (sic) for your rehearsals; it will cost you very little. Call Fricke down from Dessau too: he knows my ideas perfectly as to scenic arrangements and has served me well in these matters.

Please observe these details carefully.

With warmest greetings,

Sincerely,

Richard Wagner.

Wagner's wishes could only be carried out in part, since our decorations, as I have said, were already ordered from Lüttkemayer. Fricke was invited to attend as guest of honour and Seidl was immediately appointed as one of our conductors.

Now came the following letter as regards this:

My dear Director:

I should like to know just when you will need Anton Seidel (sic)—that is, when do your rehearsals begin in earnest. Would the end of August be time enough? Let me know directly as to this. When do your performances take place?

Then we can easily arrange the matter of indemnity. Answer at once—for your own sake as well as that of

Your devoted,

Richard Wagner.

June 29, '78.

In our answer we fixed on the last of July for Seidl's arrival. In the meantime other doubts rose in Wagner's mind. We had engaged George Unger at the Master's special request, but this tenor having lost favour during

the London concert tour through his constant refusal to
sing—"on account of indisposition"—Wagner now recommended Jäger for his place.

My dear Director:
I am writing you again to-day, as your definite programme for September has given me much food for
thought.

Since my London experience with Unger (he made me
so much trouble with his laziness and irresponsibility)
I can no longer recommend him to you.

Two years ago he sang both Siegfrieds here three times
in succession; yet in this performance (which he only
undertook out of jealousy of Niemann) he constantly
slighted the rôle of Siegfried in " Götterdämmerung,"
which I never could make him sing with thorough vigour.
My advice to you is, in case you wish your performances
to follow each other in quick succession (in view of the
rôle of Siegfried as well), to take the opportunity I can
offer, and engage a young man who is studying the part of
Siegfried with me—Herr Jäger.

I had overlooked this singer formerly in spite of his
true and sympathetic tenor (and very high too) because
I had only heard him in rôles he was not fitted for. Now
I have changed my opinion. He will make the best Siegfried and Siegmund of all the artists I have ever heard.

At all events he will go with Seidel to Leipsic to finish
his studies there. In case Unger should fail, Jäger would
be on the spot; of course it would be bad policy and extremely detrimental to Unger if it appeared that Jäger
were superseding him.

On the other hand Unger will (or at least he should) be
very glad to have part of the burden of the " Nibelungen "
rôles definitely and amicably taken from his shoulders.
Let them alternate as Siegmund, but be sure and give
Jäger the Siegfried in " Götterdämmerung."

Jäger looks upon this Leipsic engagement as an interim between his studies and his career; consequently his engagement will not be a matter of great expense for you.

Please pay special attention to these arrangements.

With hearty greetings,

Richard Wagner.

Bayreuth, July 5, 1878.

As we had closed our contract with Unger, we could no longer follow this advice. Moreover I could not quite agree with the Master. Later events will prove how correct my apprehensions were. Seidl soon came to Leipsic with the following letter of introduction from Wagner:

"Richard Wagner recommends the honourable board of directors of the Leipsic theatre to pay special attention to the demands of Anton Seidel as to corrections with regard to the ensemble of the tableaux and the music, as he (R. W.) is unable to direct there personally."

At the very first rehearsal Seidl proved his extraordinary talents in this direction, and any one with artistic sympathies could understand his wild desire to be allowed to conduct the works he felt himself so fully master of. He plead with Wagner to insist upon it I should give him the bâton for the "Ring."

One day he handed me the following letter from the Master:

My dear Director:

My young friend Seidel has given me certain information which determines me to urge you to allow him to conduct my "Nibelungen Ring"—that is, to enrol him in your company as leader of the orchestra.

I believe this would be your wisest plan, both for the present and for the future, as I hear that Sucher (for whom I have the highest regard) is about to resign his position in Leipsic.

You must realise my tremendous interest in your " Nibelungen " performances and attribute my interference to this, when I give you the following definite advice as to the casting of the great tenor parts.

Lederer it seems we cannot count on at all. Unger's voice always *was* uncertain, and he is not to be depended upon. You will have the worst sort of a shipwreck with your daring plans if you fail to grasp this providential opportunity of engaging Jäger, who, though young and hardly finished with his training, has an absolute purity of tone and a staying power that will make him invaluable. Only *he* can safely assure the carrying out of your designs.

I tell you this candidly, and I hope you will act promptly upon my advice—*or else* . . . !

It is impossible at the present time for me to direct this work personally. But all my best wishes are with you!

With hearty greetings,

Yours truly,

Richard Wagner.

Bayreuth, July 30, 1878.

To be sure, Sucher, who had conducted " Rhinegold " and " The Valkyre " with signal success, was to leave Leipsic for Hamburg at the end of the year. His wife had already preceded him. But for such a reason as this to relieve him of the baton and let another man conduct " Siegfried " and " Götterdämmerung " would have been a bitter blow indeed.

My answer to Bayreuth could only be that Seidl's appointment could merely *follow* Sucher's resignation— and this conclusion I held to, in spite of the " Or else—! " Jäger's engagement, as well, was not to be considered. Wagner wrote once more concerning this matter:

My dear Director:

I am still waiting vainly for Sucher. In the meantime I wish to repeat, to avoid further misunderstandings: Look out for Unger (I learned to know him in London!) —or else—! *He's* the one I meant by that " or else—! "

Jäger is certainly not ready yet to sing " Götterdäm- merung "—but what does that matter when you are simply looking out for your future productions? At all events you misunderstood me if you thought I meant he should be only an understudy, to be used in case of emergency. On the contrary, I beg you earnestly to cast him at once for Siegfried (number one), for Unger is never to be depended upon for the incessant high A's in the last scene of the first and third acts. These, however, are vital spots in the success of the whole, and I must insist upon their being done brilliantly. Jäger takes them with a most beautiful ease and vigour.

How much better, then, for Unger to attack the " Götter- dämmerung " (where the high notes are not so important) with a fresher voice; and prove that he can do with that rôle what he has hitherto failed to accomplish. Later (if you see fit) they can alternate in both parts. But I think you will have to handle Jäger carefully.

As to the rest—you have my unlimited confidence; but I say again on this point, follow my advice—" or else—! "

Yours devotedly,

Richard Wagner.

Bayreuth, August 12, '78.

As I was not yet ready to decide as to Jäger's engage- ment, I left his last letter unanswered—which seemed to irritate Wagner. For he sent me a message in a letter to my wife (I had previously begged him to send her an autograph for her birthday) and this was the selection he chose for her album!

My dear Madame:

As your husband has not found it worth while to answer my last letter, I will now beg you to enlighten me on the subjects aforesaid.

Yours truly,

Richard Wagner.

—In honour of August 27, 1878.

Then of course I wrote the Master a long letter of explanation so urgent and convincing that he saw our point of view. At least this " Extract from the Album " which now came down from Bayreuth seems to point to a better mood than the last.

(⅛ original size)

CHAPTER VII

" SIEGFRIED " AND " GÖTTERDÄMMERUNG "

THE closer we drew to our colossal task, the more we realised the tremendous difficulties yet to be overcome in this exacting work. For technical and artistic problems of such dimensions had never been put to us before.

It was popularly supposed in those days that the " Ring " must be presented in a theatre built especially for the purpose. Who would have considered it possible that only four years later the writer of these chronicles would tour through half of Europe at the head of the Richard Wagner Opera Company, staging the Trilogy and having in his train a complete staff of artists and a full orchestra? That he would present these gigantic works to all the different nations within the course of a year, giving the foreigners an opportunity to know these operas, for which they might otherwise have waited long in vain.

The rehearsals for the last two dramas of the cycle now went on. The energy and eagerness of our artists grew apace, for they were jealous of the triumphs of " Rhinegold " and " The Valkyre " and worked with a will to outshine their former record.

So at the appointed time the " Ring " was finally performed—to the everlasting triumph of the Leipsic stage and the glorification of the cause of Richard Wagner.

The cast was as follows:

September 21, 1878
Siegfried

Siegfried...................George Unger
Mime......................Fritz Rebling

Wanderer......................Otto Schelper
Alberich......................Julius Lieban
Fafner..........................Karl Resz
Erda........................Rosa Bernstein
Brunhilda......................Marie Wilt
Voice of the Bird...........Bertha Schreiber

September 22, 1878

Götterdämmerung

Siegfried.......................George Unger
Gunther.....................Hermann Kratze
Hagen.........................Otto Schelper
Alberich...................Heinrich Wiegand
Brunhilda.......................Marie Wilt
Gutrune...................Bertha Schreiber
Waltraute...................Rosa Bernstein
First   ⎫   ⎧   Emma Obrist
Second ⎬ Norns...........⎨   Anna Stürmer
Third   ⎭   ⎩ Katharina Klafsky
Woglinda..................Julie von Axelson
Wellgunda...................Marie Kalmann
Flosshilda......................Paula Löwy

The day after the "Götterdämmerung" Richard Wagner wrote:

My dear Director Neumann:
Although at the present writing I have had no news of the last half of my " Nibelungen " cycle, yet I feel compelled to send you a line in order that you and your magnificent staff of artists may have no doubts as to my opinion on the subject. In the first place I want you clearly to understand why I was unable to accept your

invitation, and be present at the performances; it was simply that I could not stand the strain and dreaded the excitement which I knew would carry me away. I could not resist taking the management into my own hands, for I never can be a calm and staid spectator until I am sure that matters are going absolutely to my satisfaction, both musically and as to scenic arrangements.

But this is due to a personal peculiarity of my own rather than to any shadow of a doubt in your perfect ability to conduct these performances. Even though I've not been present, I confess that my confidence in the Leipsic theatre is absolute. The success of your representations which, setting aside the merits of the " Nibelungen Ring," far exceeded the average attendance at our opera, speaks loudly in your behalf.

Truly I have only to look back a few years in my experience and remember how my " Ring " was considered quite impossible for public performances (not only in the existing theatres but even on the special stage I had prepared for the purpose) to view the achievement of the Leipsic theatre with utter amazement.

It would ill become me here and now not to recognise and express my unreserved gratitude to you and Dr. Förster for your enthusiasm and your skill.

I shall ask you to thank your entire staff of artists who have devoted themselves so eagerly to overcoming the uncommon difficulties of my rôles; and furthermore I shall ask you to tell them this one thing for me: that the devotion of the singers to their work surprises me less than the efficiency and pluck of their director; it is this last quality that I so rarely meet among theatrical managers; while on the other hand the artists and singers (though not always their *teachers*) have from the first rallied to my standards in this battle against public opinion.

So may I have a happy entry into my native town, from

which I have been kept so long by the strange circumstances of my musical career!

With deepest respect,

Believe me always,

Yours,

Richard Wagner.

Bayreuth September 23, 1878.

"The strange circumstances" of which the Master speaks, which kept him out of Leipsic, meant the strong trend of opinion in the highest musical circles there. The feeling was, as I have already observed, that the great composer of Bayreuth was not "Gewandhausfähig"— that is, not worthy to be played by their glorious orchestra!

Now that the theatre orchestra plumed itself (and with a certain amount of right) on being fit to play with the Gewandhaus orchestra, it was inevitable that the critical attitude of that conservative body should somewhat permeate our ranks. The more easily too because of the tremendous technical difficulties, quite beyond anything they had been accustomed to, which the rehearsal of the new music demanded.

How carefully I went to work is proved by the fact that I closed the opera house for fully three weeks to give the orchestra and its conductor leisure to study their new rôles.

For this, however, I needed the consent of the board of managers, which was given me by an overwhelming majority. I wish to publish here my grateful recognition to the members of the city council: Dürr, Wagner and Schilling, and particularly to the mayor, Dr. Georgi, as well as his deputy Dr. Tröndlin.

The immensity of the task which confronted our orchestra now caused some friction between them and their manager; particularly since our opponents had spread the rumour that not only the capacity of the orchestra had suffered under the burdens imposed upon them, but their artistic finish was gradually being destroyed. They never lost an opportunity to hold *me* responsible for this, and to attack me publicly and privately.

It was consequently no small satisfaction for Richard Wagner, for his works, for their interpreters, and finally for myself, when on the 1st of January, 1879, a deputation from the orchestra appeared at my door to wish me a Happy New Year and thank me at the same time for my management; acknowledging that the orchestra now stood on a higher artistic and technical plane than ever before.

The following letter from the Master concerns Seidl again:

My dear Director:

I hear you have announced Seidel's (sic) engagement at your theatre to be impossible!

However, I beg you to *make* it possible. This I urge, less in view of Seidel's artistic interests (for I could easily find him another good position) than for the success of the performance of my operas in Leipsic—and I know whereof I speak.

None of the other conductors have such a clear understanding of my tempi, and the harmony between the music and the action.

I have coached Seidel personally, and he will conduct your "Nibelungen" as no other can. If my word for this is not sufficient, then I shall *never* express my opinion to you again!

(Heaven send that Unger hold out—even without his high A's and B's:—my London experience with him was of the worst!)

Excuse the haste of these few lines—it seemed urgent to me.

Always devotedly,

Yours,

Richard Wagner.

Bayreuth, September 27, '78.

Naturally, on Sucher's account we could not agree to an immediate engagement of Seidl. Wagner then placed him in the Royal Opera of Vienna, where, strangely enough, his talents were not recognised and he had no success; they were even doubtful whether he would do for *us!* The Master, however, was justified in his praise of Seidl, and later I too came to prize him as the most wonderful of Wagnerian conductors. His special power lay in the fact that he knew how to make the singers work in harmony with the orchestra. When we began our great Wagner tour, a fairly good orchestra was placed at his disposal. What Seidl succeeded in doing with that orchestra, how their work in the course of that tour grew more and more finished until it finally reached the acme of perfection, is due solely to his wonderful talents. Even with soloists of moderate skill he knew how to urge them on, till they were capable of playing the most exacting passages. Furthermore, he had a clear manner of presenting his facts and a complete understanding of scenic effects.

The following letters explain themselves:

My dear Director Neumann:

Just a little business note for to-day!

Will you kindly remind your treasurer to enclose a statement of the amount still due on your advance payment, when he sends my half of the royalties. The deductions had amounted to more than five thousand Marks at our last reckoning and he is still deducting the percentage, though the September receipts had covered the other five thousand.

My agent is empowered to receive the back payments of the dividends suppressed by this error.

In consideration of the successful outcome of your undertaking I shall waive my claim to a further deposit, as per contract of April 1, 1879. In lieu of which I ask you to turn over my ten per cent. net from now on, in monthly payments, to Mr. Otto Eben, who will be my future agent in these matters.

Were it not for the pressure of business I should have taken up my pen and written to Leipsic in a very different cause to-day. For I feel I owe Dr. Förster the warmest thanks for his most gratifying letter. I hope soon, however, now that this business is settled, to repair my neglect.

And with the best of wishes for you both (please express to Dr. Förster how deeply touched and grateful I am, and that I send him the assurance of my highest regard),

I am yours,

Richard Wagner.

Bayreuth, October 16, '78.

My dear Sir:

In my last letter there was an error, which permit me now to rectify. I told you that Mr. Otto Ebner(sic) would be my business go-between from the month of October of this year. However, he will not fill the position until November 1.

(And Unger!—too bad!)

Warmest greetings.

Yours devotedly,

Richard Wagner.

Bayreuth, October 23, '78.

At the end of December Förster received the letter already alluded to.

Dear Sir and Honoured Friend:

It seems I owe you a good word of recognition for your charming letter announcing the success of the performances of my "Nibelungen Ring" in Leipsic.

I wish to acquit myself of it this very day, and remind you with what delight I received your first proposition to present my Trilogy in Leipsic; and that I myself, after our first contract had fallen through, took up the matter when the time seemed ripe and made a counter-proposition. Everything tends to assure me that my intuition at that time was correct. The most important victory I have ever won is the battle of Leipsic, under your generalship, and with your splendid staff!

What particularly strikes me in the matter is the spirit in which this great undertaking has been pushed to completion by all the participants. My young friend Anton Seidel, who has come up from Vienna to spend Christmas with me, has given us a glowing account of the artistic atmosphere of Leipsic compared with that of Vienna; presenting such a striking contrast that immediately the scale of my sympathies dipped again in favour of my native town.

My every wish would be gratified if you would consent (in pursuance of your course of striving for perfection) to appoint to your vacant position of conductor this young musician, in whom I have more confidence than in any other, and who would surely carry out the traditions of your former record.

Our inimitable colleague Angelo Neumann has practically given his consent, but I live in hopes of a final definite word from him on the subject. I should be sorry—yes, very sorry indeed—if my recommendation in this matter were considered in any way an intrusion; so I take this pleasant occasion, my dear sir, to thank you most earnestly for your last charming as-

surances, and to give you a further opportunity to win
my eternal gratitude.

Depend upon it, my personal regard has not the slightest atom of weight in this recommendation. I know I
am suggesting an occupant of the conductor's chair who
will be of inestimable value to your opera in Leipsic.

Again my warmest thanks—if it can be a question
between us of " thanks " for your candid and generous
congratulations. Keep my friend Angelo (this does not
mean that I mistrust him in the least) steadily up to
his former mark of enthusiasm, and I see before us a
wonderful flourishing of the dramatic arts upon a hitherto
unfruitful ground.

With deepest respect and friendliest greetings, believe
me,

Yours very truly,

Richard Wagner.

Bayreuth, December 27, 1878.

I simply reiterated my former assurance as to Seidl,
and reminded him as well of a favour I had asked,—that
he would come and direct one of his earlier symphonies
at a concert we were about to give for the pension fund
of our orchestra.

Then he wrote:

My dear Director:

You cannot know what pain it gives me to refuse, else
you would have understood my silence.

It will be utterly impossible for me to appear in public
either in Leipsic or elsewhere,—if you ever hear that I
have conducted a public performance you may call me to
account for the same. I have recently been overtaken by
a complaint that forces me to avoid all nervous excitement.

Furthermore I hold it to be the duty of the citizens of
Leipsic themselves to care for the families of those whose

performances have given them so much pleasure. I have too many personal calls upon me to take up outside burdens much as I might like to. Yet I shall not forget to send a contribution to your Benefit.

Please understand how difficult this explanation is for me, and avoid all occasion for it in future.

Yours very devotedly,

Richard Wagner.

Bayreuth, December 31, '78.

The following needs no commentary:

Dear Sir:

I should be exceedingly grateful if you would send me simply a receipt for my signature from now on. Business formalities always worry me and every one else now spares me this trouble.

Kindly excuse,

Yours faithfully,

Richard Wagner.

Bayreuth, January 17, '79.

At last the time came (so ardently desired by Wagner) when Seidl was appointed leader of the orchestra on Sucher's withdrawal. The Master expressed his pleasure at this, and commented at the same time upon our Berlin project, which had suffered some delay.

Dear Sir and valued Associate:

You have delighted me unspeakably by your appointment of Seidl, for I feel sure he will become invaluable in your theatre. You will never regret his appointment as long as you keep to the path you have marked out for yourself. Accept nothing short of absolute perfection and sacrifice everything else for this—and you may be sure that he will abet you most ably.

I regret that your Berlin project was blocked last year. Was the Leipsic board of directors the only hindrance?

If that were so, would there be no way to win them over? If I could be of any assistance let me know.

Don't think I am anxious in this matter to bring pressure to bear upon von Hülsen, for I assure you that without a complete change both in the staff and in the direction of the Berlin theatre, I should never consider allowing the Royal Opera Company of Prussia to produce my "Nibelungen." Still it would interest me to see what could be done in this field—particularly under such unusual circumstances.

With kindest regards to my excellent Dr. Förster,
I am, with heartiest greetings,
Yours truly,
Richard Wagner.
Bayreuth, January 26, 1879.

Our answer confirmed Wagner's question as to the difficulties in the way of our Berlin engagement. The Council of Leipsic exercised a certain control over the movements of the orchestra. However, we had not abandoned the plan, and I was about to leave for Berlin to follow up the matter.

At the same time I wrote for information as to the announced production by the Wagner Society of the first act of "The Valkyre." Was it authorised by the Master?

At which Wagner telegraphed:

Bayreuth, January 29, 1879.
Refused Berlin Society unconditionally.
Richard Wagner.

Then followed a letter:

My dear Director:
Again I hear that you have given up your original plan for the "Nibelungen" performances in Berlin; and in order, no doubt, to avoid insurmountable conflict, have

concluded to take a smaller theatre and give the operas with a different orchestra.

That would be fatal and would necessitate my withdrawing my consent.

I had agreed to the Berlin engagement on the understanding that you were to take your full staff. A weak simulacrum with the Bilsen orchestra, hastily rehearsed for the occasion, would be sheer madness, and not to be considered for a moment.

I beg of you then—if you have any difficulties that necessitate your weakening the quality of your representations—if you cannot get a suitable theatre at Berlin—or if the Council of Leipsic put obstacles in your way with regard to the orchestra—let the matter drop *at all costs,* as I have only taken it up again on the understanding that *your entire cast* should take part; and I felt that such a production—*in a suitable theatre* in Berlin—would be interesting and profitable.

Let me know decisively, and at once please, for I am uneasy at the reports I see in the papers. If these be true, nothing will quiet me but a complete abandonment of the Berlin project!

Best of greetings,
Yours devotedly,
Richard Wagner.

Bayreuth, February 15, '79.

To which I answered:

Leipsic, February 17, 1879.
My Honoured Master:

First a word to ease your mind, my dear sir and honoured patron. Nothing shall be done without you. Not only your *support* but your *complete satisfaction* is absolutely necessary to our Berlin project.

This matter settled, I will now, with your kind attention, proceed with my narrative.

The question of the theatre and the orchestra have held us breathless these last two weeks, and we could come to no conclusion—could not even let you know; for I wished to wait until I had something definite to write. Your letter has interfered with my plan, however, and I must explain the situation lest you worry over the half-truths and lies that you may chance to hear.

Certainly it is doutful whether this orchestra will be allowed to go to Berlin; *doubtful* I say, but not absolutely impossible. In case, however, of its final impossibility, I have communicated with other orchestras—especially the Symphony orchestra of Mannstadt, which Dr. Tappert recommends very highly and considers perfectly capable of interpreting your work satisfactorily under the proper leadership.

As to the theatre, our first choice of course is the Victoria Theatre, but events have proved that a contract with these people will be impossible.

Three other theatres in Berlin have been put at our disposal, whose stage and seating capacity will naturally determine our choice.

The main question before us is: shall we let these obstacles—the possible substitution of a new orchestra and the choice of another theatre—wreck our whole scheme or not? If you answer in the affirmative, naturally it is wrecked; for without you we can expect no successful issue of our plans.

But, my dear Master, I consider it foolish to lay such vital stress on these questions. The main thing is to give this splendid work efficiently and in a suitable spot. As to efficiency,—certainly the Mannstadt orchestra is qualified; and it will be absolutely brilliant when, after some independent rehearsals, our leader takes charge (and this shall be either Seidl or Sucher, just as you choose). We shall reinforce it naturally with a few of our best soloists from the Leipsic orchestra.

Then as to place:—as far as Berlin audiences are concerned (of this I assured myself in my recent visit)—the locality will hardly affect the success of our undertaking. The main thing will be to find a theatre large enough to stage the work and fit our decorations, machinery, etc.

To investigate this I shall leave for Berlin at the end of the week, taking our theatrical inspector with me. I shall not start, however, until I have heard from you.

Naturally, it goes without saying, we shall only go to Berlin in case we find a spot worthy of such a presentation. But as I said, I hardly consider these matters vital.

On general principles, my dear Master, don't give up your first plan—trust me in this!—My honour as an artist is at stake and the reputation of our entire company; and I pledge myself to satisfy your highest expectations, as well in Berlin as heretofore in Leipsic.

Above all, I shall keep you advised as to our course and without your sanction naturally nothing shall be undertaken.

To avoid useless expenditure and delay, I shall beg for an immediate statement of your wishes, and in case I have convinced you, shall expect your general power of attorney to conclude all preparations.

With sincerest respect,
Yours very truly,
Angelo Neumann.

Wagner answered:

Dear Friend and Ally:

I owe you sincerest thanks for your gracious answer and your capable expression of opinion. As to the thing itself, I hope you will agree with me that the Berlin project should only be considered if the plan of last year (which was hindered by the Council of Leipsic) could be carried out now in full. This plan was: for the com-

pany which had made such a brilliant success in Leipsic
to be transported *bodily* to a suitable theatre in Berlin.
This of course included the *entire orchestra*—a decided
factor in the arrangement.

It will be quite impossible to expect the Berlin Symphony orchestra (be it never so good) to play up to the
standard, with only a short time for rehearsals—and
these without the singers: for naturally the singers would
not need these extra rehearsals which, in case they were
required, would be both tedious and expensive for them.

Taking this into consideration—and all in all,—since
only difficulties seem to turn up, it is my settled opinion
that you had better stay calmly in Leipsic and let your
Berlin public come to you.

Please say you agree with me!

Please, *please* remember just this one thing—you must
keep your performances always on the same level of perfection, yes even improve them rather than let them de-
teriorate: then Leipsic will amount to something, and I
shall always take an interest in it.

I consider your plan of alternating the conductors for
these performances a very great mistake. If I could find
even one conductor in all Germany on whose tempo I
could depend with absolute security, I should be willing
to go quietly down to my grave. I hope of course that
Seidel will be that one, but—for Heaven's sake!—don't
think of letting another man take turns with him; the
whole performance would go to pieces if you did.

Best greetings to Dr. Förster! And to you my honoured
benefactor, the hope that you will always graciously be
pleased to remain my friend.

Yours very devotedly,
Richard Wagner.

Bayreuth, February 20, '79.

Now came the following telegrams:

Richard Wagner, Bayreuth:

Letter received. Orchestra gave its consent yesterday. Shall we still abandon project?

Angelo Neumann.

Bayreuth, February 22, 1879.

Director Neumann:

You must decide whether project shall go through. As to suitable stage I'm sorry to give you so much trouble.

Wagner.

Richard Wagner, Bayreuth:

Will you give your consent for Monster Wagner Concert in Berlin March 14th with Wilt, Schelper, Unger, Lederer, Bernstein and Sucher?

Angelo Neumann.

Bayreuth, March 9, 1879.

Director Neumann:

Amazed at your plan for Berlin. The Wagner Society there has my exclusive concert rights. Please withdraw immediately.

Wagner.

Richard Wagner, Bayreuth:

Understand your reasons perfectly. Can we have your permission for the Dessau theatre? Immediate answer necessary.

Angelo Neumann.

Bayreuth, March 10, 1879.

Director Neumann:

Dessau with all my heart,

Wagner.

These telegrams need no further commentary. Now follows in chronological order a letter to Förster, among other things a very valuable expression of the Master's opinion on the subject of the spirit of dramatic art.

My dear Friend and Patron:

This time I must send my receipt to you personally, for I could not trust my thanks for the delightful way in which you have remembered my birthday to your cashier —be he never so faithful! Your trial balance of the box office is the most charming of congratulations; for it assures me that your glad zest in the work has been crowned with success. What you've done willingly, you have done well. That is a great comfort—after risking so much.

But now let me beg of you not to let your anxious endeavours flag—keep your performances not only up to your present standard but—particularly with the first two operas—repair your few unavoidable omissions and improve the finish of the whole.

For I am unalterably of the opinion that dramatic unity is the greatest factor of any performance;—and this can only be reached by perfection of detail. Whosoever, —be he poet or musician,—offers a suitable vehicle for this, will surely succeed; for the public in the long run is attached and held, merely by the show!

Warmest greetings to Neumann and the assurance of my continued devotion.

Yours,

Richard Wagner.

Bayreuth, June 11, 1879.

The following was written after reading a newspaper notice of the probable failure of the "Parsifal" performance of 1881 on account of insurmountable difficulties.

Leipsic, August 13, 1879.

Dear and Honoured Master:

I have just seen a notice about "Parsifal" in Bayreuth which has inspired me with a daring and fascinating idea, the carrying out of which depends entirely upon you;— so I hope and pray you may give your consent.

Now, without further preamble:—what would you think of the notion of our giving " Parsifal " first here in Leipsic?

I ask you this question as it comes to me, and beg you to let me know at once whether I am justified in entertaining a gleam of hope as to such an extraordinary proposition. In case this were true I should of course come to you at once to arrange further particulars in person.

The reason I ask this so promptly is that our contract with the city expires on the 30th of June, 1882, and we have only this interval for our arrangements.

As I see that its production in Bayreuth is now considered doubtful for 1881, I take the liberty of proposing that we give the work for its initial performance in the summer of 1881, or between that time and June 30, 1882—and give it in such a way as to satisfy all your demands. The interest of the whole world will settle on this performance and we shall round out our term of activities here in a triumphant and dignified manner.

With deepest respect and devotion,

Angelo Neumann.

Twelve days later the Master answered:

Dear Sir and Benefactor:

As to the matter of my first presentation of " Parsifal " you have been misinformed. In case this should not take place under my direction in Bayreuth, I am pledged to the Munich opera house for its production, since they have put their staff at my disposal for the performance here.

My only question now is the *time* of my first performance at Bayreuth; as many things have yet to be done— both at home and abroad—in preparation.

At the same time I thank you for your offer, which however hardly surprised me, as you have accustomed me to expect enterprise and initiative from Leipsic.

Now turn your whole attention to the correction and development of the "Nibelungen," whereby you will win my eternal gratitude.

With best of greetings,
Yours most devotedly,
Richard Wagner.

Bayreuth, August 26, '79.

The following letter contains a final recommendation:

My dear Director:

I come to you now with a new recommendation, as much in the interests of the person concerned as for the Leipsic Opera Company. In case you have room for another conductor beside Seidel I beg of you most earnestly to take this young man from Vienna, Felix Mottl, whom I know to be remarkably capable. He is the last one of whom I can say the same; I know no others. His skill and versatility are extraordinary, as I have had ample opportunity of judging. It would give me the highest pleasure to know that your orchestra was directed by two such thorough and capable musicians,—men so lovable and practical as well.

I follow the changes in your company with keenest interest, and hope for great artistic results as soon as you have assembled your final cast.

Kindly remember me to my valued patron Dr. Förster when you see him and believe me,

With devoted greetings,
Yours truly,
Richard Wagner.

Bayreuth, October 10, '79.

On this recommendation Felix Mottl was appointed as third conductor, with Seidl and Nikisch. He came to Leipsic, and at his first performance conducted "The Postilion of Longjumeau." In the meantime the position of Conductor-in-chief of the orchestra at Karlsruhe was left vacant by Dessoff's transfer to Frankfurt, so Mottl was appointed to this position. Naturally he went to Karlsruhe, preferring this more independent post to the narrow field in Leipsic under two other directors.

CHAPTER VIII

PREPARATIONS FOR "TRISTAN"

THE Leipsic theatre had now on its repertoire all the works of Richard Wagner from " Rienzi " to " Götterdämmerung." Only one of his operas was lacking—" Tristan and Isolde "—and it was my unwavering ambition to set this final jewel in our crown. That the Leipsic theatre should be the first to present a complete cycle of the works of Richard Wagner was my definite aim at present. So I constantly recurred to this subject in my letters to the Master, and the rehearsals were to take place under his personal supervision. On the 11th of February, 1880, I wrote to Wagner, who was then in Naples, that I was pushing " Tristan and Isolde" with all my powers and asked if he would consider Therese and Heinrich Vogl the most suitable singers for the rôles, or whether, in case I engaged Jäger, he would consider him fitted for the part. I ended my letter by saying that it was the dearest wish of my heart to close my career in Leipsic with a performance of " Tristan " which would at the same time be a celebration of the Master's return to his native town.

To which he made the following reply:

Naples, February 20, '80.

My dear Director:

I thank you earnestly for your recent friendly letter. As to Jäger I had to write to Bayreuth first. Yesterday Seidel wrote me explaining the matter thoroughly. In the first place I am very much opposed to this habit of billing strangers in the cast, especially " Tristan and Isolde " with these everlasting Vogls (sic)—who do it magnificently to be sure, but who seem to have such a monopoly of it that they stand in the way of the further production of my work. Give "Tristan" of course—but not until you can give it so well that it will redound to your credit. Jäger must eventually be able to manage it: be sure and let him sing both Siegfrieds without interference.

In case you fail to find a suitable Isolde for this summer, it will agree rather better with my plans; for I have been ordered a longer stay here on account of the sea baths and consequently could not be present at Leipsic. I shall gladly give my consent for the performance, however, as soon as conditions seem favourable for our success.

Kindly present my respects to your excellent associate Dr. Förster, and with a hearty greeting to my friend Seidel believe me,

Always devotedly,

Villa Angri, Posilipo.   Richard Wagner.

P. S. If you have any money for me, kindly send the same to my banker Dr. Feustel in Bayreuth, sending the receipt for my signature however here to Naples.

R. W.

I answered this on the 28th of February:

. . . And this it was which engaged my entire attention—the presentation of "Tristan and Isolde" with our own staff!—I have cast it entirely in our Leipsic company, and I beg you now for the rights of production—as I must set about our preparations without delay.

I beg you, dear Master, to trust in Seidl and in me—set aside all your uneasiness, for we pledge ourselves to satisfy you. It is understood that the work shall continue on our own repertoire.

We never received an answer to this letter, but continued our preparations for "Tristan" on the strength of the definite assurances in former letters. Then suddenly

at the end of April came a note to Seidl wherein Wagner
spoke of a former letter having been lost, and declared
our production of " Tristan " to be impossible, as he himself could not conduct the rehearsals, having been ordered
a longer stay in Italy (until December).

" The opera must be re-arranged before it is capable of
production—and this re-arrangement I can trust to no
other hands; not even to yours, my dear Seidl, who have
shown me so clearly in your conduct in this matter that
you have not the faintest understanding of the exigencies
of the case." The Master even threatened us with a
process at law if we failed to carry out his injunctions, so
that I was forced to answer on the 23d of April:

. . . The contents of your interesting letter to director
Seidl surprised me so thoroughly, that I find it difficult to
express myself on the subject.

It was a matter of the greatest pride to us that you
signified your readiness personally to conduct our rehearsals of " Tristan "; but that the performance was conditional upon this, is news to us indeed.

According to my calculations there was nothing now
to prevent our production of " Tristan " in the latter half
of June. Yet after reading the above letter I have naturally crossed the opera from off our repertoire, even though
the greater part of the decorations have been delivered.

Even *you* may possibly be able to imagine that the
manner in which you have seen fit to withdraw your consent has been most deeply grievous to us all—especially
to me! . . .

This letter Wagner answered with the following explanation:

Dear Friend and Ally:
So you want me to spit out my venom again, in spite
of the fact that I thought I had expressed myself clearly

enough last time;—and to tell you the truth these mis-understandings drive me mad!

I do not keep a diary, consequently cannot be exact as to the date of my last letter (about two months ago)— in which I—

First. Advised you not to give " Tristan."

Second. Advised you to give it with your own staff (in which Jäger was to be included)—I reserving the right to arrange it for the Leipsic stage—hence,

Third. As I could not return to Germany before fall— I requested that the matter be postponed.

Hereupon you answered me,—not a word!—as to the main question, that is;—Simply agreed with me that " Tristan " should be given by your own staff (not mentioning Jäger either).

This letter, containing no word as to the postponement, I then sent to Seidl (sic) asking him to clear the matter up. This last unfortunately was lost—and that probably explains why I began to see constant references in the papers to your great summer programme " under my direction."

I will freely admit that this course of action has irri-tated me, as no one but myself can know with what dif-ficulties a performance of " Tristan " would be beset if (as I have already explained to you) the performers were not drilled in their parts by *me personally.*

I hope you will understand my feeling of bitterness. If, however, without my being aware of the fact, these misunderstandings should be due to my mistake, and in case I have no right to be irritated, I beg you on my part to forgive me.

Above all, I hope this will cause no further breach in our usual pleasant relations.

With sincere greetings,
Yours,

Naples, April 24, 1880.   Richard Wagner.

ERNST
SOLL
DIR
KUNST
SEIN
DOCH
HEITER
DAS
LEBEN

ANTON SEIDL
BORN MAY VI
MDCCCL
DIED MARCH XXVIII
MDCCCXCVIII

Bas-relief by Winifred Holt of New York.
Replica commissioned by Herr Direktor Neumann.

Under these circumstances our performance of "Tristan" in June was not to be considered. I dropped the plan and eagerly took up the Berlin project again. Meanwhile Wagner wrote me as follows:

Dear Sir and Patron:

Last month I had from your treasurer the enclosed receipt for royalties of "Rhinegold" and "Valkyre." As I understood that you had given the entire "Nibelungen," including "Siegfried" and "Götterdämmerung," in a most praiseworthy manner and with an auxiliary staff of visiting artists, I have been waiting for an account of the same and the royalties therefrom accruing.

As I have now waited in vain, I take the liberty of asking you concerning the matter; and remain with cordial greetings,

Yours very truly,

Richard Wagner.

Naples, Villa d'Angri, Posollon⌐ (sic), July 16, 1880.

It proved on inquiry that the amount had already been paid to one of Wagner's agents.

Finally I will give a business letter which Mme. Cosima wrote me at her husband's request.

My dear and valued Herr Director:

My husband, who is very busy, has begged me to ask you to send the aforementioned contract directly to Herr Jäger. He also wants me particularly to thank you for your consent in this matter, as he is convinced that you will find no better interpreter of the difficult rôle of Siegfried; especially abroad, where more stress is laid on the personal appearance and the dramatic talent of this most important figure in the "Ring."

If he has asked you a favour as to this contract, my dear Director, it was only because he was pledged to find a permanent engagement for Jäger, where he might hold himself free to sing for you " as guest " in case you wanted him for the " Ring." He would be deeply obliged then if you could give him a favourable answer at once.

My husband thanks you cordially for your kind congratulations, my dear sir, and I add my own best greetings and the assurance of my deepest respect.

C. Wagner.

Friday, August, 7, 1880.

The first production of " Tristan and Isolde " on the Leipsic stage took place in January, 1882, and the cast was all our own. I shall speak of its success later on.

PART III

BERLIN

CHAPTER IX

RICHARD WAGNER AND BOTHO VON HÜLSEN

On the 28th of October, 1880, I was able to give the Master the pleasant assurance that the obstacles in the way of our Berlin project had all been set aside. I had the consent of the Council of Leipsic,—the portals of the Victoria Theatre were open to us, and I had succeeded in gathering together a magnificent cast; as follows:

Brunhilda	Amalia Materna
Sieglinda	Therese Vogl
Loge / Siegmund	Heinrich Vogl
Siegfried	Ferdinand Jäger
Wotan / Hagen	Otto Schelper
Conductor	Anton Seidl
Orchestra	Leipsic-Meiningen (combined)

Early in November Wagner wrote:

Munich, November 2, '80.
My dear Sir:

I heartily approve of your plan,—but only on condition that the performance is carried out absolutely on these lines, and with the corps of singers and musicians you have mentioned. In this matter I must have a binding contract with you, however, as otherwise I should not be justified in refusing my concession to the Hamburg Opera Company, which now demands these rights of production for Berlin next summer.

If you will kindly send me, as soon as possible, the necessary contract,—with a strong prohibitive clause as to your breaking it—I shall write immediately refusing the Hamburg offer and shall give my consent to be present at your first performance in Berlin.

With heartiest greetings,
Yours truly,
Richard Wagner.

Brienner Str., 8c: c/o Fr. Schmid.

I shall quote explanatory passages from my answer of November 3d, giving Wagner the desired assurance.

. . . I stand at the head of an opera company such as the Leipsic theatre has never before assembled. In Mme. Hedwig Reicher-Kindermann and Mme. Sachse-Hofmeister I have two prima donnas of the highest rank. I can assure you—and friend Seidl will corroborate it— that Reicher-Kindermann as Brunhilda in " The Valkyre " goes far ahead of any of her predecessors.

And now you will doubtless ask why I have then engaged Amalia Materna for Berlin, at such tremendous cost? Simply because I wish to be sure of my ground and avoid all experiments in Berlin. Reicher-Kindermann (who is now working up " Siegfried " and " Götterdämmerung ") must sing these rôles first in Leipsic before I can let her appear in them in Berlin.

Mme. Sachse-Hofmeister is out of the question as well— for the present—though she is one of the most brilliant stars of the German stage,—the most stately Elsa, Elizabeth and Senta!

And now I beg you to sign and return this document, as I have all my preparations yet to set on foot. As to certain artistic details I shall have to ask your consent and your advice. It has pleased me unspeakably that you and your gracious wife have given your consent to be present.

And now we will hope that the good Lord will give us his blessing!

Wagner sent the following refusal to Hamburg—addressed to Director Sucher:

My honoured Friend:

Allow me (for to-day) to pass over the greater part of your last letter and explain,—what you probably have not yet heard—that I have just concluded a contract with the Leipsic Opera Company for May of next year, to present the " Nibelungen Ring " at the Victoria Theatre in Berlin. This is the outcome of a project taken up with Neumann two years ago, but hitherto unrealised.

So as to this, M. Pollini's idea came too late. In the meantime—what is to hinder the Hamburg Company from giving a later production in Berlin—say during the summer—as Neumann simply wishes to give a limited number of performances.

For my part I am convinced that a director with a good cast and staff could make a success of a permanent Wagner theatre, or at least a full season's performance of my works in Berlin.

As to the general performances of " Tristan "—I wish, according to promise, to make my first attempt with the Leipsic Company. If this is successful, the work will be at your disposal.

With my respects to your charming wife,

I am very truly yours,

Richard Wagner.

Brienner Str., 8c: II Etage.   Munich, November 4, 1880.

Pollini, however, did not let the matter drop. When the time came to sign the contract with the Victoria Theatre, I learned that the manager, Emil Hahn, had been suddenly called away! What had happened? Pollini had made him the tempting offer, instead of renting me the theatre, to combine with him for a production of Boïto's " Méfistofèle " in May. Hahn went to Hamburg, heard the opera—and then chose that undertaking with its attendant risks rather than the smaller definite rent I was to pay. Hereupon the Master telegraphed to promise his help and backing in case of competition:

Munich, November 9, 1880.

If you mean to carry out the plans attributed to you, you may count on my support: I also promise I shall give no farther concessions that might endanger your enterprise. So then,—go on with all your preparations!

R. Wagner.

So I went on with my work. In spite of Pollini's competition I concluded a contract with the Victoria Theatre for May, 1881. My next step was to engage Heinrich and Therese Vogl, Amalia Materna, and Emil Scaria (whom I had heard in Vienna as Wotan in a very poor production of " Rhinegold "). With greatest care we then turned our attention to the matter of the orchestra.

As soon as our plans had crystallised I considered it my duty to announce them to his Excellency von Hülsen, director of the Royal Opera, with whom I had always been on friendly terms.

In this communication I did not hesitate to express my surprise that a man at the head of the German stage should exhibit such an insurmountable prejudice against the works of such an undeniable genius.

Replying to his comment that " The Valkyre " was the only one fit for the stage, I wrote him such a detailed description of the merits of the other three that he finally said, " I admit you have convinced me. If I can no longer hinder the ' Nibelungen ' performances in Berlin, I should much rather you came to my house than to the Victoria Theatre."

After a long conference in which we went over the details of the cast (this was to be a combination of the Leipsic and Berlin companies) von Hülsen, whose interest in the plan had gradually risen to a fever heat, closed the interview with these memorable words: " And now I must lay this splendid plan before the Kaiser as soon as possible, for we need his august sanction before we can proceed."

In the course of this interview his main fears seemed to be as to the limited stage capacity of the Berlin Opera House. To settle this matter before drawing up the contract, I proposed that Inspector Römer from Leipsic should go over the ground with his theatrical inspector Herr Brandt. But in the meantime von Hülsen wrote:

" His Majesty the Kaiser has nothing against the project. As to the technical details, however, my apprehensions have increased. The conference you proposed (probably Sunday, December 5th) will settle that, however."

Presently came a letter from Wagner sending full powers for the carrying out of the Nibelungen performances in Berlin.

My dear Neumann:

In pursuance of our agreement I herewith send you the exclusive rights for the production of the " Nibelungen Ring " at one of the Berlin theatres, either this summer or in the spring of 1881; as against which you are to assure me a royalty of ten per cent. of the gross receipts, as in the Leipsic performances.

Yours truly,

Richard Wagner.

Bayreuth, November 28, 1880.

This letter in hand, my doubts were at rest until von Hülsen sent me the following:

Berlin, November 29, 1880.

My dear Director:

Saturday, December 4th, from two to five would be the best time for our inspection. The more I think of the technical difficulties the more impossible this performance seems for the Royal Opera House.

Yours sincerely,

von Hülsen.

Other questions now arose beside the technical difficulties. Though we had not committed ourselves with the Master as to any definite theatre, the idea of the Royal Opera House had never been discussed and it seemed hardly fair now to surprise Wagner with a foregone conclusion. He had never considered the Royal Opera, though acknowledging the superiority of its orchestra, and in spite of the fact that artists like Franz Betz, Albert Niemann, Lili Lehmann, and Marianna Brandt were great favourites with him.

So after the Kaiser's consent had made our project certain, I considered it my duty to get the Master's approval. I announced my coming and received the following answer by wire:

Bayreuth, November 27, 1880.

Gladly; only let me know when.

Wagner.

Thereupon I started for Bayreuth and had a long and lively conference with the Master. He absolutely refused to hear of our performance in the Royal Opera House, as he felt himself too deeply injured by von Hülsen's former attitude. In the course of our conversation he called in his wife and told her the purpose of my coming. "What do you think! Neumann wants to give the performances in the Royal Opera House—von Hülsen has '*graciously consented*' to allow the production of the 'Ring'!"

Mme. Wagner, whom I had won over by my arguments, then tried to convert the Master by saying, " Neumann is right; it will be of the greatest importance to give these performances under the patronage of the Kaiser, as will be the case if he agrees to Neumann's demands. As far as the Kaiser is concerned his support is understood, and as far as the artistic perfection of the performance is concerned, Neumann and Seidl will answer for that! " Between us both we finally calmed the Master and got his consent, which he gave by saying, " Very well. *Go* to your Royal Opera House—but without *me!* I shall not come to Berlin." " Then I shan't either," was my answer; whereupon followed a long discussion, which closed by Frau Wagner saying:

" Now, I'll tell you—if Neumann can assure us that everything shall be done according to your ideas, we will agree to go to Berlin. After we get there, if everything has not been done according to your wishes, you can re- fuse to appear! "

So I left them, on the best of terms with the Master and his high-hearted wife, to whose clever interference in our debate I owed the consent with which I now returned to Leipsic to complete our contract with the Royal Opera Company.

My first step was to write von Hülsen as follows:

Leipsic, November 30, 1880.

Your Excellency:

Just returned from Bayreuth to find your valued letter of the 29th. In thanking you for the arranged inspection of December 4th, I wish to ask you frankly—in reference to the close of your letter expressing doubts as to the tech- nical capacity of your stage—whether you still wish to appoint December 5th as the date of our final conference. The problem is of such dimensions—of such artistic, finan- cial and national importance; it is such a tremendous responsibility I am taking upon myself in answering for a

perfection of artistic and technical detail under your pro-
tecting Ægis, that it demands something more than a
hope of success, a sense of duty, and an attention to business on the part of the staff. It needs as well the spirit of
enthusiasm and the sacrifice of individual interests, from
the Commander-in-chief himself down to the meanest
workman in the ranks.

Let me speak frankly now, your Excellency—and I know
you will be too straightforward to misunderstand me. I
very much fear that this personal care, this high enthusiasm would be impossible in the case of your Excellency.
From your former opinions of the "Nibelungen Ring"
your present point of view seems to me quite natural and
easily understood. I can perfectly comprehend too that
when technical and artistic difficulties arise, as they surely
will, your former doubts will return, and you will be
only more firmly convinced that these dramas are unsuitable for the Royal stage. Especially as you will probably
have advisers who will look with enmity upon our plan
but who will be closer to your Excellency's ear than I
myself—a stranger whom you have no special reason to
trust, and whose sanguine plans might easily be made to
appear self-interested.

If that were to be the case, your Excellency—if such
a thing could be even temporarily possible in the course
of our work—our entire preparations would be hampered
and lamed, and our success compromised. Then I should
no longer be able to answer for success either to you
or to the Master, or to the great public of this mighty
German capital.

If then, your Excellency, these difficulties appear to you
as insurmountable (though I have never yet and do not
now consider them so) and you think your faith in the
ultimate success of the work has really been shaken—I
beg you to say so honestly. I shall take it as it is meant,
and never forget your cordial interest in my plan.

We have kept up the thread of our negotiations in other directions. I shall proceed on these lines, and am convinced that we shall not lose your valued interest in this great work, and that you will not entirely withdraw the patronage which I flatter myself your Excellency has extended to us.

With deepest respect I am your Excellency's humble servant,

Angelo Neumann.

Hereupon von Hülsen answered.

Berlin, December 1, 1880.

Dear Sir:

Your yesterday's letter seems to have been inspired by Bayreuth. As to my opinions, you are judging on false premises. I take the liberty of declaring my position.

The fact is, I have confined my investigation of the technical matters of these operas entirely to " The Valkyre " —for which performance I had the Master's consent. About four weeks ago I asked Inspector Brandt for his report, which he handed in some six days since. He has assisted at the Bayreuth performances and knows the technical difficulties of these works as thoroughly as he does the limitations of our opera house. Consequently his report added to my original doubts. However, our inspection of the house and our conference will either disprove this theory, or my doubts will be confirmed and you will be free. Confess now, my dear sir—for in fact it is easy to read between the lines of your letter: The Victoria Theatre suits " The Master " better and you wish to withdraw your offer.

When you make your great demands on me for " lofty enthusiasm "—I fear I can't oblige you with the article; but what I undertake I am ready to carry out to the best of my powers. I leave it completely in your hands whether the inspection shall take place on the 4th and

the conference on the 5th—or whether you will withdraw
entirely. The notices in the papers seem to point to the
latter.

Always with the visor up, my dear Director!

With all due respect,

Yours truly,

von Hülsen.

As I had just obtained the Master's consent for the
" Nibelungen " production in the Royal Opera House, von
Hülsen was wrong in his hypothesis: for it was my firm
conviction, openly expressed, that the Royal Opera was
the best to be had, because of its glorious orchestra.
Therefore I wired von Hülsen: " Your assumption is
wrong. I shall hold to the conference "—and forthwith
started for Berlin with our head machinist Römer, to
inspect the technical capacity of the stage. After our
conference on December 5th I telegraphed Förster—" Conference brilliant victory. Business concluded—subject
to final consent of Kaiser. Hülsen has just been to call.
Discreet silence as yet. Römer arrives to-morrow noon,
I to-morrow night. Keep me informed by wire as to the
news from Wagner."

One further difficulty developed in our conference. I
had to insist that Anton Seidl, whom Wagner had chosen
as our best possible leader, should conduct all the rehearsals and the performances; whereas von Hülsen gave
me to understand that there was a tradition in the Royal
Opera House that the orchestra could only be led by a
conductor under a royal appointment. Finally I proposed that Seidl should have a three months' engagement
at the opera to which von Hülsen agreed—subject always
to his Majesty's approval.

On entering my hotel that night after the theatre I
found a card from the director saying, " Just spoken to
the Kaiser. Seidl's appointment assured."

On the day of our conference von Hülsen had declared

he meant to send the following telegram to Wagner in Bayreuth: " With Angelo Neumann and Anton Seidl as directors, with combination of Royal and Leipsic orchestras, ' Nibelungen ' performances settled, if I get the rights for later productions of ' Valkyre.' "

I begged von Hülsen not to add that last clause and told him Wagner would never answer if he did. As we parted I was under the impression that he had reconsidered. But the next morning as I came into the office he greeted me with the words, " I expect that answer pretty soon." I asked, " What answer? " and he told me he had sent the despatch early that morning. " I'm sorry for that, your Excellency, you shouldn't have done it." I said, " as I told you yesterday, Wagner can't and won't answer! " " He'll *have* to answer," said von Hülsen— then added after a short pause, " Why, it would be an insult! " I asked him if he thought for an instant his own message was any compliment to the Master, containing as it did the assurance that " Rhinegold," " Siegfried " and " Götterdämmerung " were worthless trash.

Then as we returned to the office with the entire technical staff after our inspection of the theatre, von Hülsen greeted me with the words " You were right, the beggar hasn't answered yet. I'll have to inform his gracious Majesty! "

After all the technical details were arranged in our conference, Seidl's appointment confirmed, and our cast determined upon, I took my leave of von Hülsen, who grudgingly gave me permission to return to Leipsic, where my presence was sorely needed. Promising to return in a few days, I left on the 6th of December. The next day the following letters came from Berlin:

Berlin, December 7, 1880.

My dear Director:

Last night I had no opportunity to speak to his Majesty alone, the Empress and the Princess were present and

I could not introduce the subject. I shall hardly be able to manage it before my audience on Friday. In the meanwhile I send you the blank forms for the cast which I wish you would fill out and return. The Berlin papers contained a notice yesterday. The walls have ears!

With sincerest respect,

Yours truly,

v. Hülsen.

P. S. You're right, the beggar *didn't* answer.

Berlin, December 8, 1880.

Dear Sir:

After looking at the programmes I must beg you will consent to let Niemann, Betz and Brandt sing their rôles twice; or I doubt whether they will accept. Voggenhuber too should sing Fricka twice, as it is hardly worth while studying the rôle for one performance.

v. Hülsen.

This we gladly agreed to, but on the 9th of December came the following surprising telegram:

Certain insurmountable obstacles stand in the way of our plan. Definite decision Monday.

v. Hülsen.

December 11th came another:

Sorry to tell you I must withdraw unconditionally. Forgive me, but it can't be helped

v. Hülsen.

I was ready to leave for Berlin to see if personal intervention could smooth matters out. But von Hülsen refused to be interviewed and wired: " No audience to-morrow—my birthday. Sorry can't receive you."

What could have happened? The letter in which von Hülsen explained the matter confirmed my worst doubts.

Berlin, December 11, 1880.

My dear Director:-

Personally this withdrawal is most unpleasant to me in view of your cordial friendliness in the matter. But the two original points of discussion—the " conductor of the orchestra " and the " conduct of the composer " have weighed too heavily in the scale. His gracious Majesty himself has agreed with me emphatically on the latter point. I am honestly sorry, for our useless negotiations have taken up your time, your attention, etc. But I told you in the beginning there were many difficulties in the way, and I consequently kept myself free to withdraw.

One of the Berlin papers—a scurrilous sheet—has published the story, enlarged and embellished (probably hatched out at Landvogt's restaurant), but naturally I shall pay no attention to it.

I shall always remember with pleasure your kind cor-diality.

With greatest of respect, my dear sir,

Yours truly,

v. Hülsen.

CHAPTER X

ORGANISATION AND REORGANISATION

WAGNER'S perfectly natural silence after von Hülsen's telegram had so irritated the latter that he let our carefully arranged plan fall through, practically at the last moment. He represented it to the Kaiser as a matter involving diplomatic difficulties; Wagner would have to be guest of honour at this performance and they already were on rather a strained footing with him—even without this "affront"—so the kindly monarch gave him a free hand to break the contract.

My preparations, which these negotiations with von Hülsen had not interrupted for a moment, were pushed now even more eagerly. The orchestra particularly engaged our attention.

At Christmas time Wagner wired, asking a leave of absence for Seidl.

Bayreuth, December 24, 1880.
Wish you could let Seidel off for an important conference. He is to come and stay with me.

Wagner.

We consented immediately, and Mme. Cosima writes of this and other matters, as follows:

My dear and valued Herr Director:
Accept my heartiest thanks for your friendly congratulations, as well as for the lines you sent on your departure in memory of your hours at Wahnfried. The coming year will bring you a tremendous task; but you have already proved yourself so capable that I can easily wish

you good luck, secure in the thought that my wish will surely be fulfilled.

Seidl is with us, and it was the keenest pleasure both for my husband and myself to hear the good accounts he brought of you.

With thanks again and a friendly greeting from my husband, and with the assurance of my continued regard,

C. Wagner.

Sunday, December 26, 1880.

While Seidl was with Wagner, giving him all the details of the Berlin production, Maurice Strakosch—Patti's celebrated singing teacher—was passing through Leipsic. This experienced man now made me all sorts of tempting propositions for the production of the " Nibelungen Ring " in London. So I wrote the Master, asking for the English rights.   His answer follows:

Bayreuth, December 27, 1880.

Somewhat sudden! Still I've nothing against it, as I rely thoroughly upon your discretion.

Wagner.

Presently, January 3, 1881, came a question from Bayreuth by wire:

On account of other decisions please wire me at once whether you consider Jäger for your foreign tour.

Richard Wagner.

I answered in the affirmative, and was fortunately able to give the Master further information as to our plans on January 8th:

. . . If this communication has been delayed it was because I wanted definite news before writing. And now for business! I have closed the following contract with Strakosch: The London production of the full cycle of the " Nibelungen Ring " is set for June, 1882, and to run

for sixteen nights; following directly on the close of our
Berlin engagement.

Strakosch is to pay four thousand pounds sterling for
each performance of the cycle, a total of sixteen thousand
pounds—This sum represents the fixed returns for our
enterprise—no more, no less, no matter what result.

Your royalties on this basis will be the round sum of
thirty-two thousand Marks for the four cycles—according
to my mind a very much preferable arrangement to the
chance of a larger sum in view of the uncertainty of the
undertaking.

The sum of sixteen thousand pounds is guaranteed in
advance, the same to be deposited at the Bank of England
in my name no later than April 1, 1881—and I am entitled
with no further preliminaries to cne thousand pounds at
the close of each performance. I have seen fit to conclude
this contract with Maurice Strakosch as I know him to be
well informed as to conditions in London (also in America) and thoroughly to be depended upon.

And now, my dear Master, for another matter of no less
importance.

I am considering a new apparatus for the " Nibelungen,"
hoping to improve on the last by experience. I have re-
signed all my other plans for the mission to which I
feel called of spreading the fame of your wonderful works
throughout the musical world—in foreign lands and even
across the seas. I shall feel sure of achieving my task in
triumph if you, our great reformer, will only stand by
me. Then marching under your flag, I shall be proudly
certain of finally reaching my goal.

And now it seems as a first step in the right direction
that I should have a business agreement with you for the
exclusive rights of producing the " Ring " in Berlin, London, Paris, St. Petersburg and America, from January 1,
1882, until December 31, 1883;—you to have ten per cent.
throughout of the gross receipts. As to America particu-

larly, will you give me your opinion? and I need hardly
tell you I am sure to act upon it.

Another question: Can you give me the rights for
" Tannhäuser " and " Lohengrin " in Paris? For I have a
plan: Paris in March and April, 1882, with " Lohengrin "
and " Tannhäuser," then a repetition of the " Nibelungen "
cycle in London and Berlin, crossing to America in September, and finally to end in Paris April, 1883, with the
" Nibelungen."

As to my plans for " Lohengrin " and " Tannhäuser " in
Paris I should like to remark I have already had most
desirable inducements offered me.

Finally let me say I shall make every attempt to settle
the receipts for your earlier works here in the Leipsic
theatre on the royalty basis, to your best possible advantage. I can say candidly I consider this a sacred duty
for I regard your interests and those of your family as
paramount.

You must send me a written request as to this, however,
and then I shall take the matter in hand energetically.

I now concluded a contract with Jäger (at that time
Wagner's favourite singer), engaging him on the spot for
England, Russia and America, on terms which, as Mme.
Cosima remarked, fulfilled all the Master's highest ex-
pectations. The following came from Bayreuth concern-
ing it:

Dear Friend and Ally:

I have nothing to criticise in your plans and propositions, for I recognise that you are the right man for the
enterprise.

For " Parsifal " I shall need my full staff (in July, 1882,
for the rehearsals,—and in September, for the performances) ; and according to your plan they would be free

in June. One or two of your artists I should then need in Bayreuth.

As to America, you know yourself I have until lately strongly agitated the plan of going there in person to make my fortune (I need it badly!).

I have been assured that my presence would be no small attraction; but it was just the strain of this " presence " that I had cause to fear. So I shall gladly let you appear for me and carry out my intentions in a more modest way.

" Tannhäuser " and " Lohengrin " for Paris? Certainly, without reserve!—As to the concessions, I simply have to arrange with my former agents Voltz and Batz, who handled all my earlier works. You have done great things for me and secured me an income which I myself had quite despaired of.

However, as to the Leipsic theatre you can do nothing, I fear, to further my interests; though it is good of you to be so willing to help me to my rights (morally, if not legally, I am certainly entitled to this sum). According to your wish I shall send you a written appeal. So!— Accept my best thanks and continue in health and strength!

Yours most heartily,

Richard Wagner.

Bayreuth, January 10, 1881.

P. S. Here comes the other letter!

R. W.

My dear Director:

I should take it as a great injustice, or at least an oversight, that Leipsic (my native town) should be the only place whose theatre has refused me the percentage due in consequence of the recent unexpected success of my earlier works whose production has filled their treasury for over half a century.

At a time when, banished from Germany, I was glad to get anything, even the most miserable pittance for my

operas, I accepted this so-called "Honorarium" (20
Louis d'or, I believe) for "Tannhäuser," "Lohengrin,"
etc.

It could hardly be considered legal—and certainly
would not be regarded as ethical—to take these purely
personal contracts (the first with Dr. Schmidt, the second
with Herr Wirsing, etc.) as binding, and as giving the
city of Leipsic permanent rights in the works wrung from
me by the force of adverse circumstances.

My agents have only been able to claim legal restitution
where there has been a legal contract; yet in spite of
this every *other* theatre—Vienna, Hanover, Cassel, Wiesbaden—on an equally insecure claim, has recognised my
rights, *purely* from a sense of decency.

It would be most desirable, then, that my native town
should come to the same conclusion and follow their noble
example.

Hence I ask you, who have hitherto worked so well in
my interests, to devote your energies to this cause and
secure me my author's royalties for the earlier operas:
" Rienzi," " The Flying Dutchman," " Tannhäuser,"
" Lohengrin " and " Meistersinger." This would mean a
royalty on each production. I should propose (to be
quite reasonable) a modest five per cent. of the gross
receipts.

With the greatest respect,

Yours very truly,

Richard Wagner.

Bayreuth, January 10, 1881.

The same day came a telegram:

Bayreuth, January 10, 1881.

When do London performances take place?

Wagner.

The next in Wagner's hand deals with the question of
the royalty:

Dear Sir:

Was this for the first or second performance of " The Valkyre"?—Sincerely,

Rich. Wagner.

Bayreuth, January 18, 1881.

They answered from the theatre that I had gone to Munich to arrange a furlough for the Vogls for our Berlin performances and assured the Master at the same time that only one performance of " The Valkyre " had taken place in December. In a letter to Seidl (January 20, 1881) he asked if this report were correct, upon which I answered:

Leipsic, January 28, 1881.

My Honoured Master:

From your letter to friend Seidl I notice you are labouring under a delusion as to " The Valkyre " performances. Your impression may be due to Seidl's mentioning this work in November, when the performance really took place on the 25th of September.

After reading Seidl's letter I have gone through the books and found the following:

For the full cycle you received

June, 1880...................... 1266 Marks

For " The Valkyre ":

September 25....................143.50   "

December 5.....................245.12   "

The proceeds of the performance on the 9th of this month will follow at our January reckoning.

This evidence proves, my dear Master—and I hope you will understand it—that " The Valkyre " was not on our repertoire in November. I shall give " Siegfried " and " Götterdämmerung " in February, and the whole cycle I hope in March.

As regards our foreign undertaking I am strongly urged from London to present the " Ring " in June, 1881. But you yourself must judge of its feasibility. I close definitely in Berlin the 29th of May, to be in London June 6th at the latest—as the season there closes at the end of June. Do you consider this ample time for transporting that huge technical apparatus? And then, moreover, the installation? So I am inclined to postpone London till May, 1882, after our performance in Paris—for which city I ask you now for the exclusive rights of giving " Lohengrin " and " Tannhäuser."

If I have not yet answered your letter with regard to the royalties of your earlier operas, it is because the question now before the board is whether we shall continue our present lease of the theatre. When this main question has been decided I shall bend all my energies to the other matter.

I take this opportunity to explain an error of yours. Herr Batz has undoubtedly served you well in other things,—no one can dispute this; but it is *his* fault that you have failed to receive royalties for your earlier operas: " Rienzi," " The Dutchman," " Tannhäuser," " Lohengrin " and " Meistersinger,"—from the 1st of July, 1876.

Contrary to precedent I have considered it a moral duty, since my appointment to this opera house, to look upon your unofficial contracts with my predecessors as binding—and on my own motion offered your agent Herr Batz a royalty of three per cent. This offer, however, he declined so brusquely that my only resource was to break off negotiations.

My preparations for Berlin are advancing slowly but surely. I hope,—and count on your blessing for the work.

With greatest respect I kiss the hand of Madame Cosima.

Yours very truly,

Angelo Neumann.

Dear Friend and Ally,

The exclusive rights you wish for " Tannhäuser " and " Lohengrin " I must qualify somewhat. You wish to give

your German performances there in the Spring of 1882.
—If the French or Italian performance (particularly of
" Lohengrin ") either in the Grand Opera or the Italian
Opera House should be announced at that time, you would
run the risk of competition. If this production took place
(I have heard as yet of no such, and as the author's rights
are fortunately reserved they would have to apply first to
me) I should lose heavily if I were not free to convey
these rights for next winter. Consider this matter *please*,
and draw up your contract in such a form as to protect
us both. (By the way I don't really believe in any French
or Italian performance in Paris—only I hear rumours of
it continually.)

London seems to me under the circumstances rather
difficult for this year, as you would have to pay heavily for
the rapid transportation of your properties—a payment
that the two thousand pounds per evening would hardly
warrant. It would be a pity if it came to nothing—for
next year would probably be the same.

You wrote me once you meant to remodel the technical
appurtenances of the " Nibelungen " and were considering
some improvements. If you do this,—for Heaven's sake
don't fail to engage Karl Brandt! He did everything
for me here—under my direction—invented *everything!*—
It will be hard to equal and impossible to improve on
him—I am now contracting with him for " Parsifal " and
(in spite of his abrupt ways) count myself most fortunate
to have dealings with such a clever, ingenious and willing
man.

I shall leave the matter of the Leipsic royalties entirely
to you as to time.

I'm sorry, but the matter of the number of " Valkyre "
performances is still puzzling me. Early in December
two friends of mine were present at a very unsuccessful
performance of " The Valkyre " in Leipsic. Bülow was
there as well and spoke of it to Seidl in Meiningen; this

must have been the 5th of December. After Christmas you were good enough to give Seidl a few days' leave to visit me; this certainly was before the beginning of the new year; it was then that Seidl mentioned a later performance which, as he had held more rehearsals, had proved most successful. What should be more natural than that I should take it for granted there were two performances in December? If you *please!* Either Seidl was romancing, or I misunderstood. This is the explanation of my stubbornness in the matter.

As to the rest, may the good Lord keep you in his wise care and may the good work go on!

With warmest greetings,
Yours,

Richard Wagner.

Bayreuth, January 29, 1881.

In my next letter, chiefly about "Lohengrin" and "Tannhäuser" in Paris, the misunderstanding about "The Valkyre" performance was cleared up. Anton Seidl had been correct in his facts, but mistaken as to dates. The very mediocre performance, at which Bülow unfortunately was present, had been on the 25th of September, whereas the other, with which Seidl was so much better pleased, was on the 5th of December. This was finally confirmed by a letter from Bülow to Seidl.

The Master now wrote:

Dear Friend:

I understand now your plan for Paris; it is almost superhuman and I do not hesitate to give you my full confidence in the matter. Send the contract for my signature.

With warmest greetings,
Yours,

Rich. Wagner.

Bayreuth, February 5, 1881.

When I sent the contract I wrote the Master as well that Mr. Gye, manager of the Covent Garden Theatre in London, had announced his arrival in Leipsic on Tuesday. " He is coming with an agent and wants me to give the ' Ring' at Covent Garden. Naturally I shall hear what he has to say, weigh the matter, and then decide upon our best course."

A strong anti-Semitic party in Berlin had loudly proclaimed Wagner as their chief apostle; which moved George Davidsohn (a well-known political writer and friend of Wagner) to write, calling my attention to the risk we ran in our Berlin enterprises if the rumour spread that Wagner was a member of this society. I wrote Mme. Cosima asking if this were true, and received the following reply from Richard Wagner.

Dear Friend and Benefactor :-

Nothing is further from my thoughts than this same " Anti-Semitic " movement; see the Bayreuth papers for my article which will prove this so conclusively that people of *sense* will find it impossible to connect me with the cause.

Nevertheless my advice is :—Give up Berlin and go to London in May and June. How you are to do this of course is your own affair. It would be a pretty thing if your (and *our*) enterprise should be side-tracked by the sort of idiocy that seems to flourish there in Berlin!

Court intrigues and Jewish cabals—what a combination! and nothing but absurd misunderstandings after all! Both of these at once are rather too much I fear for our poor " Nibelungen "!

Believe me,

    —Unconditionally for London—

     —At once!

        Yours devotedly,

             Richard Wagner.

Bayreuth, February 25, 1881.

And I wired back:

Giving up Berlin out of question! London next year. Probably Covent Garden. Letter follows.

Neumann.

Wagner answered immediately:

Bayreuth, February 25, 1881.

Insist on giving up Berlin.   Combine forces on London.

Wagner.

If the Master thought for an instant of giving up Berlin after our contracts had been closed with the Victoria Theatre, the orchestra, the singers, etc., it was only the natural ebullition of a hasty temper. He himself forgot it directly.

On the 25th of February I wrote to Bayreuth:

Dear and Honoured Master:

The abandoning of our Berlin plan is out of the question. It would have too much the appearance of having been put to rout and would discredit us before the world so that London and Paris would fail us as well. " None but the brave shall inherit the earth." So I shall go steadily forward with the great work.

My letter to Mme. Cosima was written from precaution; —*precaution* not timidity, for even courage must be allied with precaution!

As you will soon see, London is on a very different and far more favourable footing than before. They have offered me at Covent Garden a fixed salary for a limited season of German opera—which I naturally refused. The manager, Mr. Gye, invited me to give the " Nibelungen " this year in three matinées and one evening performance —which I also refused. Now, however, negotiations are under way for next year on a most satisfactory basis. If I am to go to Covent Garden I have made it contingent upon four evening performances a week. Furthermore the " Ring " must be billed as the star attraction of the season and included in the subscription list. On these terms I shall undertake it and feel sure the matter can be arranged to the best advantage of us both. When it is settled I shall let you know. I must tell you I have engaged Mme. Hedwig Reicher-Kindermann until 1886.

In the firm conviction that victory will be ours on the field of Berlin, I call you to action! We shall meet again on the ramparts!

Yours,

Angelo Neumann.

In the meantime Strakosch sent me the following wire:

With your consent I can arrange matters perfectly at Covent Garden. Sixteen thousand pounds deposited May 1. Gye stipulates that none of your artists accept a public or a private engagement before July 1st without his consent. Am ready to engage orchestra if feasible. Wire as to cost.

Mme. Cosima then wrote me, two days after her husband's letter, as to the matter of the anti-Semitic agitation in Berlin.

My dear and valued Herr Director:

You will see from my husband's letter that I have appreciated your anxiety for us, and it only remains for me now to thank you for your trust in my judgment— which I do most heartily. We shall try to circulate the counter-rumours you have suggested, but this will be difficult since my husband had absolutely no hand in the agitation. Certainly, however, your anxiety seems justified and we hope this whirlwind of misunderstanding will have blown over before the performances, so that your difficult task may not be made more trying!

I repeat my thanks for your kind thought, my dear Director, and add once more the assurance of my highest regard.

C. Wagner.

February 25, 1881.

On sending another instalment of the royalties we begged for the loan of certain orchestral scores, to which Wagner answered by wire:

Bayreuth, March 12, 1881.

Many thanks. Send score for three parts. Hope to get " Götterdämmerung " from Munich. Will follow.

Wagner.

Anton Seidl had gone to Berlin some time in advance to drill the Symphony Orchestra before our arrival; and I went down one day to inspect some technical details and complete our business arrangements, as well as to investigate the condition of the orchestra and confer with Seidl as to the number of rehearsals needed. I was delighted with his enthusiastic report. " The Master will be more than satisfied with our orchestra! " he said. With this pleasant assurance I returned to Leipsic that same afternoon, and my surprise may be imagined when on my arrival Förster handed me the following telegram: " Victoria Theatre impossible. Not enough orchestra room. Anton Seidl."

I must explain that the orchestra of the Victoria Theatre had been considerably enlarged to accommodate the seventy instruments needed for the " Nibelungen " performance, and in the meantime our rehearsals had taken place in a hall we had hired for the purpose. That evening the first rehearsal had been ordered for the reconstructed theatre, and no sooner had they assembled than the musicians declared the space insufficient and assured the conductor they could never play there. Seidl was beside himself, and helplessly telegraphed for me. I wired back—"Arrive 12.15 to-night. Call orchestra rehearsal at Victoria Theatre 12.30. Will drive direct from station to theatre."

I took the next train back and found Seidl waiting anxiously for me at the dépôt. As we drove through town he gave me the details of the affair. On our arrival I took a seat in the front row, ordered the orchestra to assemble, and asked Seidl to lead off the first few bars. But directly there was a storm of protest. "Impossible!" They tried their bows, sounded a measure, and repeated their first declaration unanimously. From my post of observation I watched the conflict in silence, but presently the cause of the whole trouble dawned on me, and I realised why the violinists had no room to handle their bows. "Gentlemen," I called out, "would you be so good as to lay aside your heavy wraps? I shall ask you all to take off your hats and your overcoats, too." When they had grudgingly complied, I made the further request that they lay aside their mufflers, furs and scarfs, and asked Seidl as well to remove his fur coat. The orchestra received these suggestions with shouts of ironical laughter, but I was firm and very much in earnest, and continued my demands, saying, "I'll show you presently, gentlemen, what I mean. I shall prove to you just how much space seventy winter overcoats, furs, scarfs, umbrellas and sticks can occupy." So I ordered the attendants to stack them all on the orchestra chairs of the front rows in full view. The sight of the actual space they occupied was not without its effect on the men, yet still they were loath to comply with my request, and took their places with shrugs and doubtful smiles.

When all were finally seated I asked Seidl to go on with the rehearsal. He was directing the introduction to "The Valkyre," and this time—lo and behold, it went without a single hitch! At the close the men broke out in a great ringing cheer to which my only response was to point to that heap of overcoats, transferring the honours to them. This made the orchestra laugh most uproariously—not at me this time, however, but at their own lack of common sense.

The day was saved, the performance was again made possible, and I went quietly back to Leipsic, where Förster laughed till he cried at my account of the matter.

CHAPTER XI

THE "NIBELUNGEN" IN BERLIN

As we know, the Master had promised us his presence at the Berlin performance of the "Nibelungen," and it needed no prompting to make him keep his word. Quite of his own accord he wrote me (showing what an interest he took in the matter) :

My dearest Friend and Ally:

How is it going? As my presence at the rehearsals in Berlin must be published and as I see I must keep my promise, I should like to be somewhat prepared and to know when I am expected. When will the final rehearsals take place?—for I'm sure I shall be able to help you somewhat then. Will you kindly send me your definite programme, that I may arrange matters accordingly?

Hoping you are still confident of success and with the best of greetings,

I am,

Yours devotedly,

Richard Wagner.

Bayreuth, March 31, 1881.

Tremendously pleased at this, I set the 30th of April as the date of Wagner's arrival. While our Berlin preparations went on, negotiations were pending with London. Letters were exchanged with Bayreuth, one of which was from Mme. Cosima concerning the appearance of a paper called the *Nibelungen Herald*—containing notices of our performance and a portrait of Wagner by the Berlin artist, Th. Schröter.

138

My dear Director:

My husband wishes me to ask you to settle the following matter with a man of whom he knows nothing. It will be impossible for him to suggest a title for the proposed paper or to permit his portrait to be published, as he wishes to avoid any sort of advertisement—especially in Berlin.

And I am to add another matter; both of which affairs my husband wishes you to consider, and act as you see fit.

Mr. Francke, the impresario, is here on important business, namely the production of " Tristan " and the " Meistersinger " in London for May and June (1882). My husband has advised him to consult with you, as he considers that far from injuring you, these performances might be of service. Francke has already rented Drury Lane. And the way in which he conducted those earlier concerts against tremendous odds is our security for his artistic and practical carrying out of this plan.

Our friend Director Seidl gives my husband the most glowing reports of the Berlin orchestra. When you see him will you assure him that no one has ever said anything against his present orchestra, and that my husband has most pleasant recollections of a tremendous success with these same men in Berlin before they were united into a corporation.

So may a friendly star still shine upon our enterprise! My husband and I greet you, my dear Director, with our heartiest appreciation.

                                        C. Wagner.

To this I answered by wire:

Richard Wagner, Bayreuth.

Please,—no other contracts for London. If my plan should go through (and it will) we must have no competition. Am prepared to take up " Tristan " and " Meis-

tersinger" myself. Wire at once. Berlin splendid, have
engaged Scaria too.

Neumann.

Wagner answered:

Bayreuth, April 9, 1881.

Director Neumann, Leipsic.

Nothing settled, but promised since last May. There
seemed nothing against it as Francke, who knows London
well, declares that rival performances will only add to
interest, and he does not fear competition in his undertaking. Settle this matter with Francke, I can't make it
plain by wire.

Wagner.

I returned:

Richard Wagner, Bayreuth:

Have consulted London authorities, my fears confirmed.
Any competing contract dangerous.

Neumann.

In the course of a few days came the following from
Mme. Wagner:

My dear and valued Director:

My husband asks me to tell you he has received
Francke's contract but has not yet signed it. He wishes
you to weigh the following points and advise him definitely at once:

I. Strakosch is considered financially unsound and they
say the plan failed this year because he had no theatre
and had no money to rent one.

II. It is a question whether Strakosch can even get a
theatre for next year, whereas Hermann Francke already
has his. They say Strakosch has caused some surprise
and great amusement by premature announcements without regard to facts—publishing dates of performances,

theatre where the same were to take place, subscription lists, etc.

III. Many consider it possible, in fact probable, that the performances would not conflict in the least. Just as there are two Italian operas in London there might be two German companies as well.

Richter's name is very popular in England; the concerts which he led and that Herr Francke established were a brilliant success.

My husband begs you now, my dear sir, to give him the facts and figures for your opposition, whereupon if you convert him, he will agree not to sign this other contract as he would not wish to injure your enterprise.

He asks for an immediate answer as he feels bound to Herr Francke not to place any obstacles in his way.

With greetings from my husband, to which I add my best regards.

C. Wagner.

Bayreuth, April 24, 1881.

My answer was to telegraph:

Cosima Wagner, Bayreuth:

Our London plan quite independent of Strakosch. At close of Berlin engagement go directly myself to London via Paris. Further particulars when you come to Berlin. Had offer yesterday of Covent Garden for " Nibelungen " in 1882. Again I urge in both our interests—accept no other contract!

Devotedly,
Neumann.

How well founded was this anxiety will be shown by the course of events. If I remember rightly it was then forty-odd years since any German opera company had ventured to London. When my plan was published von Hülsen surprised me one day with the question: " Neumann, do you know that Pollini is getting jealous of your

Berlin laurels—he's going to run an opposition in London? It seems he's gone into partnership with Hermann Francke, and they mean to give Wagner there when you do." I smiled at the time, because I was then convinced that Wagner would never consent to have two rival companies enter the London field at once. Furthermore Francke had recently offered me his co-operation, which I had naturally refused.

During my visit to Munich, while arranging a leave of absence for Therese and Arthur Vogl in view of our Berlin engagement, I attended a rehearsal of the " Götterdämmerung," and in the final act investigated the details of Brunhilda's celebrated ride into the flames. The horse she used had once been a favourite charger of the Emperor Maximilian; and now in its old age fulfilled this last and only duty with a marvellous intelligence and an almost uncanny instinct for the rôle. It knew its cues perfectly! For, the moment that Brunhilda advanced, saying, " Heya Grane, grüsse den Freund!" it grew restless, champed the bit, and pawed; then at her final call—" Siegfried, selig gilt dir mein Gruss!"—it wheeled rapidly, and galloping straight across the stage, dashed at the blazing funeral pyre. Brunhilda, grasping the mane at the start, leaped to its back on the keen run, and so they rode— apparently into the very heart of the flames! It was wonderfully carried out, and the effect on the audience was simply overwhelming.

I expressed my awe and admiration to Therese Vogl, who assured me that, though she was a skilled rider, she could never carry out that leap with any other mount, for the creature's intelligence was nothing short of marvellous. " You might almost say," she added, " that the animal has an ear for music!" For at each performance of the " Götterdämmerung," precisely at the same bar, without a sign from her and not waiting for her to mount, the horse started on that wild dramatic plunge across the stage!

As this final act of "Götterdämmerung" was of the keenest importance both to myself and to all the artists concerned, I resolved with the Vogls to petition his Majesty Ludwig II., well known for his gracious and en-lightened patronage of the arts, to allow us to take this horse to Berlin for our coming "Nibelungen" cycle. This request was most courteously granted, on condition that he should be suitably lodged in the Royal stables in Ber-lin. Naturally that could only be arranged by application to his Majesty, the Emperor of Germany. Kaiser William I.—always kindly and generous—immediately gave his consent, and arrangements were made for the care-ful handling and housing of the horse in the royal stables.

In the midst of our rehearsals, however, just as we were preparing for his shipment from Munich, came the news of his illness, and finally of his death. Then the problem was to secure another tractable horse for the part. Where could we find a "Grane" to play that dif-ficult rôle, both in "The Valkyre" and the "Götterdäm-merung"? Day after day I hunted through Berlin, but all in vain. As a last resort I was recommended to apply to the Equerry of the Imperial stables (at that time Count Pückler), who received me most graciously, but refused my request most emphatically! He escorted me over the palace, and spared no pains to make up by urbanity for his point-blank refusal. When finally, quite in despair, I appealed to him naïvely, asking who could give me permission to borrow one of the royal horses— without which our performance must inevitably fall through—he answered with a calm candour that I shall never forget, "The only person who could let you have it would be the Kaiser. But I may as well tell you now, that even if he gave his consent, I should certainly refuse mine!" Then he ushered me to the door and bowed me out—and I knew I had failed in my last attempt!

I went to his Excellency, Minister von Schleinitz, with my tale (it was he who had sent me to Count Pückler), and he laughed most immoderately, saying, " Yes, we all know that crotchety old fellow!" He was eighty-four years old—exactly the age of the Emperor. " Let me tell you, I know him so well that I'm sure if you'd gone to him with a letter from me as you wished, he would have received you most ungraciously, for he might have considered I was meddling in his department. We all know his peculiarities and steer clear of them, on account of his age and his services."

My joy and surprise, then, may be imagined when a royal lackey was ushered in some two days later and handed me a note from Count Pückler, saying, " I shall expect you and Madame Vogl this morning between eleven and twelve at the riding-school of the royal stables. We can then pick out a suitable mount. What *could* have happened! I rushed to his Excellency von Schleinitz and told him what an unspeakable relief it was. He laughingly said, " I'll believe you!" Then he told me how it had come about. " Last night the Crown Prince gave a reception, and Pückler was invited. I was telling his Highness your troubles about the horse and your interview with his equerry, and he said, ' Oh yes, I know how impossible he is to manage! I'm sure if *I* said anything to the old fellow about it now, he'd be as obstinate as possible. But wait a bit—we'll see if I can't " bridle that horse" for Neumann by some hook or crook at supper to-night. I'll see to it directly that the old fellow is put near me at the table. But whatever you do, don't say a word to him about the horse!' " So at supper the Crown Prince had turned casually to von Schleinitz and said loud enough for every one to hear—" I'm awfully vexed at what you tell me about Neumann and his unsuccessful search for a 'Grane.' If the 'Nibelungen' performances really fall through because they can't find a suitable horse it will be a keen disappointment to us all. Every one of us—the whole family—has taken such a tremendous interest in this performance, and we're looking forward to it with such anticipation." Then he immediately turned the subject, and presently drew Count Pücker on into a long conversation, but with no further mention of the horse or of the opera!

When I thanked his Excellency for his providential intervention he said, "The Crown Prince will be so delighted when I tell him that ' the horse has been bridled' at last!"

Promptly at the given hour I arrived at the riding school with the Vogls—both excellent riders—and found the court equerry waiting for us. Here the prima-donna tried twelve or fifteen horses without being able to find one with whom she could manage that daring leap into the flames. However, we might still count ourselves fortunate to find a horse that was suitable in other respects. So the Berliners had to thank the quick wits and the genial readiness of their Crown Prince (later the Emperor Frederick) for their enjoyment of the "Nibelungen" cycle.

Early on the morning of April 30th Richard Wagner and his wife arrived at the Hotel Royal, having come to Berlin to assist at the last rehearsals. When I appeared at the hotel Wagner met me with a reproachful face—"You disappointed us shamefully! I thought you'd come on to Berlin with us, and looked for you at Leipsic." "But, Master," I said, "I had to be on the spot to hold the first rehearsals, that things might be in shape as far as possible by the time you arrived. Now I shall hand you over my staff of office, and your forces are waiting eagerly to be marshalled in battle array!"

After we had arranged a few preliminary details, the Master said suddenly to my great surprise, "Tell me, Neumann—as I drove in, I saw Scaria's name on the posters; what are you doing with a lout like that?" I answered, "Schelper sings Wotan in the second and fourth cycles, and Scaria in the first and third." "But why have him sing at all?" said Wagner. "How did you happen to think of letting that fellow sing here?" "But, Master, I wired you my plans. What makes you say that of Scaria?" "My dear fellow, he won't do at all! No, no, no, no! Give him his price and send him off." "That's utterly impossible, Master. I can't and won't do a thing like that. To announce to Scaria that Richard Wagner absolutely refuses to allow him to appear, will simply mean his ruin as an artist. And more than all that, we should be doing ourselves out of the greatest and most finished Wotan that ever sang the rôle!" "I can't see, man, how you happened to engage him!" "Because I heard him sing the part." "Where?" "In Vienna." "And you liked him?" "I not only liked him, I was enchanted with him—and I predict you will be too." "No, no, never! I tell you plainly—either you dismiss him at once,—or else *I leave.*" When I realised how utterly useless it was to try and overcome his prejudice, I made him the following proposition: "Master, it's absolutely impossible for us to condemn Scaria, or to dismiss him, without a hearing. Furthermore, if you leave Berlin before our performance, it will be a deathblow to this entire enterprise. We're to have a rehearsal of 'The Valkyre' this morning. Will you and your wife come with me now, but not to appear on the scene. Simply sit in a box and listen to Scaria. If he offends you as much as you seem to think, you may leave Berlin as soon as you like after the rehearsal."

Then Mme. Cosima added, "Listen! Neumann's proposition sounds reasonable. We'll meet him half-way!

We'll *hear* Scaria at least, and then you can give your verdict."

And so it was decided. The Master, with his wife, Countess Schleinitz, and Daniela von Bülow, took their places in the lower left-hand proscenium box. He asked me to sit in the next box beside him that he might criticise the performance as the occasion arose.

I had ordered the rehearsal to open with the second act of "The Valkyre," and as Scaria turned to leave the stage after his great scene in that act, Wagner sprang from his seat, flew down the steps, and tore on to the stage at such a frantic pace that I could scarcely follow; shouting, "Where is he? Where is Scaria? That was glorious! Man alive, where did you get that voice!" and catching the artist about the neck, he hugged him enthusiastically, kissing him and saying, "*But* you did that well—that was well done!"

From now on he took the direction of the rehearsal himself. He showed Sieglinda how to lay her head on Siegmund's lap and fall asleep. He insisted that Brunhilda, when she comes to announce the doom, must throw her right arm about the horse's neck, holding the shield and spear in her left. The fight between Hunding and Siegmund was not at all to his liking. Scarcely had they begun their sword-play when we all had a fright that made our hearts stop beating! Suddenly with the agility of an acrobat, Wagner swung himself up on to the railing and ran lightly along the high narrow ledge of the proscenium box, balancing skilfully, but too full of eager impatience to think of reaching the stage by the regular way.

Here he snatched up Siegmund's sword, and finished the fight with Hunding on the heights at the back of the stage. Then, at the given signal, he fell with a crash close by the edge of a precipice; his head brought clearly into relief by the rise of the hill behind, and his arm hanging limp over the edge of the abyss in full view of the audience. All this with a certainty and a dashing agility that a man of twenty-five might have envied.

Under his direction the scene between Hunding and Siegmund was repeated over and again until it finally went to please him. Then at length he ordered Wotan to thunder out his deadly "Go!" breaking it off short and sharp to let the clang of weapons and the crash of Hunding's fall be heard with more distinctness.

The following rehearsal—"Rhinegold"—Wagner conducted almost entirely. Then in "Siegfried" we had a scene that rivalled the one with Scaria. The Master had recommended his Bayreuth singer Schlosser for the part of Mime; but I had decided to give the rôle to Julius Lieban, an ideal Mime and a member of our Leipsic cast. At the close of the first act Wagner, who had never seen this young singer before, could hardly contain himself. With his characteristic dash he flew on to the stage, and stormed up the steps, passing Lieban, whom he did not recognise, in his hurry. The singer himself, young and inexperienced, was hurrying down the stairs, anxious to hear the Master's verdict. As he passed him by I called to Wagner, "Master, that is our Lieban," but not recognising the name he hurried on, still looking for the artist; till I finally cried, "Master, that is our Mime!" Then he stopped suddenly, wheeled, and rushed at Lieban, who stood there, trembling at the thought of meeting Richard Wagner. The Master threw his arms about him in an ecstasy of enthusiasm, and when he exclaimed, "You did that wonderfully—it was simply matchless!" the young fellow fairly cried for joy and kissed his hand in reverence and gratitude.

In the third act we had a most exciting incident. In the duet between Siegfried and Brunhilda we had introduced an effect that Seidl had formerly arranged under Wagner's direction. The latter seemed not to have

noticed, until Vogl called his attention to it as something
unusual and disturbing. Immediately Wagner began to
scold, denouncing the rendering of the scene. Mme.
Materna, who felt that Vogl had criticised her conception
of the rôle, and considered it an intrigue on his part
against her as a rival of his wife, immediately burst into
tears. It was a tragi-comic scene. On the stage the
weeping prima-donna,—in the box the angry author.
My first efforts were directed toward soothing Wagner,
which I did by reminding him that he himself had
originated that passage and approved of its introduction
years ago. Finally, when that tempest was laid, he in
turn helped me restore the injured artist—patting her
gently on the back and comforting her with honeyed
words of praise.

That same evening we had ordered the dress rehearsal
of "The Valkyre." It was to begin at six, and in order
that everything should be in readiness before the Master
came, I myself arrived at five. There I was greeted by
Major von Witte, inspector general of the fire commission, who informed me that the donkey-engine we had
set up in the court to furnish our clouds of steam, was
contrary to the fire ordinance and would have to be re-
moved. The effect this announcement had upon me may
be imagined. The final rehearsal in the presence of the
Master was to begin in just an hour; and we had no steam
for the fire scene. Nothing I could say or do moved
Major von Witte. He was cordial, sympathetic, and
deeply interested in the performance, yet as he said,
" Herr Director, I am a Prussian officer, and my duty
comes first of all."

In the meantime several of the artists had arrived,
among them Heinrich Vogl—the Siegmund of that night.
When he saw me coming from the theatre with Major von
Witte he came toward us calling out, " I say, this is a
pretty mess. There's no steam, I hear." Then he added,

pointing to the adjacent building, " I'll tell you what— if you say the word I can fix it for you next door. We'll have all we need in a couple of hours." " The devil! Where from? "—" That's a distillery," he continued, and told us he had one of his own on his estates. " They've steam enough in there for anything, and all we'll have to do is to get permission to lay a pipe in here and connect it with our stage." Then Major Witte declared, if we could arrange it with the owners, there would be no further interference from the fire department,—and I forthwith flew rather than walked into that distillery and ran up against the son of the proprietor.

I told him my troubles breathlessly, and he set my mind at rest by saying, " I'm somewhat of a Wagner enthusiast myself and if there's anything we can possibly do to help, you may rest assured it shall be done. Only I must speak to my father about it first, though I've not the least doubt that he'll be glad to help you." After a whole night's work we broke through the wall, laid our pipe, and our troubles were finally over. Indeed I may say I've never seen better or more convincing steam in any other performance of the " Nibelungen."

Herr Kahlbaum, the owner of the distillery, would not hear of any reimbursement, and even put his workmen at our disposal for the necessary connections. He asked, however, as a special favour that he might meet Richard Wagner, and the manner of his introduction was truly remarkable. I had told him to come behind the scenes, and he arrived just at the particular moment when Wagner was trying to take me aside to discuss some important technical details. Herr Kahlbaum shyly persisted in following us up, which made Wagner so nervous that he flew at the poor man in a whirl of fury, saying, " Who the devil are you? Can't we have a moment's peace to ourselves? " Naturally I immediately explained the situation and introduced him as our saviour in the late

difficulty; then Wagner soon calmed down and greeted
him with the utmost friendliness and gratitude.

In speaking of these days of rehearsal I must add that
Wagner was absolutely and completely satisfied with
Seidl, making only occasional minor criticisms, and expressing the heartiest approval in warm and flattering
terms.

His little admonition to the musicians was most characteristic and worthy to be noted by many an orchestra of
this day.   " Gentlemen," he said,—" I *beg* of you not to
take my ' fortissimo' too seriously!   Where you see ' ff,'
make a ' fp ' of it, and for ' piano,' play ' pianissimo.'
Remember how many of you there are down there, against
the one poor single human throat up here alone on the
stage! "

At the close of the cycle, on the 4th of May, he made
us a short address full of the heartiest commendation.
To me he spoke in praise and admiring recognition of all
I had accomplished;—then turning to Seidl he expressed
his enthusiastic and unqualified approval both of his conducting and his orchestra, thanking them all for their
patient efforts.

And now I must tell of the first great performance of
the " Nibelungen Ring " in Berlin—days of excitement
such as can hardly be appreciated in these later times.
Even the drive to the theatre was a spectacle in itself.
The whole length of Unter den Linden from the Imperial palace down was lined with people closely packed,
and patrolled by mounted police under the supervision of
Inspector General von Madai himself.   The windows were
black with heads watching the parade, and even the trees
were filled with curious observers.   Members of the court
were greeted with enthusiastic cheers, and the tumult
reached its height when Wagner appeared driving up the
line, his wife beside him and the Countess von Schleinitz
in their carriage.

It was a glittering audience that packed the theatre to its topmost gallery that night, apparently the rendez-vous of the entire court and all Berlin society. Notable among the audience were H. I. M. the Emperor Frederick (at that time the Crown Prince) and his wife, the Princess Victoria; Prince William, the present Emperor, and his wife, Princess Frederick Karl; the Crown Prince of Meiningen, with his wife; Count von Eulenberg (the Lord Chamberlain), the Counts Dankelmann and Perponcher, with their wives; Princess Bismarck, Countess William Bismarck, Count and Countess Rantzau, Prince Radzi-will, Prince Hohenlohe, Prince Ratibor, secretaries von Puttkammer, Delbrück and Count Rodern.

Reporters were there from the Berlin papers, and correspondents of all the leading foreign journals. The artistic world was represented by Albert Niemann and his wife, Josef Joachim, Frederick Haase, Paul Lindau, Frederick Spielhagen, Oscar Blumenthal, Julius Stetten-heim, Fritz Mauthner and many others.

As Wagner entered his box (the 5th on the line to the right) the audience rose and greeted him with a tempest of enthusiasm. He was accompanied by his wife, von Bülow's daughter Daniela, and Count Wolkenstein, the Austrian attaché at the court of Saxony. In the adjoining box sat Count Schleinitz and his wife. Among the invited guests I noted especially Director-general von Hülsen of the Royal Opera House.

The reception was most flattering, Wagner himself applauding the artists with enthusiastic delight. The audience, however, refused to be satisfied till the Master, after repeated and insistent calls, was finally induced to appear before the curtain. In a black frock coat with a light grey summer overcoat, his silk hat in his hand, he stood there beside Fricka, Wotan and Loge. Then the orchestra blew a fanfare—and the whole house rose and cheered, with scarves waving from every balcony. Finally

the Master stepped to the footlights and in a firm voice,
yet deep with emotion, made the following little speech:
" If this reception is an expression of thanks on your
part, I shall accept it—not for myself, but for these artists,
who have been brought here from far and near to interpret my work to-night.   They have so completely expressed my thoughts, and have incorporated themselves
so thoroughly into my style, that I myself can only add
my thanks to yours.   And this I do with all my heart,
and close with the wish that this work of mine, so happily
inaugurated this night, may complete its course as favourably, and charm you to the end.

" If the work has pleased you, its success is due not to
the splendour of its presentation, but solely to the incomparable magic of art itself."

At the close of this simple, earnest speech the applause
broke out in renewed thunders, and as they left the theatre the Master had a tremendous and most touching
ovation.

So ended the first day of the " Nibelungen " in Berlin,
which proved indeed a glorious victory ; converting even
that stiff-necked sceptic von Hülsen, who told me the
following day, " Now that I've seen what a success your
' Rhinegold ' is—a thing I should never have believed
possible—I no longer doubt that the whole ' Ring ' will
be well received."

In point of fact, " The Valkyre " was even more of a triumph.   Wagner on that occasion did not appear before
the curtain, but rose in his box and received the wild
applause of the public,—transferring it with a gesture of
recognition to the artists on the stage.

Between " The Valkyre " and " Siegfried " came an
evening's intermission, which we spent in a last thorough
rehearsal of the " Gotterdämmerung."   Wagner, quite exhausted by the performances and the constant rehearsals,
went to bed and sent me the following note with regard to

our somewhat inadequate arrangements for the Rhine maidens' swimming apparatus.

My Valued Friend:

As I told Feustel,* it is not a matter of the machinery but of its covering. The heavy, trailing draperies in front give an effect of massive clumsiness. They should be more transparent. See to it then, please, that this change is made. The lower part should be more solid and the upper lighter and more transparent, rising above the rocks in the foreground.

I'm not allowed to go out to-day, but should be glad to see Seidl.

Best of greetings,

Yours,

R. Wagner.

[May 7, 1881.]

Before our rehearsal I called on the Master and was received by Mme. Cosima. I told her it was doubly unfortunate that Wagner was not able to attend to-day,— first of all since we needed his advice, but more especially because I was anxious about Jäger. He had come to the first rehearsal that morning hardly recovered from his late illness, and had sung most horribly off the key. I had come to beg that he should not be allowed to sing until the second cycle. Mme. Cosima undertook to lay the case diplomatically before her husband, but he sprang from his bed and came out in great excitement, saying, " What's this?—You've always had a grudge against Jäger; I've noticed that for some time! " So I realised there was nothing to do but to let him sing.

In that performance of " Siegfried " my worst fears were justified. The first act fell utterly flat, and at the close of the second a deputation of the Wagner Society

* His banker in Bayreuth, who had suggested sending there for the machinery for this scene.

waited on me to ask that I should let Vogl sing the following night in " Götterdämmerung." Then Wagner came dashing behind the scenes in a frenzy—" What!—*That* fellow thinks he's a singer?" he shrieked.   " He's only fit to keep a tavern!" and then he ordered, " Let Vogl sing tomorrow!"   " But, Master," I said, " I warned you yesterday.   It's too late now to change.   Since Jäger sang Siegfried to-night, he must sing it to-morrow.   He can't spoil that performance so completely, for he is never alone on the stage then." And so the unlucky artist had to sing the " Götterdämmerung " against Wagner's expressed wishes.   I must admit he did far better that second night, but the following day he left us.   Wagner later forgave him and forgot his faults in consideration of his magnificent stage presence and his really wonderful acting.   He was even called to Bayreuth at one time to play the rôle of Parsifal.

I shall add here a letter I received at this time.

My dear Director:
Might I ask you to deposit my proportion of the receipts for the cycle as they come in, with Platho and Wolff, Bankers, No. 6 Breitestrasse, Berlin.   It will amount to the same thing as sending it to Feustel in Bayreuth, and will be more convenient for a certain purpose—with regard to that letter you know.
           With hearty greetings,
                  Yours devotedly,
                        Richard Wagner.
May 9, 1881.
P. S. Send the vouchers to me—in Bayreuth.

On the 9th of May we rounded out the triumphs of our first cycle with the " Götterdämmerung." The Crown Prince had sent his chamberlain, Count Eulenberg, to Wagner, asking whether he would accept an invitation to appear in the royal box at the close of the second act.

But the Master answered that he was not very well, and begged that the honour should not be pressed upon him. At the same time I myself was invited to an audience with his Highness, who had retired with his suite to the little refreshment room attached to the royal box. He received me most graciously. "Pardon me, Herr Director, you find us here at supper," said he, as he presented me to his family. "My wife, the Crown Princess,—my son, Prince William—the Crown Prince and Princess of Meiningen.

"Now let me congratulate you on the success of this stupendous work. I hear you're planning to let my connections over the water hear the 'Nibelungen' next winter; you're going to London, aren't you? I'm quite curious to know how they'll receive it there." He then touched upon the incident of the donkey-engine which had been forbidden by the police, and praised Vogl's resourcefulness in getting us a steam connection. Then finally he said, "In case you do follow out your plan and go to London, don't forget I'll gladly do anything for you that I can. I should very much like to help your enterprise." This promise he afterwards made good in the most signal manner, as I shall describe later.

During the scene-shifting for the third act Wagner came behind to see me, and expressed his unqualified satisfaction with what we had done, suggesting several minor alterations which had just occurred to him. I then took him to his box and was about to settle into my own orchestra chair, when a vague feeling of uneasiness impelled me to go back on to the stage again. I fought it down at first,—for the whole executive staff was there, the well-drilled corps of attendants, and my experienced inspectors and stage manager. Why not give myself up for once to the complete enjoyment of that glorious final act? and yet my inner consciousness urged me to go. "Just this very night, when so much depends upon it,

why not follow out your invariable custom and see that
all is well?" Finally I obeyed my instinct and went behind once more. "All in order?" "Everything!" came
the prompt response.

As Mme. Materna was not a horsewoman like Therese
Vogl, we had arranged the leap into the flames as it is
now carried out on most stages—that is, Brunhilda was
to lead Grane quickly off into the wings, and there a rider
in her identical costume should spring to the horse's back
and dash across the stage into the flames.

My next question was, " Is the false Brunhilda ready?"
Some one answered, "All ready, sir!" and I looked up
to catch sight of a Brunhilda—with long unkempt, grey
shaggy hair, and a full and flowing beard! And just outside the second was approaching when the real Brunhilda
was to dash into the wings with Grane. "What! _You're_
the man who's to ride the horse into the fire?" "Yes,
sir!" was the answer. But there was no time now to
parley, for just then I could hear Mme. Materna beginning, "Siegfried—selig grüsst dich dein Weib"—as she
started for the wings. I flew for the man, clutched at
his beard, and snatched the wig from off his head!
Then, just as I had swathed him in his long black veil,
we heard his cue—he swung himself up onto the horse,
and I sank back almost fainting against the side walls
of the stage! In just those few seconds I had been able
to save the closing scene of the first " Nibelungen " performance in Berlin from utter shipwreck.

And the explanation? The Countess Schleinitz had
begged us to engage a friseur who had been employed at
Bayreuth in 1876 and who claimed to understand " everything"! To tell the truth, his specialty had been chorus
make-up, and chancing to come across our rider in the
costume of Brunhilda, he took the opportunity to finish
him according to his ideas—believing him to be one of the
chorus. So in his eager zeal he furnished the brawny

soldier with a suitable wig and beard. Our docile rider, not knowing what it was all about, made no resistance— and inspectors and stage manager were all too busy to pay any attention beyond seeing that the man was there.

Our stage life is made up of countless unforeseen incidents of that sort, and the most carefully studied performance can be wrecked by the merest trifle. Franz Dingelstedt, from whom I learned so much, used to say quite aptly, " Each perfect performance is an aggregation of two hundred unnoticeable trifles—yet the omission of a single one of these can mar the whole! "

At the close of the " Götterdämmerung " the audience broke out into the wildest tumult of applause and refused to be satisfied till Wagner, pale and overcome with emotion, appeared on the stage to make a farewell speech.

" I should indeed be lacking in appreciation," said the Master, " if I failed to speak the few words that come to me at this moment.

" . . . I thank you, my friends [to the singers]—I thank you, my kind patrons [to the public]—for your applause, which I take as a sign of your hearty approbation! I am both delighted and astonished at your unqualified approval,—for in my first conception of this work I had in mind only its performance before a small and select circle of friends. Out of that grew my undertaking at Bayreuth. I had no thought of presenting it to the critical and pampered public of a large metropolis, whose audiences are accustomed to another order of art, and whose main object is merely to be amused.

" Even in Bayreuth I have been astonished at the general comprehension of my work, for I realise it to be both strange and unusual. Still more I am amazed at its reception here.

" I promised my presence and my assistance to this daring man who, with his band of finished artists, has undertaken to present these works to so critical a capital as

Berlin. We have brought to our enterprise the greatest
singers of the world, but they too have been trained in another school of art, and I marvel at the manner in which
they have grasped the meaning of my ideas.

"First of all let me thank the indomitable man who
stands at the head of this undertaking—Come out here,
Neumann—Let me thank you from the depths of my heart!
And then that other young man, M. Seidl" (here the
Master gave his other hand to Seidl)—"I must thank
him for all the wonders he has accomplished. And all
my artists as well. You have given me such an inef-
fable pleasure. I must thank you all—*each and all!*"

Then the Master accepted a testimonial that was
presented in my name and in the name of the entire company. It was a richly chased bowl made in the Wagner
workshops after a design by H. Zacharias (silversmith to
his Majesty). From among the flowers with which the
bowl was filled rose a slender pedestal on whose four sides
were engraved the dedication and the names of all the
participants. Surmounting this was the graceful figure
of a Fortuna bearing a golden laurel wreath. I am elabo-
rating these details because they are mentioned in later
letters.

Next morning came the following note of thanks from
Wagner:

My dear Director Neumann:

I must beg for leave of absence to-day, for pressing
affairs are calling me home. No one who was present at
the Victoria Theatre last night could have the least shadow
of a doubt that I am leaving you with the most perfect
confidence in your ability and your artists' skill in carrying out the many difficult details of my exacting works.

I feel that it lies with me, however, to express my deep
appreciation of your dauntless spirit of sacrifice for our
Art,—my admiration of your courage and enterprise, and

my heartiest thanks for all you have accomplished in my behalf. But my future confidence in you, and my complete reliance upon you from now on, will speak more loudly for me than any mere words.

If you continue true to the course you have marked out for yourself, following consistently my new departures in stagecraft, and keeping at its height the spirit and integrity of my style, I shall feel that you are doing the greatest possible service not only to myself, but to the sacred cause of art in general.

With the wish, and the hope, that I may be able to return at least for the fourth cycle in Berlin, I will close for to-day.

And with warmest greetings, believe me,

Your devoted

Richard Wagner.

Berlin, May 10, 1881.

On receiving this letter I hurried eagerly to the Master, who met me, saying, " I am going home now to get my children and bring them back with me for the fourth cycle. My young people must hear these performances. I doubt if such a finished presentation can ever be repeated."

That same day Wagner and his wife went with me to see Niemann, to secure him for the rôle of Siegmund in the next cycle,—for we could hardly expect Vogl to sing Loge, Siegmund and both Siegfrieds! Unfortunately he was not at home, but hearing of our visit he hastened to Wagner's hotel. Other engagements, however, obliged him to refuse our request; but Vogl expressed himself as ready and will g to sing Loge and Siegmund as well as both Siegfrieds in all three performances of the " Ring." And I wish to say here that, thanks to his perfect physical poise and the phenomenal endurance due to his temperate life, he was able to carry out this difficult undertaking, and scored a brilliant victory.

Dr. Förster now received the following letter from Madame Wagner:

My dear Dr. Förster:

Will you kindly tell your wife how very sorry I am to have missed her and not to have been able to return her call in those last few days in Berlin; I hope, however, soon to have an opportunity of telling her this myself.

Another favour I should like to ask as well. Would it be possible for you to lend us from your property rooms the paraphernalia for a magician's cell—(kettles, mirrors, etc.)—for a performance on the 21st of this month? *

I will see to it that they are sent back on the 22d. If this is out of the question will you kindly wire me? Thanking you in advance, my dear Doctor, I remain, very respectfully,

C. Wagner.

[Bayreuth], May 12, 1881.

On the 16th came a note from the Master with the superscription: For Seidl.

Hagen's heavy walk suits me to perfection,—but when he turns from Brunhilda to Gunther in the 2d act of the "Götterdämmerung," he must do it with a nervous alertness which—in contrast to his usual slouching gait—will be all the more gruesome!—Don't forget from there on— a quicker tempo than last time.

Gunther must be more demonstrative in his lament; Hagen must always stand close by him.

Congratulations!

R. Wagner.

[Bayreuth, May 15, 1881.]

The same day Mme. Wagner wrote:

* A rehearsal of "Parsifal."

My dear and valued Herr Director:

I had no opportunity that evening of our departure to say many of the things I had intended. But first I must ask you kindly to send the silver your artists presented to my husband, to our care—C.O.D.—as we had no time that last day to pack it.

I left it with the porter in our hotel to be delivered to you. I also asked Herr Dohm to hand you a letter with our architect's plans for the new theatre; they may possibly be realised some time in the near future.

Thanks for the telegram of yesterday. You say "The Brave shall inherit the earth "—and I hope it will prove true indeed, and that this evening's " Siegfried " performance will be a perfect success.

With the kindest remembrances to those among your valued staff who have not forgotten us—and with a warm handclasp for " The pearl among women "—my husband and I wish to assure the " Bravest of men " of our heartfelt devotion.

C. Wagner.

Sunday, May 15, 1881.
P. S. My regards to your wife.

The Master now telegraphed:

Bayreuth, May 15, 1881.

Don't forget, in the lesson in fear (Mime)—the tempo must be somewhat quicker, with livelier gestures in pauses of Siegfried's song.

Congratulations and thanks,

Wagner.

The papers of the day show that the second cycle in Berlin was a more triumphant success even than the first, which had been hampered by Jäger's indisposition. As I have said, Vogl sang Siegfried also in the second production; and the next day the report was—" Berlin had

never before heard 'Siegfried' as it should be given!"
The Crown Prince, and his son-in-law the Crown Prince
of Meiningen, were both present at the second cycle as
well.

During the third cycle Kaiser Wilhelm returned to
Berlin from Wiesbaden. The papers announced that he
had ordered a libretto of the "Nibelungen," and if his
doctors consented, meant to be present at one of the performances. As a matter of fact, a court lackey had appeared one day asking, in his Majesty's name, for the
official text of the whole "Ring." Even Bismarck, who,
as is well known, never went to the theatre, told Emil
Scaria, who had the honour of meeting him, that he should
like very much to hear "The Valkyre." The Italian Er-
nesto Rossi, who was at that time playing an engagement
in Berlin, was one of the most devoted of Wagnerites, and
was heard to declare after the performance of "Siegfried,"
"Mais, après cela il n'y a que le déluge!"

During the third "Siegfried" performance, at the opening of the second act, a buzz of excitement ran through the
house as the venerable Kaiser entered his royal box with
the Crown Prince and listened attentively till the end.

It is well known that this excellent monarch, brought
up in another school, had never had a leaning toward
Wagner. Yet it spoke for his fine tact and his noble
feeling of national pride that he wished to share the
enthusiasms of his people and preside at the triumph of
the highest flower of our German art.

The following day—Sunday, May 22d, and Richard
Wagner's birthday—was celebrated by the head of the
firm of "Bote & Bock" * with a memorable "Nibelungen"
dinner. In the course of the meal we noticed a certain
embarrassment in our host, after receiving a message
from one of the servants. Conversation presently flagged,

* Famous music publishers in Berlin.

until finally Hugo Bock came over and told me nervously that " The chief of police, von Madai, was in the drawing-room and wished to see me!"—Consternation among the guests!—While they consulted and debated as to the reason of this unexpected call I went calmly smiling into the drawing-room, where von Madai greeted me with, " They told me at the Hôtel de Rome I should find you here." Then he asked whether we had any plan for a public demonstration at the theatre that night in honour of Wagner.

As I answered in the negative, he told me he had nothing against such a celebration, but in case we had such an intention His Majesty of course could not be present at the performance as he had planned. On my further assurance that nothing of the sort would take place, he announced His Majesty's official presence for the " Götter-dämmerung," stipulating of course that the curtain should not go up until the advent of the Kaiser. " I can assure you there will be no delay! His Majesty is always punctual."

You may imagine the pleasure when I returned to the company with these joyful tidings. I then went directly to the theatre, where the artists received the news of the official visit with the greatest enthusiasm.

.   .   .   .   .   .

We had sent the Master a birthday telegram composed by Förster :

" We, beneath your great victorious banner,
    Have fought full many a field in sorest plight.
Now triumphing at last in royal manner,
    We crown you once again our King to-night!
Your loyal forces faithful now are meeting
To send to-day a hearty birthday greeting.

" To further triumphs, our belovèd Master,
    We beg you lead us on—we'll conquer all!
    ' Woe him who hath no foes! '—we'll fight the faster.
    While Germany applauds we cannot fall!"

That very evening came the Master's answer:

"' While Germany applauds '! how proud a boast!
    And this I owe to you, my valiant host!
            In triumphs of our Art
            You've done a yeoman's part.
    You've served me well,—we've won the game,
    And Wagner's proud to own his name!
    My greetings, then, to great and small;
    Thank Römer *—yes, and thank them *all!*
                              " Richard Wagner."

        * Romer was one of our stage directors.

CHAPTER XII

THE "NIBELUNGEN" IN BERLIN (CONTINUED)

In sending our congratulations, we had added the announcement of our private decision to recognise his claims for a five per cent. royalty on the earlier operas. Wagner's agents, Volk & Batz, had lost their suit against Frederick Haase and the city of Leipsic, so that Wagner had no legal claim on us for these first operas. His pleasure then was all the greater at our spontaneous action. He telegraphed:

Bayreuth, May 24, 1881.

Best thanks to you and Dr. Förster for your joyful announcement, which unfortunately by some accident I did not hear until to-day. We are coming with all the children to the fourth cycle,—to-morrow (Wednesday)— either at six in the morning or at eleven. Please ask Lang of the Hôtel Royal to reserve good rooms—for me, for my wife, four daughters and one son,—as well as for two friends who are coming with us. We surely want the Hôtel Royal if they will make us a reduction.

The rest I'll tell you when I see you. Hearty greetings for you and all the "Nibelungen." (Good seats for nine people.)

Richard Wagner.

Late that night came this other wire:

Bayreuth, May 24, 1881.

We're coming at 12:30—Hope we're all welcome and everything ready for us.

Wagner.

As the Hotel Royal had no suitable rooms, Wagner and his family went to the Hôtel du Nord. Then the last cycle of the "Nibelungen Ring" went on most satisfactorily under the Master's eye. Again Wagner sat in the right-hand box of the first tier, surrounded by his children; again the orchestra sounded the fanfare, and the people cheered as he entered the box and came forward bowing his thanks.

Even the indisposition of Reicher-Kindermann did not subtract from the perfection of the whole, for Orlanda Riegler took her place at the last moment and sang Fricka. At the close of " Rhinegold," Wagner expressed his astonishment that we were able to carry out this work, —which had been the despair of other great opera companies,—in spite of the sudden failure of one of our chief supports.

After the final curtain the Master and his family were about to withdraw; but the enthusiastic audience refused to be satisfied until he had come forward twice to the edge of his box and had bowed amid storms of applause and a tumult of glad shouts.

The " Siegfried " performance, with Vogl in the title-rôle, was one of the most successful this opera ever had. The Crown Prince, Prince William (the present Kaiser), with his wife and members of her suite from the court of Mecklenburg, occupied the three first boxes in the lower tier. The audience raved and shrieked for Wagner!— Mme. Cosima, who sat with her children in the Countess Schleinitz' box, sent the little fair-haired Siegfried again and again to find his father, but it was fully five minutes before Wagner appeared, to be greeted by a hurricane of applause and thundering hurrahs. It was as if their enthusiasm could find no bounds.

Accordingly we were not a little disturbed to know how to conduct the arrangements for Wagner's final triumph at the close of " Götterdämmerung," in order to exceed this last demonstration. Our thanks must include the royal family (particularly our revered Kaiser, who had signified his wish to be present on that momentous occasion), as well as the Berlin public and the press. As an instance of the diplomatic difficulties of this task, I shall mention that the speech I was to make on this occasion was composed with the assistance of Paul Lindau, Frederick Spielhagen and August Förster. The latter even offered, to my amazement, to sit in the prompter's box himself and help me out from there; so great was our enthusiasm and so perfect our attention to the details of this crowning effort of the "Nibelungen" season in Berlin.

But how differently it all turned out!

At first everything seemed to go according to our wishes. A brilliant house was assembled. Kaiser Wilhelm, Princess Bismarck, Countess Rantzau (her daughter), Count William Bismarck and others were present. The members of the orchestra had laid a laurel wreath on Anton Seidl's desk, and as a special mark of their appreciation blew a solemn note on the trumpets as Wagner came down among them in the last intermission. But we all noticed unmistakable signs of uneasiness in Wagner's manner.

At the close of the performance when, at my request, he appeared on the stage and we were about to bring him our testimonial, he looked strikingly pale and ill. Nevertheless he promised to make a little speech. The curtain meanwhile had fallen, and while the audience shouted their acclamations, the members of the cast pressed forward to surround the Master. Then the curtain rose again, to reveal him in their midst. I had time to notice that not a soul in all that crowded house had left his place —that Förster's head was bobbing up in the prompter's box—and then I stepped forward and began my speech:

" On this momentous occasion, at the close of this magnificent work, which has held us in your midst these last
few weeks, allow me to express my deepest gratitude to
all who have contributed to the success of this undertaking.

" First, let me thank the august members of our reign-
ing house——"

Hardly had I spoken these words when Richard Wagner
turned and left the stage. Wounded to the quick,—in the
face of all the court and the swarming witnesses of this
rebuff,—I still went calmly on, as though nothing strange
had happened.

——" Let me thank the august members of our reign-
ing house who—always the generous patrons of our
sciences and arts—have now extended their gracious pro-
tection to this wonderful new flower of the German stage.

" Thanks then to you, the discriminating public of our
great capital, and to you the representatives of public
opinion, for the continued and growing enthusiasm with
which you have followed our efforts, and for your encour-
agement which has never failed us.

" I thank you next, gentlemen of the orchestra, and particularly I thank your great conductor, my honoured
friend and colleague, Anton Seidl.

" And finally, I thank you _all_—my friends and fellow-
artists. You have worked together with an unexampled
devotion to your art and a noble spirit of sacrifice for
the great cause which has brought you here—whether
from Vienna, from Munich, or from Leipsic.

" Especially let me thank our dear and valued Heinrich
Vogl, whose enthusiasm and unselfish devotion (as we all
ungrudgingly admit) have been among the prime causes
of our successful completion of this tremendous task.

" And now, what can I say to you, our mighty Master "
(this last I had to shout into the wings)? " How can I
express my thanks for your trust in me—that you have

found me worthy to produce your works in this great capital of Germany—the royal place of residence! If we have failed to carry out some of your ideals, let us hope, I beg, that you will consider the difficulties, and remember that we are but human and therefore frail.

"And so I quote to you, ' Meister Richard Wagner,' the very words you used toward that other Master-singer:

> " ' Dein der Preis !
> Keiner wie du zu werben weisz.
> Ja, holder Sänger ! Nimm das Reis,
> Dein Sang erwarb dir Meisterpreis ! ' "

The thunder of cheers and applause that followed upon these words forced the Master at length to come to the front of his box and bow his thanks.

Meanwhile the most awful hush of embarrassment had settled over the participants on the stage. It was as though a stream of cold water had been dashed on our festive excitement. There stood Vogl and his wife, foolishly holding the tremendous laurel wreath we had intended for Wagner; and there stood all the cast of the " Götterdämmerung " in their costumes, and the other members of the company in full dress—Mme. Materna in her trailing satin robes, Scaria with all his orders on his breast—all stood there thunderstruck and disappointed; and, if the truth were known, with the conviction in their hearts that it was no sudden indisposition, but an unaccountable " tantrum," that had ended our well-planned and hitherto triumphantly successful performance with a note of bitterness.

So in a spirit of righteous—though perhaps hardly justifiable—indignation, I wrote to Wagner declaring that, after these late events, I thought best that all further personal intercourse between us should cease.

The next day Wagner sent Seidl first, and then Vogl, to assure me that it had really been a heart attack that had

made him leave the stage. But I knew better! Even
Lindau, Spielhagen and the others tried in vain to convince me. Finally, when all other means had failed, Wagner himself wrote:

My dear Neumann:

I can hardly say whether it was my own excitement or
the surprise of your sudden tribute that caused the violent
spasm which drove me from the stage last night: I only
know that every one spoke of my paleness—and the feeble
condition of my heart is well known. You should have
known better than to count on me under such circumstances, especially as my wife has told you of these attacks, though I begged her not to. I am sorry that you
refuse to take our word for this matter.

The "insult" you speak of vanishes utterly as soon
as you accept my word for this, as I have tried by every
means in my power to have you see.

I have given every possible evidence, both in word and
in deed, of my sentiments toward you and your entire
staff; and no momentary spectacular action could call
this now in question.

First, I wish to calm your feelings on this vexed question,—and I for my part see no reason for breaking off
our personal relations,—and then presently I shall have
something further (thoroughly friendly) to tell you.

With warmest greetings,
Sincerely yours,
Richard Wagner.

Berlin, May 30, 1881.

Not even this written statement was enough to heal
the bitterness of the wound. I left my card on Mme.
Cosima, avoiding all further meeting with the Master,
who left the following day, for Bayreuth.

That Wagner had taken the precedence of our royal
patron, in my speech of thanks, as his cue for leaving the

stage had naturally not passed unobserved. The many
opponents of his dramas, who had hitherto not dared
make any open attacks, now seized the opportunity to
enlarge upon this sign of his dislike for the Hohenzol-
lerns, and a number of prominent papers took it up as
well.

In spite of the fact that Count and Countess Schleinitz
were unremitting in their efforts in his cause, it had to
be admitted that the Kaiser's interest *was* purely impersonal, on the strength of the national importance of the
works, and that the performances—a strain on even the
most enthusiastic music-lovers—were rather a bore to
the kindly monarch. And add to this Wagner's real or
fancied affront, which was hardly calculated to conciliate
an important power!

In this critical situation Kaiser Wilhelm showed himself again the man of noble mould. On May 31st we
had advertised a special performance of " The Valkyre."
Promptly at seven, with the first long notes of the violins,
appeared the venerable Kaiser (eighty-five years of age)
with his sister, the Dowager Duchess of Mecklenburg (a
woman of eighty-seven), and these two sat through, not
only the entire performance, which lasted until midnight,
but stayed for the final applause, joining enthusiastically
from the front of their box until the artists, after countless recalls, had finally left the stage. He wished thereby
to show publicly how little Wagner's slight had touched
him; and he parried the rudeness of that genius (if rudeness it were) in a most courtly and dignified manner.

Wagner finally (and with perfect right) was disgusted
at my stiffness, and wrote Förster a letter on the subject
quite different from his former genial communications.

Dr. Förster, Honoured Sir, Patron and Friend:
I still regret not having been able to call on you and
your charming wife before leaving Berlin; I also regret

not having answered Herr Neumann's letter and visit.
To my great sorrow, however, I realise that you were
not disposed to believe my reasons for leaving that
night.

You neglected as well, my dear sir, advising me as I
asked, whether there were any one close enough to Herr
Neumann to entrust with the delicate task of explaining
my conduct on that final night in the Victoria Theatre;
hoping in some way to make him understand it.

Now, however, that I have given up this hope, there
seems nothing further for me to do but to avoid all future
possibility of such occurrences. As this would mean no
further participation on my part in any performances
under your direction or that of your colleague, the nature
of my interest in these performances compels me, for the
sake of my art, to make some firm stipulations in this
connection.

As far as that is concerned I have always loudly proclaimed Herr Neumann's skill in drawing together an
irreproachable cast: his determination to remodel the
stage arrangements after the Bayreuth pattern has pleased
me as well, though I could wish he would call in Fritz
Brandt (an experienced technician and son of my mechanical expert, Karl Brandt) for the work.

My only stipulation now is, that Herr Neumann shall
appoint a new and competent stage manager who shall be
thoroughly conversant with my methods. The utter lack
of style and finish in the staging of my "Nibelungen"
cycle has surprised me continually in view of my constant
remonstrances on the subject, which Herr Neumann has
seemed not to comprehend.

In case Herr Neumann can assure me he will comply
absolutely with these demands, I shall not refuse him the
further concessions he has asked;—if not, however, I shall
feel it incumbent upon me to adopt the same tactics which
Herr Neumann recently employed with me,—stand on a

point of dignity and preserve my artistic honour by refusing him future concessions.

Should my exactions, or the necessary consequences of the choice I have laid before him, seem to Herr Neumann to endanger his undertakings I stand more than ready to realease him from all engagements to me.

With the best wishes for your health and kindly regards to your estimable wife, believe me,

Yours truly,

Richard Wagner.

Bayreuth, June 15, 1881.

PART IV

HOPES AND PLANS

CHAPTER XIII

FRIENDS AGAIN

I SHALL now quote Förster's answer to the above letter.

Marienbad, June 16, 1881.

My dear and honoured Master:

Your letter of the 15th inst. (you dated it wrong—it *reached* me on the 15th—so again you see you find your-self ahead of your times) was forwarded to me here in Marienbad. Consequently I cannot confer with Neumann on those same vexed questions. I thought it wise then to send him the letter and let him answer himself; for it was undoubtedly meant for both of us, and he certainly will best know what to say to your propositions, stipulations and judgments—whether to agree, to assuage,—or else to defend himself.

As to the technical points raised in your letter, I am unfortunately not in a position to carry on a detailed correspondence on this subject. Where should I find time for such an interchange of thought? It might do if we met face to face, and could settle the matter *viva voce.*

Yet I am perfectly willing to express my opinion on the subject as a *whole,*—which is that you have gone rather far, my dear Master, in mixing the personal with purely technical questions—perhaps *too* far.

I fully realise that " A straw may cause a mighty war where honour is at stake "—but you, my dear Master, are far too " mighty " yourself to " Rear and rage without sufficient cause."

You have often publicly acknowledged, and you repeat the acknowledgment in your letter, the importance of

Neumann's contributions in the field. As to the remodelling of the scenic apparatus—you already have his consent. And Fritz Brandt? Certainly an exemplary man! But to make him a condition in the affair—my dear Master, I fear that is a mistake. Let me tell you—we can't be sure there's not a Mr. X. Y. Z. somewhere who could even do *better!*

Our interests in the enterprise are certainly the same as yours. Then why not give us some latitude?

Let me remind you of Jäger. " And Patroclus is fallen, —no longer is himself."—But the main thing is that Troy was conquered!

Something of the same tenor I might say with regard to your stipulated stage manager. Where shall we find this paragon of a manager, who is he,—this man who is so " perfectly acquainted with the ins and outs of your works "? I know only one such man, but he lives in Bayreuth and his name is Richard Wagner. If you are able (and willing) to unite the professions of poet and composer, impresario and stage manager—and possibly like Sophocles be your own actor too, I think we should probably reach the ideal presentation of the Richard Wagner dramas. *Probably*, I say, Master! For " Close packed our heads with seething thoughts, while deeds accomplished few and far between." I mean to say, that the theatrical profession is simply a series of compromises. Experto crede Ruperto!

And may it comfort your wounded artistic sensibilities to know that the power of the whole thing is so great that it takes hold of the people and overwhelms them, even if there *is* a little defect here and there in the performance.

Have " the lack of style and lack of finish " which you have noticed in our performances prevented in any way the artistic triumphs that seem to have been accorded to your works at the Victoria Theatre in Berlin?

No, my dear Master—stand at your exalted post; be *you* the King—the builder—and let your labourers, carpenters, masons and draymen do the work that is apportioned to them. Small things must still be small even in the hands of the great!

One phrase in your letter, thank Heaven, I can't quite understand! It is where you say that in a given cause you will " resort to the tactics that Neumann recently adopted." I only gather from the following phrase—where you speak of Herr Neumann's future undertakings suffering in such an event—that this is a *threat* of some sort, that proceeds no doubt from your attack of ill humour.

And this hurts and saddens me. I should think that considering the loyalty and the devotion to your cause of the Leipsic Opera Company under my management and that of Herr Neumann, you might sing the personal note and judge the technical question more fairly. Content yourself on your Olympian heights with a calm and Jove-like smile at the fallibility of earthly things;—remember the many proofs we have given of eagerness in the cause and watchfulness for your interests, and consider that Neumann's attitude on that fatal evening was decidedly human and certainly most natural.—With the best possible intentions and in a mood of noblest exaltation a great ovation was planned—and it ended in a fit of temper!

Now, Master, I am of the opinion (and I know that all your genuine friends must share it with me) that your greatness would only prove itself the greater if you should rescind your hasty action *as* hastily,—and overlook what might have been considered a tactlessness in our demonstration, in view of the undeniable tribute that was intended.

Neumann will probably write to you in the next few days, and I hope the dismal dream of these last few weeks

will soon be over and that " when we awake our sky will
be quite clear, with not the slightest cloud on its horizon."

With hearty greetings for you and all your family, in
which my wife joins me,

I am,

Devotedly yours,

Dr. August Förster.

Förster then urged me to write to Bayreuth, which I
did, suggesting that the matter could hardly be smoothed
over without a personal interview, and proposing that as
I was to be in Aigen for July, I might come to Wahnfried,
as it lay quite near.   To which Wagner answered:

My dear Director:

I shall be ready and glad at any time to greet you and
talk things over.   In the meantime let me announce my
consent in the matter of the concessions you ask for Berlin, Dresden, Breslau, Belgium and Holland in our contract till the end of 1883.   As to your purchase of the
Bayreuth properties for the " Nibelungen," nothing stands
in the way except a small reluctance on my part; even
the King of Bavaria had the generosity not to ask for
these properties for his Munich performances, considering that they belonged exclusively to Bayreuth.   And I
mean sooner or later (before I end my days) to give the
" Ring " once more in my own way.   But as between now
and then many a good set of properties may go to de-
struction, my agent advises me to accept your offer.   We
will talk this over when you come.

Until then you may rest assured that it is clear as day-
light to me now that nothing was ever *intended* in the
matter that came between us.   What happened shall never
be repeated, and so—let's drop it!

With the best of greetings,

Yours truly,

Bayreuth, June 20, 1881.   Richard Wagner.

To a business question I asked came this answer by wire:

Bayreuth, June 23, 1881.

Gladly give you Prague, but am closing advantageous contract with Frankfort.

Wagner.

Now arose an unexpected matter in Leipsic, the details of which are unnecessary here. At the meeting of the city council on the 29th of June Max Stägemann was appointed director of the Leipsic opera by a majority of one.

The following letter as to this explains itself. I insert it, as it makes later events more clear:

Leipsic, July 6, 1881.

My dear and Honoured Master:

As you have probably seen by the papers, Max Stägemann takes the control of the opera here for the next seven years from August 1, 1882.

This matter concerns you as well; for you know, my dear Master, the royalties you have received for your earlier works have been paid at my personal instigation. Now I want to suggest a plan to make these permanent. I ask you to give me the exclusive rights of performing the " Nibelungen Ring " in Leipsic until June 30, 1889.

In case Stägemann takes a genuine interest in your works and is willing to continue their production in my spirit and with my ideas I should turn over these rights— on condition that he recognises your claims for the early operas as I have done.

In case he refuses I should withhold my concession for the " Nibelungen."

If he agrees, however, I must be in a position to offer him the properties; and now comes my opportunity to plan for our great undertaking.

In greatest respect,
Yours,
Angelo Neumann.

As to our interview, Wagner now sent the following invitation:

Bayreuth, July 18, 1881.

Tuesday, at one o'clock. Dine with us.

Wagner.

On the morning of the 21st I went to Bayreuth. I dined at Wahnfried—Franz Liszt being present as well. We had planned an inspection of the properties at the theatre for that afternoon. Toward five o'clock Wagner and his wife called at my hotel (The Sun) in their little covered carriage so well known in Bayreuth. It looked like a perambulating tent. They were to drive me over to the theatre. The heat was suffocating, and when he drove up Wagner called immediately for a glass of beer.

After our inspection, which went most smoothly, I declared my perfect satisfaction and announced that I wished to take possession of the treasure in time for my London production. Wagner then said he would make the necessary arrangements with his Majesty's Chancellor of the Treasury in Munich.

The Master appeared unusually gay and loquacious. We were in a great state of hilarity. Wagner was unflagging in his anecdotes, particularly the comic ones in Saxon dialect, which he imitated to perfection. I remember he told us of the manager of a travelling opera company in Saxony who was about to give the "Freischütz." He apportioned the rôles as well as he was able (all the members of his family cast for the star parts), but the trouble came when he wanted to find a Hermit. Every one who had a bass note in his voice was already cast three deep. He himself sang the Duke. In this emergency the bright idea struck him of having a deaf and dumb messenger, who was to enter and hand the Duke a scroll. "Ha!" says the latter, "a missive for me—and from whom? Oho! from my dear good old friend the

Hermit! Ah! Now let us see what it is he wishes." Here
the orchestra plays the motif which is the cue for the
Hermit's entrance—whereupon the Duke himself sings
the whole rôle out of the letter—"Who dares to lay so
stern a ban," etc.

Then he told a most delicious tale of a Berlin cabby—
this last had really happened to himself. But naturally
the tale is nothing without Wagner's wonderful drollery
and mimicry. I can only say that all who were present
that evening broke out again and again in inextinguish-
able laughter at the inimitable way in which Wagner
played the cabby.

It was a hot summer night in Berlin—so he told us—
and Wagner took a cab at the Döhnhofsplatz, telling the
man to drive to a street quite at the outer edge of the
tariff limit. He noticed as they started what a touching
farewell the cabby took of his fellow Jehus—how he
leaned down from the box and wafted a regretful "Ah
well, good-bye, Bill, farewell—ye won't see me for a while
yet!" After they had gone some distance the carriage
suddenly stopped. The driver dismounted, and coming
round on the right side, solemnly opened the door and
then closed it again. Then he went round to the left
side and repeated the same performance—and finally
mounted his box and drove on.

When they arrived Wagner asked what in the world
it was all about—and the cabby answered with a sly
wink, "You see, I wanted to fool the horse a bit, sir—
he never *would* have believed that any single gentleman
could ask us to go so far on *one tariff*, and he might
have refused to budge!—So you see I let him think
that one gentleman just got out and another one got
in!"

The man's original method of getting an extra tip
amused Wagner unspeakably.

But the nucleus of our more earnest talk was naturally

the change of directorship in Leipsic. The unexpected result of the election seemed to worry Wagner.

"But, Neumann," he said reproachfully, "I asked you in Berlin at the first cycle to let me know if there were anything I could ever do for you. If you'd said a single word about what was going on, I should have taken a hand in affairs myself—*that* would have brought them to terms." When Förster's name came up he said, "I tell you what,—he can write a good letter,—that colleague of yours!" and he went on to express his admiration of that famous epistle.

Towards evening our party broke up. After I had said good-bye to the family, Wagner went with me to the garden gate. Nothing had as yet been said of the Berlin affair. But now, as we went down the shady path together, he stopped, and began of his own accord:

"Neumann, you have misjudged me. I can only give you my word once more that I left the stage that night in Berlin for no other reason than the one I've already stated—I really felt that I should faint if I stayed there a moment longer." Then he took my hand and laid it on his heart: "If you only knew how it beats in here, how I suffer with it!"

He looked at me with his deep, earnest eyes: "Will you believe me now?" But even then I could not say "I do." Then he flung my hand away with an angry jerk, clasped his forehead in despair, and said in pained and bitter tones, "Ah! why should it be so impossible to find a trusting soul!"

We went on in silence down the leafy path to the gate, stood there a while, and then, without another word, Wagner kissed me and put his arms around me. So we parted.

It was fully two years later, when the sad news came up from Venice of the Master's sudden death from heart

failure, that I was finally convinced of the tragic sincerity
of his words.

          .   .   .   .   .   .

At the Master's suggestion I had arranged to drive
from Bayreuth to the next station, where I should catch
the late express from Munich. This gave me a longer
time at Wahnfried; and so ended that memorable day
for me—July 21, 1881.

          .   .   .   .   .   .

In August Wagner wrote to Seidl with an enclosure
for me—saying that according to my letter of July 6th
he now sent me the exclusive rights for the "Ring" in
Leipsic and the contract for the same. I sent him the cor-
responding form on September 1st, having arranged the
further details partly by letter and partly by wire.

CONTRACT

I

Between Richard Wagner, residing in Bayreuth, and
director Angelo Neumann the following contract has been
agreed upon and signed:

§ 1

Richard Wagner concedes to Angelo Neumann the exclusive rights of production for his musical drama "The
Nibelungen Ring" in London, St. Petersburg, Paris and
the United States until December 31, 1883.

§ 2

Richard Wagner concedes to Angelo Neumann the exclusive rights of his "Lohengrin" and "Tannhäuser" for
the whole of France until December 31, 1883.

§ 3

Angelo Neumann is empowered to give these works
either in German, French or Italian (quite as he sees fit).

§ 4

Angelo Neumann is pledged to make over to Richard

Wagner (or to his legal heirs) a royalty of ten per cent.
(10%) of the gross receipts of each and every performance taking place in the above time-limit.

§ 5

The royalties are to be paid at the end of each month.

§ 6

Richard Wagner is entitled at any time to inspect the
books of Angelo Neumann in as far as regards said undertakings.

§ 7

Should this contract not have been revoked by either
of the contracting parties six months before its expiration, i. e., on the 1st of July, 1883, the same is then to
hold good for a further term of three years.

§ 8

Whichever of the two contracting parties breaks or dis-
honours this contract, is to pay the party of the other part
an indemnity of fifteen thousand Marks—payable at the
current rate of exchange.

This document is carried out in duplicate and has been
read and signed by both contracting parties.

Richard Wagner.
Angelo Neumann.

Bayreuth ⎫
Leipsic ⎭ February 16, 1881.

Contract

II

Between Richard Wagner of Bayreuth and Angelo Neumann of Leipsic, . . . etc.

Here follows a duplicate of the above except that clause
1 substitutes Berlin, Leipsic, Dresden, Breslau, Prague,
Belgium, Holland, Sweden, Norway and Denmark until
December 31, 1886, and clause 2 is omitted.

As soon as he received these contracts the Master
wrote:

Dear Friend and Ally:

It is all very well arranged—*but*, we must add a little codicil—something on the lines I have sketched out in the enclosed. Your pride is quite commensurate with the trust I have in you and your capacity: the exclusive rights I have given you in recognition of this, you are under no circumstances to convey or (pardon me!) to sell to any one else!

I received to-day at the same time with your letter, a Musical Weekly published by Fritsch, where I saw in the Dresden notes a statement that certain conditions and circumstances had arisen which might cause us trouble with our contract there. For instance, the management of the Royal Opera House (*as such*) must under no circumstances be allowed to produce my works. If you were to rent their opera house and give the " Nibelungen " with your own company, that would be another matter and quite within the limits of our agreement;—otherwise —not.

I shall return now to our late discussion on the occasion of your negotiations with von Hülsen about the Berlin Opera, when we had arranged that the performances were not to take place there. You know how I felt about it. But now—let us be square with each other and work on a basis of mutual trust which on my side is built up on admiration for your energy and capacity, and a perfect confidence in your sense of honour.

If you will put this small codicil to the contract I shall add my signature at once.

With warmest greetings,
Yours devotedly,
Richard Wagner.

Bayreuth, September 2, 1881.

I instantly made the changes he suggested and sent the contracts for his signature on the 4th of September.

Shortly afterwards I was to have the pleasure of greet-

ing Wagner in Leipsic. He had been to his dentist in
Dresden and made a short trip from there to Leipsic on
September 13th. Our plan to give " The Valkyre " on this
occasion was unfortunately frustrated by the indisposition of one of our stars (Reicher-Kindermann, I think it
was).

Nevertheless Wagner and his wife, with little Siegfried
and Eva, came to the theatre that night and sat in the
director's box. The performance was " The Cousin " by
Benedix—and the Master and his family seemed to enjoy
it tremendously. Wilhelm Eichenwald, who took the part
of the Cousin, pleased Wagner immensely. In watching a
tiny little actress who took one of the rôles he expressed
this judgment: " Any one as small as that should certainly keep off the boards! "

Returned to his rooms in the Hôtel Hauffe we then
talked over our plans for the near future, and on the
following morning Wagner returned to Bayreuth.

By the end of September my new project, after many
preliminaries, had arrived at the point when its details
must be discussed with the Master. It was a question
of uniting the newly founded " Deutsches Theatre " in
Berlin with the Richard Wagner Opera Company, so that
in their immense theatre building they could arrange for
a smaller stage for their plays and a larger one for opera
—modelled after Bayreuth; both to be united under one
management.

The propositions which I laid before the Master were:

(1) We will form a company of ten whose head and
front must be Richard Wagner.

(2) Each member contributes twenty-five thousand
Marks of the capital and is entitled to ten per cent. of the
net profits.

(3) On the payment of the twenty-five thousand Marks,
each member enters into possession of one-tenth of the
entire property.

(4) You concede to me the exclusive rights of producing " Parsifal " in Europe and America.

(5) At each performance of any of your works, no matter where, you are to have ten per cent. of the gross receipts.

(6) This royalty is to be quite independent of your ten per cent. net profits as member of the society.

(7) This payment, both the percentage and the royalty, will be continued, in case of your demise, to your legal heirs.

(8) At the end of ten years your heirs shall be free to claim the original investment of twenty-five thousand Marks and withdraw from the company.

(9) At the end of thirty years the above-mentioned company, as well as your heirs, shall be entitled to claim the return of their original investment.

(10) The terms of years in clauses eight and nine (ten and thirty years respectively) are to be reckoned from the day of your demise.

I have only this to add to the above outline of my project—that in case the deposit of twenty-five thousand Marks should be inconvenient for you, I will gladly undertake it in your name, taking your personal note for the payment of the same.

My opinion is that the profits from this venture will be so tremendous that I should not hesitate to quote your income on the investment as probably sixty thousand or seventy thousand Marks a year. Consequently I consider this an opportunity not to be despised of assuring your own future and that of your family.

The answer to this proposition was the following letter from Mme. Cosima:

My dear Director:
My husband asks me to say that before he definitely

answers your letter he wishes to make sure of certain points.

He feels that your contract is one-sided and decidedly to his detriment, my dear sir.

For instance it gives you the *exclusive* rights—but deprives him of the right to make other arrangements in case you fail to bring your productions to a successful issue. And for these rights you have given neither a guarantee as to the date of your performance, nor arranged for a deposit to cover the payment.

In order that you may thoroughly understand how detrimental this might be to him, my husband begs you to consider the case of Dresden.

In the course of affairs we hope that the director of the opera there will comply with our demands (of which you may have heard) and will conclude a contract for the performances there.

On the other hand, *you* would be able to do nothing at all in Dresden; so what a sum you would have to pay to indemnify him for the loss he would undergo when these other matters shall be settled—as they soon will be.

Consequently he asks you to give up the rights for Dresden, and to add to your contract a time clause and a considerable advance deposit—for it is quite probable that others will want concessions and he would not wish to bind himself without any security nor any indemnity.

As soon as these questions are settled, my dear sir, we will go on with the matter of the Wagner Theatre in Berlin.

My husband joins me in the warmest greetings and the greatest respect.

C. Wagner.

Bayreuth, September 30, 1881.

I now wrote a further explanation of these specifications, whereupon the Master answered:

My dearest Friend and Fellow-worker:

You take the matter too seriously. It's not a question of mistrust but of settling a mooted point in our contract which might (possibly) cause me a great deal of loss.

The rights I concede you (and mark you well—they are *exclusive* rights!) can only be useful to you in a place where you can guarantee a performance. This you can do in nearly all the towns for which you wish to acquire them (even Leipsic, should you decide to use the so-called Carola Theatre). Circumstances, however, have proved that it would be impossible for you to give a performance in Dresden.

How can you ask me, then, to refuse a theatre like the Royal Dresden Opera House which has a most adequate staff for presenting my " Ring," simply because I have promised you the rights for a term of years—which you are not in a position to use there!

This is all I shall say on the subject—however, I fear you seem not to believe me in this case again—for I take it you are under the impression that I am negotiating with the Dresden Theatre as to the production of the " Nibelungen." Even though this is far from my thoughts, yet it is quite possible that my relations to Dresden will change in the course of these years for which you mean to acquire the rights. Should I, then, be forced to hold to that purposeless contract with you? Of course you'd not expect that, and—as I do not doubt for an instant your inviolable rectitude—yes, and your great personal devotion to me and to my cause—so I rest in the assurance that you would not mean to injure me. Why, then, hold fast to this one—*useless*—point?

If, furthermore, I consider it necessary to demand a guarantee for the dividends due me from the concessions I am to give (for, as a matter of business, I must say our contract leaves me with very little foothold) it can hardly be considered unusual in such strictly business dealings.

At the same time I must admit that my financial condition is such that I should be glad of any additional income from my works, not so much in the uncertain future as in the immediate present. So I will gladly accept your offer of a deposit on the royalties due me and stipulate that it shall be as considerable as possible. If twenty thousand Marks does not seem too great a burden to you, I should be able immediately then to plan a much needed tour for my health and recreation with a calm and cheerful mind.

I believe I have now stated all my views and fully reassured you as to my sentiments.

Hoping that this is the case and with the best of greetings,

Yours most truly,

Richard Wagner.

Bayreuth, October 11, 1881.

I accepted Wagner's proposition of the advance, by telegram. Considerable funds had been placed at my disposal for the erection of the Wagner Theatre in Berlin. I wrote the Master that our plans had been fully worked out on the Bayreuth model and asked for his immediate decision. He answered:

. . . But, my dear fellow, how you do beset me! How *can* I decide such a weighty question so suddenly? I devoted twenty years of my life to founding ' Bayreuth ' because I had a great and far-reaching plan in my head with regard to it. A Wagner Theatre in Berlin?—nothing could have been easier for me: years ago I had the offer of the means for it. But that was not the fitting place for the creation I meant to give to the world. What I finally achieved in my secluded spot, where the world is forced to come to me, may now (if it is required) be carried further on; but this requisition must come from the *other side:* may *you* represent the other side! You know from experience that I trust you.

But this is entirely your own affair; I've nothing to say on the subject whatever—except that I should rather trust you with my works than any other man who would undertake them.

You do not need my money, but—my—name! In giving you my works I give you my name as well for your theatre —but not for your list of shareholders—not even for the head of the list. Berlin must be your undertaking, not mine. How much more so, however, if you are to be associated with other men in the founding of the theatre; which from a practical point of view I consider thoroughly justifiable, but which would utterly preclude my personal co-operation.

My dear friend, if you cannot found a purely (shall we say) " Wagnerian " Theatre—an exceedingly difficult matter, I'll admit—then rather give up this thing entirely.

" Parsifal " is to be given *nowhere else* but in Bayreuth; and this from private and personal motives that my gracious benefactor the King of Bavaria so thoroughly understood, that he even waived his privilege of having it given at the Munich theatre. In view of this, how could I dispose of " Parsifal " to you as you propose? I cannot and will not ever allow it to be given in any other theatre; unless it were that I fitted out a real Wagner theatre—a stage sacred to the Drama which (wandering of course from place to place) should spread throughout the world the creations which I have so far tended and brought to their full and stately perfection in my own theatre at Bayreuth.

In case you are steadfast in your ideas for your great enterprises, the time may yet come when I shall be glad to entrust my " Parsifal," not to any " court theatre " or a municipal theatre, but to the great Wandering Wagner Opera Company.

I shall simply add now my deepest thanks for your immediate and willing consent to my wishes as to the deposit.

To-morrow I shall send the letter for Minister Ferry.

Do not be angry, but think well of me. Then everything will go smoothly!

With heartfelt greetings from

Your devoted
Richard Wagner.

Bayreuth, October 16, 1881.

This weighty letter needs no commentary. The letter to Minister Ferry in Paris had been written by Mme. Cosima in view of the coming " Lohengrin " presentation there.

The following letter from the Master deals with a mistake in the acquisition of the Bayreuth "Nibelungen" properties. I had taken it for granted that the lighting apparatus was included. Shortly before leaving for Paris, to arrange for " Lohengrin," I had written Wagner that I must regard his manager's refusal to send me the complete apparatus as a breach of contract. Whereupon the Master enlightened me as to the disputed point.

My dear Friend and Associate:

I am racking my brains to find out what you mean— when you've given only fifty-two thousand Marks for a paraphernalia that cost us one hundred and forty thousand, and that is in perfect condition—as we have only used it three times;—and then you demand our lighting apparatus besides! This it would cost us about thirty thousand Marks to replace, as we need it in all our other performances as well as for the " Nibelungen Ring."

Can this really be your idea? Certainly you could not have thought that we wished to be rid of this apparatus *à tout prix*—there would be no sense in that—especially as I only consented to the sale of these same properties simply out of deference to you and to help out your—yes, and *my*—very weighty enterprises.

Tell me truly now—what was your notion? Do you regret the whole undertaking? Do you mean to try to supplement with the Leipsic properties?—which would not do at all! Certainly an entirely new apparatus would be very much more expensive. Or—shall we let the whole thing go for something like twenty-two thousand Marks when the new instalment of the lights would cost us an immediate thirty thousand Marks? As little as the financial side of the question touches me here at Bayreuth, I could hardly consent to that!

In short: I am racking my brains!

My wife is writing you that letter to-day for Ferry.

Now accept the most cordial greetings of

Your devoted

Richard Wagner.

Bayreuth, October 23, 1881

Although the lack of a lighting apparatus (especially for London) make me rack my own brains, I let the matter stand, though our contract had expressly said " . . . All the appliances for the ' Nibelungen Ring.' " In London it caused me great anxiety. For I never should have considered it possible that a leading theatre (as Her Majesty's Theatre then was) could have such meagre and insufficient lighting arrangements.

I shall speak later of my remarkable experience there.

CHAPTER XIV

PARIS AND "LITTLE PARIS" *

AT the end of October I went with my Leipsic machinist Edward Römer to London to make preparations for our performance of the " Ring," and especially to investigate the stage arrangements of Her Majesty's Theatre.

Von Hülsen had long since called my attention to the fact that Pollini had gone into partnership with Francke to give a Wagner season in London at the same time, and this I now found to be true. So Wagner—not heeding my warnings—had given the double concession, and led to a rivalry that would undoubtedly wreck both enterprises not only financially but artistically as well.

Under these circumstances I should have preferred to resign for the time being, but the contracts were signed and it was out of question. My only alternative was to fight the matter out as manfully as I might.

After we had made all possible arrangements for the following May I sent Römer back to Leipsic, while I went to Paris to conclude matters for our great German " Lohengrin " performance in February.

My first impressions were most favourable. My plan developed;—not only to give " Lohengrin " in German but later " Tannhäuser,"—and with the best artists of our German stage. The Elsa should be sung alternately by Anna Sachse-Hofmeister of Leipsic and Therese Vogl of Munich; Ortrud, Hedwig Reicher-Kindermann of Leipsic and Amalia Materna of Vienna; Lohengrin, Heinrich

* Neumann speaks of Leipsic as "Little Paris."

196

Vogl, and Gudehus from Dresden; Telramund, Otto
Schelper of Leipsic and Theodore Reichmann of Vienna;
The King, Henry Wiegand of Leipsic and Emil Scaria
from Vienna. The orchestra I should engage in Paris and
the chorus as well;—supplemented by certain selected
members from Germany. Anton Seidl naturally was to
be my conductor and Felix Mottl his second in command.
The decorations, costumes, weapons and properties had
been ordered in the leading ateliers of Paris and all was in
train for a sumptuous and brilliant performance. As this
became known the general public enthusiasm seemed most
propitious.

I had important introductions as well. Through the
Bismarck family I had letters to Count Hohenlohe (then
ambassador to France and afterward Chancellor of the
Empire) and to the Austrian ambassador Count Beust.
Mme. Wagner had written in my behalf to M. Ferry,
Minister of Foreign Affairs. Nor did I lack introductions
to prominent artists such as Camille Saint-Saëns, Charles
Gounod, etc.;—and important representatives of the press
as well, like Albert Wolff of the *Figaro*, Lalo, etc.

After a thorough inspection of the Théâtre des Nations,
which we had chosen for our performances, and a final
revision with its director of the last details of our contract, I felt that before signing I should consult with
those political officials whose dictum would be final as to
the possibility of our undertaking. One must remember
that these were the unsettled days of 1881-82.

My first visit was to Prince Hohenlohe, whom I had
already met at the studio of my friend Paul Lindau in
Berlin, and who had promised his support in my Paris
venture. As Prince Bismarck had written him of my
coming he received me with utmost graciousness and
asked for details of my plan. After assuring himself it
was to be an artistic performance of the highest rank, he
again offered me his services. At the close of our con-

sultation, during which I had implied that I relied upon his judgment in the matter, the Prince made this final statement: " Go on with your contracts in perfect security, and our German ' Lohengrin ' shall have a triumphant entry into Paris under your leadership! "—His Excellency had received me in his study and led me to the drawing-room when we parted. As I was about to leave the house he called me back once more to say, " Listen, my dear Director: don't sign your contract yet; it might be as well if I sounded the government as to their feelings on the subject of a German performance. Day after to-morrow I am giving an official dinner for the President and all his Cabinet, and shall bring up the subject and find out. So wait till I send you word."

And so I did. In the meantime I went on with my preparations; looking at sketches and estimates for costumes, decorations, armour and all sorts of properties; calling on Minister Freycinet and other important personages. I went to see Gounod, whom I had known in Vienna when he came there to direct the rehearsals of his " Romeo "; and made the acquaintance of Saint-Saëns, who took a tremendous interest in our German performance and united with several other artists and the publishers Durand and Schönwerk to give me a congratulatory breakfast where he himself toasted our coming triumph.

I must now add an incident giving the trend of the political situation of those days. I had naturally called upon the Austrian Ambassador Count Beust. After hearing my purpose in coming to Paris he looked at me quietly for a moment and then said, " My dear fellow, I consider this project of yours decidedly dangerous—in fact I think these Frenchmen will pull your theatre down about your ears! " My report of the manner of my reception elsewhere left him still sceptical and quite of his original mind.

A singular occurrence took place on the 4th of November. The celebrated conductor Lamoureux appeared with the publisher Durand, and announced that they must protest against my performance of " Lohengrin," as the firm Durand and Schönwerk (Wagner's publishers) possessed the exclusive rights for all of France and could not sanction a German production. When I demanded to see their contract they waved the question aside. From this as well as from Durand's whole bearing—for it seems to me that my performance would have been of profit to him—I gathered that there was a cloud on the title somewhere. So I gained time by declaring I should consider the matter carefully, and asked again to see their contract.

We then fixed a meeting for the following evening in Lamoureux' apartments, where I was accompanied by a lawyer my friends had recommended—Dr. Reutlinger.

I first tried to convince Lamoureux it would be impossible for him to give a French performance of " Lohengrin " in 1881 as he had not the artists for it, and then my lawyer and I both dwelt upon the matter of my legal rights, proving them by my contract with Richard Wagner. Here Lamoureux broke in excitedly with the declaration, " You'll never find a French court here in Paris that will give judgment against a Frenchman, even if the German that opposes him should have the law on his side!" Whereupon I answered, " I have a higher estimate than you then, monsieur, of French justice: for I'm convinced that even a *French* judge would render a decision in favour of a German if he were convinced the Frenchman had no rights!"

This answer made a tremendous impression; all present (friends of Lamoureux) agreed with loud applause. But our conference nevertheless came to no result.

So I turned in my predicament to Bayreuth and asked

for Wagner's testimony, and immediately Mme. Cosima
wrote me the following:

My dear and valued Director:

Enclosed you will find a letter which will clear up the
Paris difficulties. I shall add as well a card to a friend
who will be of assistance to you.

The London affair is more complicated; for the competition of Richter and Francke, which seems to you the
stumbling-block, is not the difficulty at all, and my husband does not know who is interested in the " German
Opera Company " there. I wrote to ask our friend Mr.
Henry Schlesinger (Kensington Park Gardens, 5) to find
out for us, but without success. I think you would find
him a valuable ally; he knows the conditions and is devoted to our interests.

My husband sends you his best greetings, my dear
Director, to which I add my own, and the assurance of
my regards.

                                        C. Wagner.

Palermo, November 16, 1881.

P. S. My husband means to write you a letter for
publication in which he regrets the difficulties arising
from the competition. It would hardly be the thing just
now, however, to let this appear.

My affairs in Paris progressed. Two days after my
call upon the German ambassador, as I was coming home
at one o'clock from a performance of " Don Giovanni " at
the Grand Opera, I found a note from Prince Hohenlohe
appointing an interview for the next morning; he had
something important to tell me. After a troubled night I
appeared at the Embassy at the appointed hour, to be met
with the glad announcement from his Excellency, " I
brought your topic up at the dinner by asking if there
would be any political reasons for not giving a Wagner
performance with German artists in the German lan-

guage;—adding, as you had told me, that the orchestra
and the chorus were French and the scenic effects had all
been ordered in the Paris ateliers."

President Grévy answered promptly: " On one condition! That the first box subscribed for at these performances shall be mine!" " And the second," said
Gambetta, " shall be for me!"—and so, said the Prince,
it was taken up all about the table, each member of the
Cabinet ordering a box.

After some further conference, the Prince dismissed me
with these words, " Now sign your contract and be sure to
reserve a box for me!"

It is not necessary to say with what gratitude I left
the Embassy, or how high were my hopes when I telegraphed home that all was definitely settled.

I closed the contract with the Théâtre des Nations by
paying a first deposit of fifteen thousand francs; then paid
my first instalment in the Paris ateliers, and completed
all preliminary arrangements.

Naturally the *Figaro* and all the other Paris journals
had commented freely on my presence and my purpose.
So I was besieged in the Grand Hôtel by musicians who
wished to join the orchestra, and by singers who wanted
an engagement in the chorus and clamoured for the score
to learn the German parts. Finally I was able to leave
Paris in the calm security that everything was in order for
a successful performance of " Lohengrin."

I went first to Munich to arrange a leave of absence for
the Vogls, for which the King's consent was necessary. I
was even prepared to ask an audience of Ludwig II. My arrangements with the other artists were being concluded as
well, and nothing was needed now but the final signatures.

Fancy my amazement, then, when Vogl announced on
my arrival at Munich that he had had messages from
Paris which indicated that our " Lohengrin " venture had
gone to the wall!

The King had even received a personal despatch advising him not to grant the furlough for the Vogls, as it was feared the theatre might be mobbed and the artists' lives endangered.

Though I smiled at first at these reports, I finally resolved to drop the idea of the audience and go to Vienna to get the signatures of Materna and Reichmann—the contract with Scaria was already signed.

On my arrival here, the Paris news seemed more threatening. The papers clearly showed that such a violent opposition had arisen that our performances were no longer to be thought of. The German artists I had engaged all trembled for their lives.

What could have happened since my departure from Paris to change the temper of the people?

The Chauvinistic press had started such an active campaign against us that even the more conservative journals dared make no defence. A number of these as well had gone to the enemy,* and others, the *Figaro* among them, advised us to abandon our project.

The signed contracts, however, were binding. I sent the whole paraphernalia (costumes, weapons, etc., which had been partly paid for) to Leipsic and let my contract with the Théâtre des Nations go by default, losing my deposit of fifteen thousand francs.

But the question was, who had sent that telegram to the King? None but the German ambassador himself!

.   .   .   .   .   .

Now I meant to delight the Leipsigers with the performance I had intended for Paris. On the 19th of February, —in Leipsic then instead of Paris,—took place the performance of " Lohengrin " with this all-star cast.

* Many journals even published extracts and translations of Richard Wagner's " Farce of the Ancient Mariner" and his amusing "Capitulation," written late in 1870.

King Henry................Heinrich Wiegand
Lohengrin...................George Lederer
Telramund.....................Otto Schelper
Elsa.................Anna Sachse-Hofmeister
Ortrud...........Hedwig Reicher-Kindermann

Conductor......................Anton Seidl

The crowd was tremendous. The box office was closed the day of the performance and not even standing-room was left. The house was as enthusiastic as possible.

This evening something unusual took place. Shortly before Lohengrin's entrance in the boat I remembered I had planned a new effect for the swan boat with the French scene-painter, which had made an unusually good impression even in our rehearsals. As I could not see this entrance from the director's box I hurried over to the balcony in the centre and stood by the door (there being no vacant seats) to get the effect of the scene. It was magnificent. Charmed by the picture, I resolved in spite of my uncomfortable position to see the act out from that spot. But at the first words of Ortrud in her great duet I noticed that Kindermann's voice was decidedly hoarse. This grew more and more noticeable and at the close of the scene I hurried on to the stage, quite prepared to have the artist tell me she could not go on. Not so, however. She declared she never had felt better in her life. Yet still I feared an accident to the performance, for I did not see how she could sing out her rôle with her increasing hoarseness. With no further remarks I sent a carriage directly for her under-study Orlanda Riegler, telling her to come at once with her costumes for "Ortrud."

On my way back to my box at the opening of the second act I met the man I had sent, and asked if Riegler were already in the greenroom. Judge of my horror when he answered that Director Seidl had asked him to tell me that my fears were all imaginary—Mme. Kinder-

mann was in the best possible voice this evening. With
a sharp reprimand I sent him off again, and as the singer
lived in the neighbourhood she was soon there, and
presently they were dressing her.

In the meantime the act had proceeded on the stage.
With every note that Kindermann sang I saw—no, I
heard—the hour of catastrophe approaching. I hurried
to the greenroom and grasped Riegler by the hand (she
was calmly putting the finishing touches to her costume),
and while we made our way to the further wing,—our
entrance not being possible on that side,—the property
woman added the final details. Suddenly she exclaimed
" I'm losing my petticoat, pin it on quick! " But there
was no time for that. I jerked it off from her myself—
and then rushed my Ortrud No. 2 to the spot from which
she could make her entrance, expecting every instant to
see Ortrud No. 1 end her career.

We were not a moment too soon. The manager had
already given the order to darken the stage, and just as
we came down into the wings I saw Ortrud No. 1 falter.
Seeing me, she hissed out in a quick whisper, " I can't go
on! " Then not knowing of my precautionary measure,
she begged, " Send for Riegler." What a shock she must
have had to catch sight of Riegler herself, ready and on
the spot.

As the stage was thoroughly darkened, the audience
never knew when the one went off and the other stepped
on, and the illusion was kept up for some time by the
similarity of the costumes. Finally, however, they noticed
a difference in the voices and perceived the change.

This incident made a tremendous impression on the
people of Leipsic, who are great theatre-goers. The
papers spoke most flatteringly of my careful management
and presence of mind. The charge circulated by the disgruntled element, that it had been a " coup " planned and
carried out between ourselves, was received with derision.

This, as well as another incident which I can hardly quote here, proves the truth of that old saying of Heinrich Laube: "A director who plays the game sitting at his office desk is no sort of director at all: he makes you think of a general who fights his battles in the office of the Secretary of War. The place for a director is on the stage!"

We next rehearsed Weber's "Euranthe." Reicher-Kindermann came to me one day, complaining that I had not cast her for the title-rôle but had given her the Eglantine. She declared she could not sing the great aria in that rôle,—that it lay too high for her voice,—and contradicted my assurance that she would make a tremendous hit in just that part. However, I soothed her by saying I would have the aria transposed. When the time came, however, for that scene in the general rehearsal, I was called off the stage. A very influential member of the board wished to speak to me just as Kindermann began her song. I could hardly listen to what the member had to say; my whole attention was centred on the prima-donna.

At the close I was convinced that the thing lost all effect in the transposition. Excusing myself as best I could, I hurried back to the stage, saying, "My dear Madame, now let me ask you to sing that aria as it was written." She insisted it was impossible, and assured me that Seidl had agreed it was too high.

I then begged her as a personal favour to *me* to try it just once as it was written, and then to-morrow at the performance she might sing it in the lower key:—so she consented. I can hardly describe the storm of applause that broke out on all sides at the close of that aria—chorus, orchestra, soloists and all! The artist, overcome with emotion, tried to kiss my hand in grateful recognition.

Our conductor for these rehearsals and for the final performance was Arthur Nikisch.

Our new and brilliant " Lohengrin " in Leipsic consoled me then for my Parisian failure. The French press grew so vituperative that we were forced to resign all future plans. It only remained for me to carry out all my contracts with a faithful celerity. As far as I was concerned, the newspaper talk would not have hindered my enterprise, for I had more faith in that intelligent public than to fear it could be dictated to by a venal press in the matter of such a masterpiece.

But the Royal Operas of Vienna and Munich were afraid to risk their Scaria, Reichmann, Vogl, etc., etc., and withheld the permissions at the critical moment. Without these well-known stars I could hardly expect to make a success in Paris, so I decided, in spite of the tremendous losses it entailed, to give the matter up entirely.

In relating my Paris experience and the Leipsic performance that was its outcome, I have not strictly followed the course of events as they occurred, and have omitted the account of our performance of " Tristan and Isolde," January 2, 1882. The Master had not been present at the rehearsals as he had wished, for he was still in Italy.

The cast was:

Tristan......................George Lederer
Isolde.............Hedwig Reicher-Kindermann
King Mark.................Heinrich Wiegand
Kurwenal.....................Otto Schelper
Brangäne..................Katharina Klafsky

I was able to send Wagner, who was then in Palermo, a most enthusiastic report by wire, which I followed up later by a letter:

My dear and honoured Master:
Though I have had no word acknowledging my telegram

HEDWIG REICHER-KINDERMANN.

I hope you got my news of the glorious triumph of our
" Tristan and Isolde."

The splendid work brought their enthusiasm to a white
heat and pleased the public tremendously. One might
have thought that we children of the colder north had
caught in a measure the ardent spirit of the south, a dash
of Italian warmth;—to have called forth which, my dear
Master, must have been a source of most pleasurable
gratification to you. Our capable Seidl did wonders with
the orchestra, and the ensemble of the performance—
though *I* should not be the one to praise it—was unanimously said to have been magnificent.

Schelper as Kurwenal had his usual ovation and
Lederer as Tristan quite surpassed himself and gave an
impersonation which, according to Oscar Paul's judgment, places him among the first tenors of the German
stage.

But   Reicher-Kindermann's   magnetic   performance
brought down the house with frantic applause. I do not
in the least doubt, my dear Master, that even you would
have agreed with us in our verdict had you seen her passionate intensity, her dramatic abandon, and heard her
glorious voice.

Our second performance took place on Sunday, repeating the success of the first evening. All the singers,—
Klafsky as Brangäne, Wiegand as Mark, Lieban as the
Shepherd, Caliga as Melot,—had their share as well, of
the applause. To this joyful announcement I can add
another no less joyful,—in fact even more important in
its consequences. The outlook for the London campaign
is brilliant. We already have as many advance sub-
scriptions as we had in Berlin up to the day of the final
rehearsal. With that in sight it strikes me our success in
London is beyond any question. This success at our first
great bivouac along the line has encouraged me tremendously, and I am now ready to announce to you that your

plan of the " Wandering Wagner Theatre " is rapidly approaching completion.

I have now resolved to engage my own orchestra and my own chorus; and have the definite assurance that not only Scaria but the Vogls as well will associate themselves with our enterprise. I have not yet closed the contracts with the latter, but matters have taken such shape that I no longer doubt their consent. These engagements naturally have been exceedingly costly. But my faith in the triumphant qualities of your works has given me the courage of my convictions—but greater than all is my faith in your powerful support, my honoured Master. This I now demand on the following lines:

Until the close of our tour (from September 1, 1882, until May 31, 1883) will you promise to refuse all concessions for the performance of the " Nibelungen Ring " both at home and abroad (naturally not including the rights already conceded) ?

When you consider that I can only undertake this venture, with its tremendous risks, on condition that it is a *first performance* in every place where I am to appear, you will find my request most natural.

The management of the Königsberg theatre, for instance, is about to ask you for the rights. If you were to grant them I should have to cross this town off my list,— as well as every other place that had the same rights. That would be a death-blow to the Wagner Theatre.

So, my dear Master, I beg you most urgently either to refuse or to postpone all such offers, and keep these rights to yourself until after the 31st of May, 1883.

Only under such circumstances can I go into the work with any hope of success. Then, however, my hope will be a certainty, and neither you nor I will be disappointed.

I shall give thirty-six cycles within the course of nine months. That would give you, according to my calculations, one hundred and fifty thousand Marks in royalty.

My outlay will be gigantic, but it will be more than covered if I can be assured of your support on these points.

Respectfully and devotedly,

Angelo Neumann.

In a few days came Wagner's answer:

Palermo, January 16, 1882 (Hotel des Palmes).

Incomparable Friend and Ally:

It was most thoughtful of you to wire me of the success of "Tristan" at your theatre,—but what answer was there for me to make? Had you asked me a question? The question I asked myself remained unanswered because I am still in doubt as to the matter.

You know it was my desire that this work, still in its problematic stages, should not be given again until I could personally direct the rehearsals. Now, however, it has been given without me,—and that fills me with amazement. And now,—Long may it prosper!

Of course I recognise in Seidl a born genius who needs only a little added warmth to astonish even me: and so I beg of you, for the good of the *whole,* to give him a freer hand in the matter of the scenic arrangements than is usually given to the conductor, *for herein lies his specialty and what he has particularly learned of me!*

I have not yet found time—I am far from well and need the rest—to answer the letter from the Königsberg management: I shall naturally refuse, however. I thought our last agreement had fully assured you that I should give no further rights for the N. R. as long as our contract holds for your difficult undertaking. (Frankfort applied just before the signing of our agreement.)

Though I consider it unnecessary to send the further agreement you have asked for,—simply to quiet you I hereby announce that it is soon to follow.

For London as well, I shall give you all the assistance within my powers.

As to Paris,—I wish indeed you would give it up. I can
hardly see now how you induced me to give my consent.
Had you not spent so much money on it, or if I knew
where else you could use these properties to reimburse
yourself for your outlay there, I should beg you to cancel
our French contract entirely and should then turn over
the rights to the " Commission d'auteurs dramatiques "
of which I am a member, with the permission to give them
in any language whatsoever.

You are too young, and really as yet too inexperienced,
to understand fully the diplomatic difficulties of " arriv-
ing " in such an arrogant centre of culture as Paris.   For
myself—the very thought of *contact* with it, disgusts me!
I fear that after another such experience you will agree
with me.

Content yourself, my dearest friend, for to-day with this
feeble evidence of my existence, and may this request explain all the rest.

Hearty greetings for Seidl and his valiant guard!
Devotedly yours,
Rich. Wagner.

The next letter shows how eagerly and heartily Wagner
in Palermo followed the further course of my plans.

Best of Neumanns:

A few words of advice!   This Königsberg letter (which
I don't intend to answer) may interest you.   In case G.
has not published my letter (concerning your project),
it might be a clever plan for you to give this copy to the
papers (leaving out perhaps the name of the writer) : for
to my mind it is the best possible commentary on the
purpose and the character of your undertaking.

Even if I don't always follow up your glad announcements with an answering shout of triumph (as in the
case of your late Leipsic success) you must surely know
what pleasure your news invariably gives me.

Kindly give this enclosed answer to Dr. Görres after
reading and sealing the note.   You see I am always ready
to smooth the way for you.

Warmest greetings—*if* you please—to Dr. Förster and
" *Antonio* " Seidl, and don't forget that I emphatically
recommend you to rely on his judgment and give him the
control.
With warmest greetings,
Your devoted

Palermo,   Rich. Wagner.
Villa del Principe Gangi,
   Piazza Porrazzi,
     February 19, '82.

I shall quote the enclosed letter to Dr. Martin Görres
concerning the refusal of an invitation.

Honoured Sir:

Herr Neumann knows how he stands with me, and how
highly I value his services in the presentation of my works.
Just where I stand, however, with my native town of
Leipsic,—which has withdrawn from him the privilege of
fostering their production in that place,—is a question I
am not so certain of.

Hitherto the demands of my work have prevented my
enjoying the pleasure I had promised myself,—something
in the nature of a fifty years' anniversary in Leipsic of
the first performance of one of my youthful operas; if,
however, I renounce this idea now, it is because I should
have an uncomfortable feeling on seeing my works in the
hands of strangers, with a board of directors who are
quite indifferent to me;—and if I should thus give them
my countenance, I should be publicly doing a grievous
injury to those who formerly directed the opera in Leipsic
and in whom I have every confidence.
Yours truly,

                          Richard Wagner.
Palermo, February 20, 1882.

The second enclosure in this same envelope was a letter to the director of the Königsberg theatre.

Honoured Sir:

It would never have entered into my head to allow the production of my " Nibelungen " Trilogy in our theatres had I not ample security and binding promises, such as you have recently given me in offering to popularise my works upon our German stage.

All such attempts, however (aside from the Royal Opera of Munich, which continues under special patronage), have failed,—with the single exception of the Leipsic theatre, which has been invariably successful; while Vienna, for instance, could not even find a suitable tenor for the rôles. Hamburg was a most signal fiasco,—and Mannheim, Cologne, and even Schwerin and Braunschweig made brief but unsuccessful attempts.

This continued success at Leipsic I owe entirely to the great energy and the ready attention to my views and methods which I have always found in the late director of that theatre.

This, as well as his recent signal success in Berlin, has led me to entrust Director Neumann with the further production of my entire cycle in those German cities which have not yet had the opportunity of hearing them; giving him my support and full power of attorney,— within certain time-limits.

While I give the public of such towns the advantage of hearing my works in their entirety—and given in a superior manner—at the same time I give the *directors* an added advantage;—for when their audiences are acquainted with my works as a whole, so that the production of a single opera would be understood and appreciated, I should gladly dispose of the rights for a single performance, which could then make a successful run in the regular theatre repertoire.

I now ask you to weigh this advantage well, and instead of considering it an insult that I should send you a model production of the "Nibelungen Ring" for your stage, rather take it as a genuine assistance which, far from injuring your enterprise, will be of inestimable benefit; as I will then gladly turn over the rights for a single performance—for you to rival the original—*if you can!*

Respectfully,

Richard Wagner.

Palermo, January 30, 1882.

To these copies the following note was added:

Dear Neumann:

If Goldberg hasn't done it, I will gladly allow you to make use of this answer for publication.

R. W.

The letters which I now quote are chiefly concerned with Paris and give a remarkable insight into Wagner's thoughts and opinions.

Dear and valued Friend:

I cannot understand why you should always be asking me questions which you could answer for yourself if you had made the proper use of the letters I gave you for Ch. Truchet (Nuitter). This friend has long been my agent in Paris and knows all about my position and my rights, —of which I have not abrogated a single one.

For some time he has been negotiating with the former director of the Grand Opera (Perrin) concerning "Lohengrin," and thereby has learned that I was quite within my rights in refusing my permission. The same is true in the case of Pasdeloup, to whom I had given the rights for "Rienzi." Then why this legal circumlocution?

At the same time I call your attention to the fact that I have resolved *never*—so long as my powers are left me— to allow my operas to be produced in Paris; and I intend to use the concession I have already made you (as long as it lasts) as a means to prevent other such attempts.

You yourself must certainly see before long that Paris will have to be given up: I wish you might see it now and simply give me back my contract.

I know Paris thoroughly, and find it incompatible with my honour to appear to lay any stress on a Parisian success.

The properties for " Lohengrin " you can probably turn to account elsewhere.

And this last is final—the translation of the " Nibelungen Ring " must be NORMANN'S, NOT Corder's! *

For important reasons!

Yours,

R. W.

(Palermo, February 26, 1882.)

My dear Friend:

Monsieur Reitlinger (sic) seems somewhat eccentric: beware!—Why does he continue to harp on those tiresome questions, since my friend Truchet set him right on those points as long ago as last November? I cannot endure it!

The enclosed letter will advise you as to affairs and you too will certainly find it strange that your Paris agent should still be in doubt as to these facts.

With best greetings,

Devotedly,

R. Wagner.

Piazza Porazzi,
Villa Gangi,
Palermo, March 7, '82.

P. S. Moreover I want to repeat my most emphatic wish, that you *give up* Paris—as I have.

* This refers to the libretto for London. These words are heavily underlined.

I should like to end this chapter with an account of an invitation from the Grand Duke of Weimar. I was asked to bring our entire company for a performance of "Tristan" at the court theatre there. The interest in the work and its production was tremendous—Hedwig Reicher-Kindermann especially received a wonderful ovation, and the Grand Duke's orchestra under Lassen was splendidly drilled.

At the close of the second act Baron von Loën, the director of the theatre, came to conduct me to the Grand Duke's box. The august gentleman expressed his enthusiasm and satisfaction at the artistic treat we had given him; and decorating me with the order of his house, he said, "Kindly accept this little token, my dear Director, as a reminder of this pleasant evening."

This production in Weimar, and our continued success in the further performances at Leipsic, were a source of deepest pleasure to the Master.

CHAPTER XV

LONDON

On the 1st of April, 1882, I left Leipsic for London with my whole technical staff, to instal our Bàyreuth appurtenances for the " Nibelungen" in Her Majesty's Theatre. These last, as well as all the costumer's properties, had lain for six years in the storehouses of the Bayreuth theatre.

My contract with Director Mapleson set forth that he was to—" turn over the theatre in perfect condition, with a full technical and administrative staff; with light and heat for rehearsals and performances; with an orchestra according to my stipulations; with a male chorus for the 'Götterdämmerung' (about twenty-eight strong), with the necessary advance agents, bill posters and advertisements "—this last a very important and costly item in England.

When I landed in London and called at the director's office I found that Mapleson was touring America with an opera company. After inspecting the theatre and making some preliminary arrangements, I had a notice from the proprietors (a well-known London bank) giving me the amazing information that Mr. Mapleson was in their debt for his lease and not legally entitled to sublet the theatre. If I intended the performances to take place at Her Majesty's Theatre in May I must make my terms with them.

I shall not soon forget that moment! I went directly to Mapleson's agent, demanding an explanation.

" Mr. Mapleson," he said," " was at present in America—

216

or possibly in South Africa—he hardly knew which!" I then asked about the chorus and orchestra—to which he replied, "You could hardly expect us to furnish those!" Then he finally told me I was to provide my own staff of workmen as well. Imagine my state of mind! I had come to London with my technical staff to arrange the Bayreuth apparatus,—all my contracts with the artists were signed—a withdrawal now on my part would mean an utter and complete confession of failure!

But then,—no theatre, no orchestra, no chorus, and no workmen,—and the performance to begin in four weeks!

I closed a quick contract with the owners of the theatre, and I must say they treated me most honourably,—though naturally upholding their own rightful interests. I paid their deposit and then set about engaging my staff.

Finally I arranged the matter of my placards and announcements. But first of all I wired to Leipsic, sending Anton Seidl—who was to have joined me for the rehearsals in a few days—direct to Hamburg to engage the Laube orchestra, which he was to drill there during the month of April. Then I hired the chorus of the Cologne Opera Company.

And now at last I could turn my attention to the immense technical difficulties before me in London.

When finally at the end of April all our members appeared and our rehearsals began, my arrangements proved to have been successful—for all the parts neatly dovetailed.

But I had failed to reckon on one adversary—the carpet man.

As is well known, the foyers, boxes, stairs and halls of the London theatres are fitted out with gorgeous carpets and most tasteful draperies. As I entered the theatre one day just before the final rehearsal, I noticed to my dismay that carpets and tapestries had vanished. On questioning I discovered that these valuable articles belonged to the upholsterer, and would be restored to their proper places—*only* on payment of a certain sum!

Here was a new business deal—a new contract to sign. But men are fortunately amenable where money is freely used;—and so at the final rehearsal our walls and floors were again fitted out with their gorgeous coverings, all fresh from the cleaner's hands.

So finally I find myself in a condition to catch my breath and wait for the opening performance on the following night.

At eight o'clock on the 5th of May as Seidl stepped to the conductor's desk, took up his bâton, and gave the signal for the introduction to the " Rhinegold," Albert Niemann came to me, saying, " Herr Director, none of us considered it possible that you could settle all these tremendous difficulties so smoothly and that we should open so favourably on the very day you set."

I never saw Mapleson but once. One day, during our rehearsals, he suddenly walked into the theatre, greeted me cordially as though we were old friends, seemed in the best of moods, and said: " Well, you're getting on famously, I hear—you're the devil of a fellow—I don't mean any offence! Won't you lunch with me? I'd be awfully glad if you would." I refused politely, saying I was needed every instant at the theatre, but asked him to set a time when we could have a business talk.

" Ah! " said he. " To-morrow, day after to-morrow,— any time you say." With a hearty handshake and a cheery " Good-bye " he went off, and I never saw this talented impresario—and still more talented *insolvent*— again! He soon went into bankruptcy, and for the two thousand six hundred pounds he owed me I received a check for fifty-one pounds some eight years later.

My first day in London left no doubts in my mind as to the rival performances of Francke and Pollini, for their placards were everywhere.

It is well known that in London, especially at that time, no theatrical enterprise like ours could be assured of good houses without the countenance of the court, particularly the Prince of Wales (now Edward VII.), for the aristocracy and the whole mass of English people blindly followed his lead. Remembering the gracious offer of our Crown Prince (the late Emperor Frederick), I had gone to Berlin to ask for the letters of introduction he had promised me.

Count Eulenberg, who received me, said he was very sorry that his Highness was off hunting. He himself remembered perfectly the interest the Prince and his family had taken in our Berlin performances and added: " Make your mind easy. Go back to Leipsic and I'll arrange it for you at my first opportunity when the Prince returns. I'll send you word at Leipsic, and I'm sure I can get you the letters." A few days later I had a message saying that on my arrival in London I should find at my hotel a letter of introduction to the Prince of Wales.

When I appeared for my audience the Prince received me with gracious urbanity, offered me a cigar, and asked me to explain my plans, saying he had just had a personal note from his brother-in-law, Prince Frederick. He assured me he was most keenly interested in the success of my venture and begged me to let him know if he could be of any assistance. I said I had come to request the honour of his presence and that of the Princess at the first cycle of the Richard Wagner operas. " How many performances does this make that you want us to attend?" " There are four evenings in the cycle," I answered. Instantly he said, " That's impossible—utterly impossible!"—and asking me to sit beside him at his desk, he opened a ledger and showed me. " You see for yourself. There are the dinners my wife and I have accepted for the season—and here are the dinners we give ourselves." The list reached well into July. Then he continued, "Now how can I possibly get four evenings free?"—to which I answered: "In that case, your Highness, the Richard Wagner Opera Company is doomed, as far as London is concerned!" "You horrify me!" he declared. And after he had run through again in *sotto voce* the letter from Prince Frederick—"'I hope you'll do all you can for Neumann in his undertaking. I shall be eternally grateful to you if you will;'"—he asked, "And now, how will this look to my brother-in-law?" Then he added, "At what time do your performances begin?" "At eight o'clock." "There, you see! And our dinners begin at 7.30."

Then he made further minute inquiries as to the details of our arrangements, and finally dismissed me with the following words, "I'll have to write my brother-in-law about it. The first night, yes:—but *four* nights in one week? Well, I'll see what we can do!" And he kept his word.

Not only four nights, but actually eleven, the Prince and all his suite attended our performances of the "Nibelungen Ring"! As well as the Duke and Duchess of Edinburgh, Princess Beatrice, the Crown Prince of Denmark, the Grand Duchess of Mecklenburg-Strelitz, and a host of other important dignitaries.

During the performance of "Rhinegold" the Prince came behind the scenes, where the swimming apparatus for the Rhine maidens interested him especially. We gave him a practical demonstration of their use, but I think he would have preferred to have the fascinating young Augusta Kraus (later Mme. Anton Seidl), who was standing there in her street dress, put on her nixie costume again and show him how it went. Instead of this, however, one of our machinists got into the little car; but the Prince turned away with an indifferent "What the devil!"

·   ·   ·   ·   ·   ·

As I have said, the Master had repeatedly promised his presence at our London rehearsals, and as the time of our first performance approached Mme. Cosima wrote:

My dear Director:

My husband asks me to say that he has hesitated a long time before announcing that circumstances have compelled him to give up the London trip. He will be perfectly satisfied if his forces prove themselves worthy of the place in Bayreuth that is waiting for them.

As for you, my dear Director, he feels he has given so many assurances of his high esteem for your capacities that you can no longer doubt that only stern necessity compels him to refuse your request.

He sends his most cordial greetings, to which I add my warmest regards.   C. Wagner.

Venice, Hôtel d'Europe,
    April 17, 1882.

Förster now, at my instigation, wrote Wagner one of his famous persuasive letters, describing the glittering triumphs that awaited him in London, the Doctor's cap at Oxford, etc., in most glowing colours.

Wagner answered:

My honoured Friend and Benefactor:

That's what one gets for living in this world of lies!

Yesterday my wife wrote directly to Neumann that even if I wished to (and I never actually promised!) — the state of my health absolutely forbids my coming to London. Even in this mild climate I am forced to recognise that I must avoid all nervous excitement from which, in consideration of my approaching seventieth year, I have long been shielded. You've had experience enough—*I should think*—with me in that line!

Organically I am normal and sound, but at the least excitement, even a moral excitement, comes a congestion of the heart with many alarming symptoms which only absolute and immediate rest can control.

If under such difficulties I still attend to the artistic details of my coming " Parsifal " performance, it is only made possible by the strict and well-established order with which everything there is carried out, and by the fact that in Bayreuth I am at home and can be cared for, isolated and shielded from all outside demands on my person.

Those very triumphs which you picture so alluringly are precisely what would place me in the most awkward predicament,—where I should do Neumann's cause more harm than good. For these reasons I have declined the Doctor's cap at Oxford with thanks—you are mistaken about Father Haydn, but it has recently proved most becoming to Joachim and Brahms!

All I can do now for the furtherance of our " Nibelungen " cause is to hand over to Neumann (for publication?) an assurance of my presence in London, and at the time of the performances to circulate an announcement of my illness; and finally to have my wife send a note, like that of yesterday, expressing regret for my absence and emphasising my confidence in his management.

You know I am always ready to testify in his behalf; particularly in view of the difficulties arising from this competition with the Francke-Richter-Pollini Company— which I tried from the first to prevent but found I could not hinder.

Do *please* have a little faith in my sincerity!

Greetings from the heart,

From your devoted

Richard Wagner.

Venice, Hôtel d'Europe,
April 19, 1882.

So in consideration of the effect of a nervous excitement on his health, and in view of the coming " Parsifal " performances in July, the Master could not be present in London. Among the propositions he made, I chose the simplest way of accounting for his non-appearance, merely giving the above reasons. Naturally, however, this announcement caused a decided shrinkage in our receipts, which up to now had prospered famously.

I must mention here an amusing incident. It was at a performance of " Rigoletto " in the Covent-Garden Theatre, in the course of which one of the city council of Leipsic, Herr Nagel, who happened to be there that evening, came into my box. I asked him to stay, and presently he remarked how tremendously popular I had grown in London,—for every glass in the house was levelled at our box. In the next intermission we made a startling discovery! It was not I who seemed to be the centre of attraction, but my guest—and as we left our seats a crowd soon collected about him in the foyer. Asking the meaning of this singular performance, we found to our amazement that the audience had taken Councillor Nagel—for *Wagner himself!* And really, when my attention was called to it, there was a certain undeniable resemblance for a moment!

A most tragic occurrence at the first performance of " The Valkyre " must be reported now, as it has to do with one of the finest exponents of Wagner's art, and was a dismal presage of this singer's clouded future.

Emil Scaria, who sang Wotan that night, ended his long narration in the second act in triumph. But when the same man came out for " The Valkyre " scene in the third act, timid and shy, creeping like a hunted soul, with drooping shoulders and a trailing lance;—when we saw him make his entrance from the wrong side, Heinrich Vogl (Niemann was singing Siegmund that night) sprang forward as suddenly as I, exclaiming, " My Heavens, Scaria has gone mad! "

Imagine our horror as Scaria, all through that most

important scene, transposed his entire part,—singing the high notes all an octave below, and the low notes an octave above the score; and casting timid and appealing glances into the wings meanwhile, as though some danger threatened him from there.

As I had witnessed the last tragic appearance of Alois Anders in Vienna I could not rid my mind of the striking similarity, and the hideous impressions of that awful night I shall never forget.

Even Niemann, Seidl and others remarked at the time that Scaria must have been quite insane.

The next day was an intermission. Scaria, who seemed to have no recollection of the occurrences of the night before, complained of a violent headache and asked for two extra piano rehearsals for his rôle of the Wanderer in " Siegfried " the following night. Seidl's report of these rehearsals was not exactly reassuring. He had utterly forgotten the text and the music—the whole rôle seemed absolutely new to him! Poor Scaria!

I shall speak later of this strange pathological incident.

In the " Siegfried " performance it was finally demonstrated that we should have to dismiss this magnificent artist; for, as though Hagen had handed *him* the cup of forgetfulness, whole pages of the score, which he had formerly mastered with consummate ease, were now absolutely blank.

Once off the stage he seemed to have no recollection of these lapses and was furious at me for giving his rôles to Schelper and Reichmann. I soothed him and suggested a vacation, which seemed to have helped him. For four months later he appeared at Bayreuth, where his Gurnemanz in " Parsifal " amazed the world and roused even the Master's artistic approval. To be sure, they had to detail a special prompter to whisper every word at him!

After his Bayreuth engagement his condition improved

so steadily that he again became the favourite Wotan of
the Richard Wagner Opera Company for its tour of 1882-
1883 in Rome, Brussels, Amsterdam and other cities.
Later, in Prague, at the opening of my direction there in
1885, he came and sang at our invitation.

It was not until 1886 at a performance of " Tannhäuser " in Vienna that the latent trouble broke out in a
most frightful manner. In the course of the second act
he came to Elizabeth and whispered, " What opera is this
we're doing? " He could hardly keep his feet, and had to
be led from the stage. That was the end of this glorious
singer!

Aside from that gruesome episode, the course of our
performances was smooth and brilliant. I shall mention
one singular occurrence to emphasise the inexhausible
genius of Hedwig Reicher-Kindermann.

At the final rehearsal of " Rhinegold " I was not at all
satisfied with the tenor who sang Froh. Reicher-Kindermann (our Fricka) had noticed this, and coming up to me,
said in her delicious imitation of the Bavarian dialect,
" Say, Director, you don't like Froh—what? I'll tell you
now,—I'll sing it for you—I'm sure I can! " It was just
at that song after the storm—" Wie liebliche Luft wieder
uns weht," etc.

I grasped at her offer, stepped to the footlights, and
asked Seidl to stop a moment. Then I turned again to
ask if she felt absolutely sure of the rôle. " Well! " said
the star reproachfully; whereupon I informed Froh that
Fricka was to sing those lines, and quieted his remonstrances by saying it was by Wagner's order!

That performance showed the full powers of Hedwig
Reicher-Kindermann. Those bars were a revelation to the
audience and to us all. Such a storm of applause followed as none of us had ever heard before in that apparently unimportant part. At the close of the performance the Prince of Wales remarked, " My dear sir, your

Fricka is the most remarkable dramatic soprano I ever yet have heard!"

Great as was the London success of the Richard Wagner Opera Company, I shall not try to hide the fact that the Francke-Pollini venture ended in most dismal failure. It was not that these performances under Hans Richter were any less artistic, but at the close of the season their chorus and orchestra could not be paid, and their sad adventures were long a scandal in the theatrical world. Pollini left abruptly—he gave out he had been called to Hamburg—and the chorus and orchestra were to be paid off after his departure!

How correct I had been in my premonitions when I warned the Master not to give concessions to two such enterprises at once,—even though both should be fitted to advance the cause of German art in London!

Richard Wagner now sent us the following telegram of congratulations:

Bayreuth, May 30.
" You've played your part
For Wagner's art.
Accept these thanks
With all my heart."

CHAPTER XVI

" PARSIFAL "

RETURNED from London, I began at once my preparations for the great Richard Wagner tour to open in the fall. On the 12th of June I wrote, repeating my request that Wagner should give me the exclusive rights for " Tristan " and the " Ring," as this would simplify my arrangements.

Wagner answered:

Dear Benefactor, Sir and Friend:
If there were anything on this earth that could still astonish me, it would be *you!* Heavens, what energy, what faith, and what courage! Well, I'll never leave you in the lurch!

As to " Tristan " there's only one difficulty,—but that can be arranged as soon as I've smoothed down Batz.

For the " Nibelungen," haven't you every concession you ever asked for? Is there anything *more* you want? I shouldn't wonder!

Then it's settled that you and Seidl will come! Till then.

Yours in breathless devotion,

R. Wagner.

Bayreuth, June 13 (???) (sic).

The allusion to Batz concerns an old lawsuit we had with Batz and Valtz (former agents for Wagner) in the matter of our dealing directly with the Master and not through them. Wagner had suffered at their hands and had written rather a sharp letter, of which he sent me a copy for publication.

Venice, April 26, 1882.

My dear Mr. Batz:

I can scarcely believe you could have so little consideration for the age and dignity you lay such stress upon, as to arouse my " octogenarian " blood to that condition of nervous circulation which men commonly call wrath, in this matter of my control of the fruit of a lifelong labour!

You seem to feel you have sufficiently proved your attachment to my person by a touching and minute inquiry as to my health. This is only *one* of your many mistakes which have forced me finally to break off our connections and entrust my affairs to another agent.

I am pained now to hear that this step has led you to further anxieties as to my welfare. To clear up this misunderstanding in a friendly manner I should like to appoint a meeting here in Bayreuth at your convenience, any time within the coming month. I hope hereby to arrive at a pleasant termination to the relations that have heretofore existed between us.

At present, however, I shall content myself with asking you not to interfere further in the matter of my disposal of the rights for " Tristan and Isolde "—according to the terms, (which I distinctly recall,) of our contract.

If you were to proceed against the directors of Leipsic in this matter, you would necessarily be acting not against *these directors,* who were fully authorised in their production of " Tristan," but against *me* who gave them this authorisation.

Hereby you would probably find yourself playing rather a singular rôle! Events would prove that according to the contract you would have to produce,—not you, but *I* would be found to have the power of conceding these rights; and you could only give such a consent after obtaining my special permission. The rights you fancy you have acquired will soon be investigated, and will prove somewhat flimsy as the basis for a contract.

Such investigation would also prove the true value of your services to me in the past with regard to these so-called "rights." It will be a simple matter then to contradict your claim—" that when,"—after long consideration and many hesitations due to my conscience in artistic matters, " I finally decide to give a certain theatre the rights of presenting my ' Tristan '—' I am not to forget' forsooth ' to give *you* due notice,' and to let you draw my Royalties "—a proceeding for which you charged an unwarrantable percentage and which the postman now manages for me quite as satisfactorily.

As I say, after my repeated demands on this subject, I can hardly believe it possible that you have so utterly ignored my wishes and have calmly proceeded behind my back to swindle these most capable men who have proved themselves so genuinely devoted to my interests. Hence I take it for granted that you cannot be in earnest in this attempt, but that you still wish to continue your connection with me on a footing of respectability!

In view of your tremendous services with regard to the lapsed copyrights of my earlier operas and the unflagging zeal of your efforts in my behalf in this matter for the last ten years,—I now repeat my invitation to Bayreuth and offer you a new opportunity to show your zest and devotion;—reserving the right,—to the best of my ability,—of judging and then rewarding your conduct.

Hoping you will agree to my proposition in a friendly and amenable spirit, I remain,

Respectfully yours,

Richard Wagner.

Gradually our term as directors of the Leipsic theatre drew to a close. We could end our career in Wagner's

birthplace in no more fitting manner than by giving the
full series of his works from " Rienzi " to " Götterdämmerung." I shall omit the account of the magnificent
ovation given to Dr. Förster and myself on this occasion,
but I shall never forget that thrilling moment when Dr.
Georgi, the head of the Leipsic council, stepped to the
footlights after the close of the " Götterdämmerung " and
made us a little speech before the audience, saying that
their theatre had never reached so high a plane before.

Then followed a delegation from the Wagner Society,
acknowledging our services in the Master's behalf and
handing me a testimonial, which is one of my most
cherished possessions.

I freely admit the parting from Leipsic was a sad one.
In all my public experience I have never found more enthusiastic or more discriminating audiences. Even those
who, as I have said, opposed me most fiercely at first when
I came there unknown and unheralded,—I still hold in
grateful recollection. For it was these very adversaries
that steeled my energies and doubled my capacity!

But the die was cast, and I now accepted a call from
the German National Theatre in Prague. It was not my
first visit to the Bohemian capital, and the place made the
same charming impression on me as always. In those
days German was almost the universal language, shops
and streets still having German signs.

.   .   .   .   .   .

Early in July Dr. Förster and I left our families together at the little villa " Fantasie " in the neighbouring
summer resort of Donndorf and started ourselves for Bayreuth. We announced our presence with an early call at
Wahnfried, which was promptly returned by Mme. Cosima
in person,—yet in these first days we saw nothing of
Wagner, as his time was completely taken up by the " Parsifal " rehearsals.

We were not to see him until an evening reception at
Wahnfried. He came directly up and took me off into a
little room where we could be free to talk things over.
A certain Countess, whose name I have now forgotten,
was blissfully hovering in the vicinity of the great man,
and followed us to the little anteroom—not noticing in
her rapt daze that Wagner wished to be undisturbed.
But she soon regretted her rash step—for turning suddenly, the Master thundered at her with the voice of an
outraged god, " Can't you see I want to be alone with this
gentleman?—we have important matters to discuss! "
Then he took me by the arm and shouldered me into a
further corner, while the poor trembling creature crawled
meekly away in silence.

" Neumann," he began, " I'm quite convinced now I
was wrong in granting that second concession for London. It would have been better if I'd taken your advice." And then the explanation which followed as to
his breaking his promise of coming to London was touching in the extreme. He spoke so warmly and overwhelmed
me so with glowing praise that every trace of my vexation
must needs have vanished—even if I had not already understood that his absence, which was such a bitter blow
to me at the time, was absolutely unavoidable, owing to
the tremendous demands of the " Parsifal " preparations.
In short I was completely disarmed, and the relations between us were more cordial than ever.

The first performance of " Parsifal " took place on the
29th of July and was an epoch-making occasion to all
those present. The audience itself naturally on such an
evening was tremendously interesting. Interest and expectation were at their greatest height.

Förster and I had seats in the third row of the parquet
and, as chance would have it, Albert Niemann, the great
Wagner interpreter, and his wife sat directly behind us.

Words fail me to express the deep impression this work

made upon us all. A lofty ecstasy came over me and I
felt I had taken part in a sacred service.

As to the interpretation,—Amalia Materna and Hermann Winkelmann were marvellous; as was the orchestra too under Hermann Levy. But above all Emil
Scaria's Gurnemanz was a masterpiece, and without ex-
aggeration I may say it was the perfection of art.

This singer, who had triumphed so as Wotan in Berlin
and then failed so lamentably in London, had risen under
Wagner's guidance to such an interpretation as to en-
rapture the audience and even delight the Master himself.

After the performance we drove home in a pouring rain
to our supper at " Fantasie "—where we were joined by
the Klingsor of that evening, Siehr from Munich, with
his wife and daughter. And what a remarkable coincidence! This famous basso, who later was to sing Gurnemanz, had always been one of the most violent public adversaries of Wagner's school, and remained so until the
close of his days.

Eduard Hanslik sat next to me at supper. That re-
doubtable critic was evidently still under the spell of
" Parsifal " and was noticeably silent and thoughtful.
Naturally the sole topic of our conversation was the
wonderful experience of the day. Hanslik joined eagerly
in our enthusiasm, making no caustic comments, and we
felt he had been quite converted.

During our talk, each giving his impressions of the day,
Förster made a statement that struck us all with terror:
" You'll see,—Wagner's not long for this world! " Our
animation faded at these words and we sat there unspeakably shocked, till I managed to stammer, " What makes
you say a thing like that? " Förster answered, with quiet
conviction, " A man who is capable of producing a thing
of that order *cannot* be long for this world—his work is
finished! " Earnestly he spoke, almost with tears in his
eyes,—and his words impressed us with such a weight of

horror, that it was long before we recovered from their effect. But our earlier light, gay mood was gone for that whole evening.

That season I heard seven performances of "Parsifal." It was at the close of the first,—when Wagner amid the thunders of the audience appeared on the stage surrounded by his artists,—that he begged the public not to applaud again as they had during the course of that performance. So the second production passed with a calm and reverent hush. This called forth another speech from the Master. He must explain, he said, that it was only *during* the performance that he objected to applause; but the appreciation due the singers at the fall of the curtain was quite a different matter. So, at the next performances, the people expressed their enthusiasm at the close of each act.

I do not know if an incident of the third production of "Parsifal" has ever yet been published. Some hitch having occurred in the scenery, Franz Brandt at the risk of his own life climbed up the swaying side wall, and clinging to a post at that dizzy height, took out his knife and cut the obstruction. It seemed hours before they could get at him with a ladder and help him down from his precarious perch.

During the performances the report was spread that trouble was brewing between Wagner and Marianne Brandt. One day the artiste came to me, crying bitterly and complaining of the Master's violent temper. Naturally I tried to soothe her, but she assured me she had already told Wagner she knew he would gladly be rid of her, but that she refused to be forced from the cast as her artistic honour was at stake.

What could I do but reassure her—though I remembered distinctly having advised Wagner a year ago not to engage her for Kundry, as I felt her incapable of singing

the second act. And her performance now justified my
fears; for, great an artist as she was and wonderfully as
she gave the first and third acts, the second was quite
beyond her powers.

Here I shall mention a dinner at Wahnfried. Those of
us who were present will never forget how charmingly,
how sympathetically, and how appreciatively Franz Liszt,
Mme. Cosima, and above all Wagner himself, spoke of
Hans von Bülow. And whoever had the rare good fortune
to have known this remarkable man must certainly admit,
as I am glad to do here, that Hans von Bülow was not
only a matchless artist and a peerless man, but a genial
friend as well.

Our talk at the table touched upon Scaria's singing of
Gurnemanz, and I must have expressed myself with great
enthusiasm, for the Master suddenly sprang from his
chair, rushed around to me and embraced me, saying over
and over again, " No, Neumann—you can't know what a
joy it is to hear you acknowledge this! I was afraid you'd
criticise him because of that little contretemps in London.
You certainly are a capital fellow! You've put Scaria to
the blush to-night—for he at all events could never sink
the personal note." " But, Master," I answered, " it
goes without saying that Scaria's Gurnemanz is simply
unsurpassable! " Wagner wrung my hand eagerly, and
turning to Liszt, he said, " What do you think of that,—
haven't I always told you that he was the one to depend
upon? " He was as pleased as a child; and I have felt
that since that day the Master's confidence in me was
perfect.

In the drawing-room after dinner the talk went on in
lively banter. At the table I had refused all alcoholic
stimulant, and now they observed that I took neither
coffee nor cigars. Mme. Wagner expressed her astonishment at my abstinence, but the Master said laughingly,

"That's not so remarkable! Neumann very evidently is fond of good living—and as he seems to fancy that *high* living—wine, coffee and cigars—interfere with *long* living —he simply refrains! But that only goes to prove that he's very fond of good living!" And amid the general laugh I had to admit the truth of this paradox.

Later, when I had a moment alone with the Master, I referred to the subject of our suit with Batz and Voltz about the rights for " Tristan," and to our plans for the coming tour of the " Richard Wagner Opera Company." Wagner gave his consent for a contract ceding me the exclusive rights for the " Ring. I was to bring it next day for his signature.

Then I again touched upon the subject nearest to my heart,—that he should entrust to me his most sacred treasure, " Parsifal "! To my own great amazement his answer was fairly favourable; he even promised to consider it at our next meeting, and I was to bring a proposition for " Parsifal " at the same time with my contract for the " Ring."

The following letter touches upon this:

Dear Friend:

Can't you stay over till Monday, as I can see you more quietly that afternoon at five. To-day I must even bar my own family, as talking is impossible; I need absolute rest for my poor nerves. To-morrow comes another performance—so Monday is the only day left for our interview, and late on Monday too out of regard for my health.

By the way I want to add that T. W. Batz is the only one with whom I've no dealings; Carl Voltz & Co. still handle my affairs.

  With warmest greetings,
    Yours devotedly,
      Richard Wagner.
Bayreuth, August 5, 1882.

On the given day I appeared at Wahnfried with my contracts for the "Ring" and "Parsifal." The Master seemed quite disposed to grant my eager wish. The tedious business details of the Bayreuth undertaking, which not even the cleverest of managers could quite relieve him of, probably influenced this decision. "Neumann, help me out of Bayreuth," he cried from the depths of his recent trials.

As we proceeded to business he signed at once my contract for the "Ring"; and now came the turn of the "Parsifal" agreement. Would the Master consent, as he had informally offered, to have the thing produced outside of Bayreuth and to hand me over the exclusive rights? He was just about to sign the contract, when suddenly he paused. With his pen poised over the paper he sat there lost in reflection; then turning slowly to me, he said in a low, gentle voice: "Neumann, I *did* promise you,—and if you insist, I'll sign the contract. But you would be doing me a great favour if you should not insist this time. I've pledged you my word—no one else shall ever have 'Parsifal' but you!"

I answered: "Master, if you say I should be doing you a great favour, then naturally that is quite enough for me!" Wagner wrung my hand and kissed me eagerly, saying with touching emphasis, "Thank you, Neumann, thank you!" and so closed one of the most important incidents of my life.

My little son was waiting for me in the shady walk leading down to the gates of Wahnfried, and as he came to meet me I told him of our interview, and added, "Karl, my boy, to-day, when I relinquished 'Parsifal,' I abandoned the prospect of many millions!"

"Father," said the little fellow (he was then just seven), "it's worth more than millions, isn't it, to have Richard Wagner thank you like that!"

Our "Nibelungen" contract ran as follows:

"I concede to Director Angelo Neumann the exclusive right of producing my Trilogie (sic) 'The Nibelungen Ring' for all of Germany, (with the exception of the court theatres which have already produced the same, and the directors who have already purchased said rights), as well as for all of England, France, Denmark, Russia, Italy, Austria, Hungary, Belgium, Holland, North America—in short, for all continental and foreign countries; with full power of granting said rights to other concerns; on condition that I am to receive for any such performance at least the same royalty as Director Angelo Neumann is now pledged to pay me. That is, ten per cent. of the box office receipts and five per cent. of the subscription price. For these payments Director Angelo Neumann gives me his personal security. The above concession of exclusive rights to Director Angelo Neuman is valid until December 31, 1889.

Richard Wagner.

Bayreuth, August 7, 1882.

Wagner now handed me the following letter regarding our suit with Voltz and Batz.

My dear Director Neumann:

At the solicitation of Messrs. Voltz & Batz I left the matter of my musical drama "Tristan and Isolde" in their hands, giving them their so-called "Copyrights"—but with the express condition that my consent was absolutely necessary for their transfer of the same. I therefore, having reserved this power of conveyance, give you now my permission for the said production in various places, and direct you to apply to the above firm for the final rights in the matter.

As it seems quite probable that you will have difficulty in maintaining your rights of conceding "Tristan and Isolde" to such managers as should make you suitable offers, I hereby give you my full and absolute permission for this same; to be used in such an emergency, on the terms of our former contracts, and needing only for its validity the signature of my original agents Voltz and Batz.

With deepest respect,

Yours very truly,

Richard Wagner.

Bayreuth, August 7, 1882.

After some further discussion of our plans for the future, and the details of the Richard Wagner Opera Company, I took my leave of the Master with his blessing and warmest wishes for the welfare of our coming tour. I was to see him two weeks later for the final time on the occasion of a business matter which had arisen at Breslau, the first halt on our tour. My business manager wired me on the 10th of August that the box office receipts for the first 3½ hours of advance sales for the cycle of September 2d had amounted to over forty-one thousand Marks, for four performances. Knowing that this news would gratify the Master, I arranged to postpone my trip till the following day.

Wagner therefore was completely surprised when I appeared that night at a reception at Wahnfried to which I had already sent my regrets, and announced: "Master, I've brought you good news." He led me aside to the anteroom and I handed him the telegram, saying, "Here's a good omen for the successful issue of our plans,—the first report of the treasury of the 'Wandering Wagner Theatre.'" Laying his arm over my shoulder, the Master said with his charming smile: "Neumann, it *is* a good sign: and I'm glad you brought me the news to-night. You've undertaken a great and overwhelming task—but it's a beautiful work as well. It will take not only all your energy and capacities, but also a firm trust in the Lord,—and that I feel you have. So may Heaven bless you and all dependent upon you, and keep you in its sheltering care!"

PART V

THE RICHARD WAGNER THEATRE

CHAPTER XVII

GERMANY, HOLLAND AND BELGIUM

By way of Vienna I went from Bayreuth to Breslau, where our " Wagner Tour " was to open with the " Nibelungen Ring." The business and technical staff had begun preparations there on the 15th of August, and on the 24th began our full rehearsals with the splendid orchestra we had engaged for London under Anton Seïdl, a magnificent staff of singers and a fully equipped chorus.

My main concern had been the engagement of Therese and Heinrich Vogl for this tour. As I had closed at once with their demands for thirty thousand Marks a month, Vogl had gone to his Excellency Baron von Perfall, and explained that it was a question of a competency for himself and his wife. Nevertheless it was a difficult matter for him to get that leave from September, 1882, to March, 1883. Baron von Perfall, to be sure, was quite ready to give his consent, but the difficulty lay with the Cabinet of King Ludwig of Bavaria. Vogl thereafter asked me to come to Munich and interview the chancellor of state— which I did, with the result that his Majesty, to our great relief, gave the desired furlough,—on condition that their names should be starred as: " Therese and Heinrich Vogl of the Richard Wagner Opera Company, on leave of absence from Munich by gracious permission of his Majesty King Ludwig II."

The dates set for the " Nibelungen Ring " in Breslau were: September 2d, " Rhinegold "; on the 3d, " The Valkyre "; (on the 4th, an intermission); on the 5th, " Siegfried," and " Götterdämmerung " on the 6th. The demand was so great at the box office that I was urged to give a second cycle. This I refused, but announced a great Wagner concert for September 1st, which was a triumphant success, taking in nearly twelve thousand Marks. This concert was arranged in two parts: the first on the programme,—vocal numbers conducted by Seidl,—given in the theatre; and the last half an instrumental concert given in the well-known Liebig Gardens, where crowds of people soon gathered, standing silent and attentive till the music was finished.

On the day of "The Valkyre" when hundreds were turned away from the box office, I was petitioned to repeat it the following night,—the day of our intermission. Out of consideration for Heinrich Vogl, however, I had to refuse, for this artist had not only taken part in the concert but had sung Loge in "Rhinegold," Siegmund in "The Valkyre," and was to sing Siegfried in both the coming performances. George Unger, who was to alternate with him, had not yet sung the Siegmund, and I did not care to let him substitute as Siegfried, though he had created this rôle in Bayreuth and been very well received. But the bills had announced Vogl, and I did not mean to make a change so early in our venture.

Vogl then assured me that, as far as he was concerned, if we chose to pay him extra for the added performance, we need not hesitate. I agreed to this, and the second "Valkyre" (which netted us twelve thousand Marks) was announced for the following day.

I mention these facts to illustrate the marvellous endurance of Heinrich Vogl, showing what an artist *can* do, if he lives carefully and manages his voice. At the outset of our tour Heinrich Vogl here made a record that I think hardly any other singer has ever touched.

On the 7th of September we took a special train to Königsberg, stopping at Posen on the way to give a monster Wagner Concert. On the 8th we reached Königsberg, where the following night Vogl again sang Loge and on the 10th gave a vigorous and masterly performance of Siegfried.

As time was an object, our trips were generally by special train. Hitherto the largest wandering theatrical troupe had been that of Meiningen; but they had only a third as many persons and appliances as we—to say nothing of their having no orchestra, with its instruments, etc. Our special train carried one hundred and thirty-four people, five freight cars full of properties, and the instruments for an orchestra of sixty. From Breslau to Königsberg cost us six thousand six hundred Marks, and from Posen on an added three hundred; for there we were made to take a guard for the freight, which I had to pay in spite of all my protests.

My petition to the department of transportation for reduced rates elicited the reply that such rates could only be made to managers of circuses and menageries. So if I had only added a few elephants, lions and tight-rope walkers to my staff I might have had the benefit of this reduction! From the rates we got for our special trains, however, I am still somewhat in doubt as to whether the minister of transportation in Germany took the Richard Wagner Opera Company for something greater or less than a circus. In Italy this matter had a very different aspect, as we shall see.

In Königsberg, as well, we played to crowded houses and the "Ring" was received with interest and enthusiasm. We also gave a concert with a programme devoted (as all our concerts were) exclusively to Wagner's music; and a special performance of "The Valkyre" was added.

Here I shall relate an episode to illustrate the amount of energy it takes to prevent any one star in such an assemblage from feeling that the whole theatrical firmament revolves about him as a centre. It was Heinrich Vogl who put my capacities to the test. As I have said, the two Vogls drew a monthly salary of thirty thousand Marks. Heinrich Vogl one thousand two hundred Marks each for fifteen extra performances, and Therese Vogl the same for ten.

At our first concert in Breslau I made the arrangement with them that for extra performances beyond this contract, they should receive six hundred Marks apiece; naturally the concerts within the contract were reckoned at one thousand two hundred Marks.

The Vogls were glad to accept this extra proposition as it seemed useful to them, as well as to myself, to appear on these programmes. But after the first payment of six hundred Marks they began at Königsberg to raise objections—they wished to receive the regular honorarium for the extra concerts. When I refused and held them to their contract, Heinrich Vogl threatened that in case George Unger sent word the next day that he was unable to sing (Unger was famous for refusing to sing) he, Vogl, would absolutely refuse to take his place, though that had been specially stipulated in our bond. I calmly told him that his threats did not move me in the least and that the performance would still go on even if Unger refused (though I knew I'd not another arrow in my quiver). Vogl frowned and declared he always kept his word—" I might ask the six hundred peasants on his estates if that were not so!" But I answered, "My dear fellow, possibly you have always kept your word to the six hundred peasants on your estates, but you seem to be about to break it to the director of the Richard Wagner Opera Company!" Then he left my office, declaring most emphatically that, come what might, he'd not sing Siegfried to-morrow! I knew his fondness for money, so his threats had small effect on me, since every performance meant twelve hundred Marks in his pocket. I was not surprised then, later at the concert, to receive a note from Vogl assuring me, with many expressions of devotion, that I might absolutely count on him for the next day if Unger failed.

At that very moment Unger stepped up to inform me how sorry he was not to be able to sing Siegfried to-morrow. He said he had heard of Vogl's refusal to substitute, so he wanted to tell me in time that I might announce the postponement of the performance. To his amazement, however, I answered with a placid smile, " Don't worry on my account, my dear Unger: even if you *don't* sing Siegfried we shall still give the opera to-morrow." My calm assurance quite convinced him and he probably spent a sleepless night racking his brains as to how I would manage it. But that next evening he sang Siegfried as a matter of course; while Vogl waited in vain to be summoned as his substitute.

I shall not go into minute details of our success, which is now so thoroughly well known, but shall mention a few of the most striking incidents. And right here let me correct the general erroneous impression that the manager of the Richard Wagner Opera Company simply coined money in this undertaking. Our tremendous, and hitherto unheard of, receipts at the box office were balanced by the costly and complicated apparatus we were obliged to maintain and by the expenses of rapid transportation.

Our good friends and colleagues (Pollini of Hamburg, for instance) had shaken their heads over the undertaking and calculated that such a new departure in the theatrical world on such a huge scale would surely fail before the month was out.

.   .   .   .

The following telegram arrived on the 11th of September:

Director Neumann—Hôtel de Prusse, Königsberg— Hail Angelo! Greetings to all those pledged to my in-

terests! Thursday night we leave for Venice, Palazzo
Vendramin, Grand Canal.   Am writing you a long letter.

                                                    Wagner.

Meanwhile our triumphant progress continued, our
next success being Dantzic. Here we encountered some
difficulties as to the size of the stage, my stage manager
declaring it ridiculously inadequate. This impressed me
with the fact of the tremendous advance in stage construc-
tion in the last few years. I remember in 1860, when the
celebrated baritone Beck was sent for to sing a short engagement at the Dantzic theatre, the Vienna papers expressed their fears that even his great voice would be
lost in that immense new auditorium. The delight of
the Viennese was unspeakable when they heard that their
favourite had taken Dantzic by storm. When I myself
early in my career was engaged there, my doubts as to the
size of the stage were justifiable; for my voice was never
of the most robust order. Yet the magnificent acoustics
of the place soon set me at my ease.

That was twenty-two years ago and many new theatres
had since been built; at Breslau, Magdeburg, Frankfort,
Leipsic—as well as the new Royal Opera in Vienna—to
say nothing of Bayreuth and its marvellous stage.

But when my inspector announced the conditions, I
could hardly credit the statement and went to verify his
word. What! *That* was the stage that had seemed so
colossal early in the sixties, and that every one was
afraid of?

To show its inadequacy I shall state that our scene-
shifting had to be done from a circus tent which we set
up out on the square by the theatre. Decorations and
properties were transferred with lightning rapidity from
tent to stage and back again at each necessary change.
This same process had to be carried out again at the Royal
Theatre in Hanover, and it was only due to the cleverness

and capacity of my stage manager Schick (one of the finest pupils of Lautenschläger) and of Inspector Sperling, that we were able to accomplish this with such rapid precision.

Here in Dantzic took place an event of some importance in the musical world—I had given the rôle of Sieglinda for the first time to our Katharina Klafsky, a young and untried singer.   A well-known Berlin critic who was there hastened to warn me not to risk my reputation with this rash step, but to let Therese Vogl sing the part. Though I assured him I knew what I was doing, he gave me no peace till I let him think he was to have his way— and he left, serenely confident that Therese Vogl was to sing Sieglinda, as he had suggested, and that Klafsky would be one of the Valkyre—Waltraute perhaps, but *never* Sieglinda! When he saw the bills next day with Klafsky's name in the leading rôle, he was furious and prophesied a complete failure. How far his prophecy was false all the world knows; and even he, the anxious critic, came to me later and confessed she had surpassed all his expectations.

Here in Dantzic we had a great concert after the second day of the "Ring" and at the close of the cycle took our special train again for Berlin, where we went through the same programme in the Residenz Theatre. From there we steered our course for Magdeburg and Hamburg, where we gave only concerts.   Wherever we went we had the public interest and most enthusiastic audiences.

In Hamburg on the day of our concert I lunched with Pollini.   He told me he'd been watching our venture, expecting a failure at any moment, for such a gigantic speculation could never last very long.   He said in his friendly way he'd give us just a little more time.   My calm security, however, in the face of his dismal prophecies, almost took away his appetite for that very excellent lunch. But when we parted he asked me anxiously if it were true, as Batz and Voltz informed him, that I had the rights of concession for " Tristan and Isolde," and would I make an arrangement with him for a performance; which I was glad to do.

From Hamburg our orchestra and concert staff went to Lübeck, while I with the technical staff hurried on to Bremen to arrange for the performance of the " Ring " on the 2d of October. Here we had some trouble with the manager of the theatre, another one of those friendly colleagues who would gladly have seen us fail.

Often at the beginning of our tour it was difficult to get the proper theatre for our performances. Sometimes the managers were afraid of our complicated technical apparatus,—especially the installation of the steam and fire effects. Again, of course, it was simply a case of jealousy at my being trusted by the Bayreuth management. All these circumstances combined to make the manager of the Bremen theatre (Emil Pohl, who afterwards turned out a very good friend) demand the most impossible terms for our lease. Such terms that Wagner angrily declared, when he heard of it, he wondered at my accepting them at all.

Our advance agent was Hans Förster, the oldest son of Dr. August Förster, and he it was who made all our preliminary arrangements, travelling always ahead of the company. He had wired me in Breslau that Bremen was out of the question, as Pohl demanded twelve thousand Marks for the cycle. Since I could not put in that week elsewhere, my time being all arranged for in other places, and as I knew that Pohl was in an unassailable position, —in which after two days of effort on our part we could find no breach,—I sent the following message: " Close contract on Pohl's terms." My agent thought this proceeding somewhat startling, but later events fully justified my action.

After our performance of " The Valkyre " Senator Alfred Schulz, a man of remarkable cultivation and the chief patron of the Breman theatre, expressed his delight at our wonderful presentation and his amazement at the daring of our enterprise. He finally asked if I would accept the management of the Bremen theatre, as the old lease was soon to expire and the new arrangement lay almost wholly in his hands. I answered that as a guest of the present direction I could only refuse; for I could hardly enter into competition with Pohl under the circumstances. Whereupon Schulz asked if I would consider the proposition, were the offer made directly by the Senate. This I agreed to, and the results we shall see later.

In Bremen I received the " long letter " the Master had announced in his telegram.

My dear Neumann:

Since you left Dantzic I've had no news of you. I hope Hanover was a success. Did you have the Royal Theatre? How did you manage von Hülsen? You must take my praise and approval for granted in advance for all your efforts; you know what confidence I have in you and that if I express any doubts they are for your interests primarily.

So I counsel you, at least for some time, to leave Paris out of your calculations: even London could hardly pay you; but America *certainly*, however, in case you follow out your German programme and announce one complete cycle in each place.

I lay particular stress on Berlin. I am sure you could have a full successful winter season there; only here the great thing is attention to detail and minute care for the finish, art and style of your performances. No makeshifts in the decorations, and the greatest care in the scenic and dramatic effects. Your model for this should not be the traditions of Vienna or Leipsic but my late performance of " Parsifal " at Bayreuth.

As far as I can gather you have already leased your theatre in Berlin. Brückwald the architect tells me he is drawing you the plans for a Wagner Theatre in Berlin quite on the lines of Bayreuth. In this connection it strikes me as a good idea to add a second tier of boxes to our so-called Prince's gallery, and to make a break in the Parterre, arranging for a small step-up between the seats of different prices.

You know of course that I stand ready to support you in such an undertaking. Yet I scarcely know what to answer to your urgent request that you should be allowed to give " Parsifal " at the opening of this new theatre— after *all* our talk on the subject!

" Parsifal "—once and for all—belongs exclusively to my Bayreuth theatre and it is at our yearly festivals that this work is to be presented. This segregation is due to the lofty character of the work itself. My creation of " Parsifal " shall stand or fall with Bayreuth. At least this shall be the case until my death; for who then will carry out my intentions is still a problem with me. In case my powers, which are put to such unspeakable tests by these performances, should be exhausted before my life, and I should no longer be able to attend to these details, I should have to think of some other plan for carrying out the traditions of my work. If by that time your Wagner Opera Company has reached that perfect plane toward which you are constantly advancing with my other works, I might then find it feasible to turn over to you my " Parsifal " for certain festival performances at stated occasions;—and it is only to *you* and on these terms that I shall ever consign my " Parsifal."

Of this you may assure your partners in the theatrical undertaking for their satisfaction;—but with the proviso that I take it all back if ever you should make this statement public. You know what the reporters are, and can hardly blame me for trying to keep this last great task at Bayreuth,—my final creation,—out of their clutches.

Would you kindly ask your secretary to notify me as to the condition of my balance since our last account? I simply wish to know how I stand financially.

And now, all good wishes, my highest praise and warmest thanks! I am still suffering from a nervous exhaustion which only an absolute rest can cure. This I do my utmost to arrange for, although a few lines from that crazy Batz, for instance, are enough when they come to upset my whole equilibrium.—But we'll hope for the best!

Greetings to you and to the whole Nibelungen kingdom under your sway!

Yours,

Richard Wagner.

Venice, September 29, 1882.
  Pallazzo Vendramin,
    Canale Grande.

Before we left Bremen Heinrich Vogl made another attempt to claim his twelve hundred Marks for that Breslau concert. Since that night, to avoid such conflict, I had billed him only for the regular contract performances and naturally, as our Breslau agreement was definite, I refused his unjust demands. Whereat he threatened me with a lawsuit. I told him to go to court, and if he won, he'd get his money; but he answered, with another allusion to the eight hundred peasants on his lordly estates, "Yes, but in the end when I've won my suit, who'll be responsible for my twelve hundred Marks?" I looked at him inquiringly, and he went on, "By that time the whole concern will have gone to pieces and you'll have nothing left to pay!" Now at last I understood him.

" My dear Vogl," I observed, " I have never had reason
to be sensitive as to my personal credit. But your proposition that I should pay you now what you'd have to
return at the close of your lawsuit is quite impossible,
as I should have to start another suit then to collect it.
However, I shall set your mind at rest as to my personal
responsibility."

So the next morning my secretary sent Vogl a draft on
the Bremen bank with the following conditional clause:
" This draft is payable to Heinrich Vogl on the successful
conclusion of his suit against Angelo Neumann, director
of the Wagner Theatre."

Vogl naturally, knowing he had no case, did not press
the suit, and my draft was paid back without a murmur.

From Bremen we went to Barmen to give the cycle in
their beautiful theatre there. In Elberfeld and in Cologne
we also gave a concert. It was in this latter place that
the celebrated critic Ferdinand Hiller came into the
concert hall saying, " Now we'll have a treat!" It was
Hillier, it may be remembered, who once wrote in the
early days of the " Tannhäuser " performances, " The very
overture itself is full of disgusting passages, etc.,"—and
he had come to triumph in our defeat.

To my amazement, however, this same man came into
the green-room in the intermission and asked me to present
him to Seidl. Then turning to grasp his hand, he said,
" I've come to tell you that I never heard that Tannhäuser
Overture before!" The sudden conversion of such an
eminent man and his noble and courtly acknowledgment
of the same was the greatest pleasure and most perfect
reward of that whole performance.

That night we left for Frankfort-am-Main to give a
concert there the following evening; and then on to Leipsic. Here we were welcomed with great enthusiasm. We
had already arranged for a complete cycle of Wagner's
works. At our first concert there was a huge and most

natural excitement, for the Leipsigers were greeting their old favourites—Anton Seidl, George Unger, Julius Lieban, Orlanda Riegler, Anna Stürmer—and, first and foremost in the ranks, Hedwig Reicher-Kindermann—that ornament of the stage, who had made her beginnings there. The enthusiasm of the audience, then, may be imagined on that evening of the 18th of October. After our concert was held a banquet of the leading citizens in Leipsic with Dr. Georgi, the mayor, presiding.

Our next stop was Berlin, where we opened our "Nibelungen" cycle on the 21st of October. As Bote and Bock had already wired me in Barmen that the advanced sales were tremendous, I announced an extra concert in the Philharmonic Hall for the 20th. Our programme and its rendering seemed to have made a tremendous impression, for I was besieged with requests to repeat it. This I was ready to do in the intermission of our "Nibelungen" cycle, which, as on the former occasion, was a most glittering success. Hermann Wolff, a connoisseur of parts and himself a concert manager, wrote me at the time: "My dear and valued friend, you have killed the entire season for me with your Wagner concerts—every one is talking of them, and everything else is a side issue."

As I came to my office the day of that concert, my secretary handed me a telegram which I opened carelessly: and yet that telegram was to affect my whole future. It read: "You are called. Will you accept? Senator Schulz."

I handed it to Förster, who happened to be there, and he seemed quite as pleased as I. This feeling of joy lasted till that evening when, the Bremen papers having brought the news, friends crowded round to comment on it. First came Oscar Blumenthal, saying: "Neumann, what do you mean by going to Bremen? It's no place for you! We need you in Berlin. The Victoria Theatre is just made for your Wagner performances, and later on we'll build that new one on the Bayreuth plan!" Then Paul Lindau said, "Nonsense, Angelo! You'll never go to Bremen. It's far too small a field for you. If you won't stay in Berlin, then take some other famous theatre! Bremen is a charming town of course—but!" The third was Frederick Spielhagen, who gave me the same friendly counsel. Then came Fritz Brandt, the technical engineer of "Parsifal," and representatives of the press like Ehrlich, Davidsohn and others. Each and all made the same remark. Berlin was the field for me. This naturally cooled my interest in Bremen, and to follow up the process Fritz Brandt and Oscar Blumenthal came to my office two days later, to propose uniting to lease the Victoria Theatre and give a series of Wagner productions, alternating with some great spectacular play, such as "The Black Venus" for instance, which was then the sensation of the hour. Even August Förster was inclined to go back on the original plan.

In the meantime came a wire asking me to come to Bremen to sign the contract. I certainly went off pleased, though not as elated as I had been at first. And now I must explain my change of attitude.

At my first arrival in Bremen, on ordering rooms at the hotel, I found I was paying Paris prices. On questioning the landlord as to this, he said, "Certainly, Monsieur Neumann, but this is Wagner week in Bremen, and the town is so crowded that we can't make you any better rates." And now, only a few weeks later, I arrived at the same place to find it a small sleepy town with empty streets and a placid little square before the theatre, lined comfortably with baby carriages. What more natural, then, than that I should remember the warnings of my Berlin friends?

As soon as he saw me, Senator Schulz, whose keen insight was remarkable, detected my change of mood; and when I asked if I might take the contract back to Berlin

and consider a while before signing, he said: "My dear
Director, you know I gave my word to the Senate that if
you were called you would accept. I should be placed in
quite a false position if you were to go back on your
pledge." That *settled* it. I promised to sign the contract
and send it back from Berlin. And so I did.

During this time trouble had arisen between the two
leading sopranos of our company. Hedwig Reicher-Kindermann had become such a rage that all Berlin turned
out for the evenings when she was billed. Her performance of Brunhilda called up an enthusiasm that I never
have seen equalled on the boards. It is most natural that
this gradual triumph of a young and rising artist should
cause a little jealousy in Therese Vogl, who had hitherto
been considered unsurpassed in this part and who really
was a wonderful singer.

Presently a third factor arose to heighten the feeling.
Katharina Klafsky continued to be the favourite Sieglinda, although that had always been one of Therese Vogl's
star parts.

So on the days when Kindermann sang Brunhilda and
the Sieglinda was Klafsky there was a clamour for seats
and every spot in the house was taken.

It is hardly surprising, then, that Madame Vogl's husband should be more and more disgruntled, and finally
come to ask me to release his wife from her contract on
the 1st of December. Any one knowing Heinrich Vogl's
passion for money would certainly think well of his devotion to his wife, for this meant a sacrifice of one hundred
and twenty thousand Marks—to say nothing of the extra
performances. Their departure almost decided me to end
my tour in Berlin. But the interest and the eager readiness of my staff finally overpersuaded me. So I resolved
to carry my plans through, filling Heinrich Vogl's rôles
(notably the Loge in "Rhinegold") with other members
of the cast.

Though no one could ever quite take his place, our company was so good, every individual so capable, and the ensemble so perfect in each detail, that Vogl really was hardly missed—except by myself.

Here I shall add an account of a performance of " Fidelio " under the patronage of the Empress Augusta, and for the benefit of the sufferers in the flooded Rhine country. The cast deserves a special mention.

Leonore...........Hedwig Reicher-Kindermann
Marcelline....................Augusta Kraus
Florestan.....................Albert Niemann
Rocco............................Emil Scaria
Pizarro................Augusta Kindermann *
The Prime Minister..........Dr. Franz Krückl
Joaquino......................Julius Lieban

Conductor.......................Anton Seidl

An incident connected with Kaiser William I. made the evening a memorable one. On his entrance, his Majesty was received by a committee and the director of the Richard Wagner Opera Company. After a few pleasant words the gracious monarch turned to me, saying, " I had hard work to get here to-night. You know one of the princesses of the house of Prussia has died: but I knew how to manage it. Do you know what I did? In order to come to-night I had to postpone the order for the court mourning until to-morrow!" This deliciously human remark impressed the hearers, as one may imagine, most tremendously.

But suddenly some one in our midst called out, just as he had ended, " How is her Majesty? Well, I hope?" (She had been seriously ill a short time since.) I can see the Kaiser yet as he stood there before us, slightly stooped (he was eighty-five years old then), and wearing his well-

* The father of Hedwig.

known military cape and helmet.   He drew himself up at the question, growing taller and taller until he stood there in all his dignity.   Turning sharply to the speaker, he thundered out, " What's that you said? "

The man who had made the blunder, a great tall fellow, now dwindled and shrank, and with shaking knees and trembling voice he answered huskily, " I only asked if her gracious Majesty was quite well! "

Turning away without another word the Kaiser strode down the hall, signing to me to follow.   And so, chatting of affairs of the theatre, I accompanied his Majesty to his box.

After the performance, when our committee again waited on him, he was full of the most gracious words of praise. " Tell me where did you get that Kindermann?   She's a most wonderfully dramatic singer."   " In Leipsic, your Majesty."   " And where did your Joaquino come from? " " From Leipsic, your Majesty."   " And the Marcelline? " " From Leipsic, too, your Majesty."   " But your conductor, Seidl? "   " He was also in Leipsic."   " And you? " " I come from Leipsic, too, your Majesty."   " Good gracious! you must have had a wonderful opera company in Leipsic! " and hereupon I escorted his Majesty to his carriage.

The blundering questioner of early in the evening had meanwhile disappeared—not to appear again until the Kaiser was safely gone.

At my instigation Hermann Wolff had opened negotiations with the Brussels theatre that now seemed to promise well; and with the People's Palace in Amsterdam at the same time.   We signed contracts for concerts as well in Cassel, Detmold and Crefeld.   Before undertaking the northern trip, however, he went to Dresden, where we gave a great concert, and on the 19th and 20th of December two performances of " The Valkyre," in which Scaria was invited to sing Wotan.   He had recently come to me acknowledging his former fault and begging me to forget it—which I gladly did.

Back again from Dresden we celebrated Christmas in Berlin, before taking up our new duties with the new year. Hermann Wolff himself, to be sure, had very little leisure for celebration that Christmas. On the 24th came a telegram from Brussels. Difficulties had arisen with the city government as to our performances of the " Ring," which only a prompt personal intervention could arrange. There was no time to lose, so Wolff decided to go on Christmas eve. His wife and the children were so disappointed that even I advised him to wait, but the plucky fellow insisted on going directly—and it was well he did. On Christmas day came a telegram: " Contract signed. You play at Royal Théâtre de la Monnaie by order of the council and directors Stumm and Calabresi, and get forty-two thousand francs down."

After the holidays the technical staff, chorus and business corps went direct to Amsterdam, while our artists with the orchestra gave a series of concerts in Cassel, Detmold and Crefeld. On January 2d came our first performance of the " Ring," quite an event in Holland. We stayed some three weeks in Amsterdam, giving concerts on our off nights in Arnheim, Zwolle and Utrecht.

It was in Amsterdam that our Kindermann contracted the germs of that disease which was to lay her low in Trieste and cost us her life. One of our young singers, after a long and tedious illness, was ordered to take the air. Kindermann, who had always been very fond of her, sent for a carriage and took the convalescent out in the Park one Sunday afternoon. They drove about for a while, but presently, tempted by the wintry sunshine, sat down after a little walk on a stone bench that cold January day. The immediate result of this was a severe case of peritonitis for Kindermann. We called in Dr. Herz, the most celebrated specialist in Amsterdam, and thanks to his skilful care she was soon able to join us in Brussels. As a safeguard for her however, as well as for ourselves, I had sent for Amalia Materna to substitute in her rôles, but Kindermann's strong will and intense craving for money spurred her on to take her own place in " The Valkyre " and " Götterdämmerung." At the close of the prelude to the " Götterdämmerung " she was carried half unconscious to her dressing-room, yet she still insisted she could sing the rôle and would not hear of any substitute. But knowing her voice and her style too well to be deceived, I was horrified with the consciousness that she was no longer the old Kindermann.

We had been urged to give an extra performance of " Fidelio " in Amsterdam, and I had already agreed when her sudden illness forced us to give up the plan and return the seven thousand Gulden of the advance sale for seats.

Here in Amsterdam our tour ended for a while, as outside of this city no theatres were found suitable for the presentation of the " Ring." So we spent the time from the 11th to the 22d of January in giving concerts at The Hague, Rotterdam and Leyden as well as several in Amsterdam.

Before we left here came an important letter from the Master.

My cherished Friend and Fellow-Worker:

I am much pleased at your asking my advice, but it is with a heavy heart that I answer your letter. I am hardly satisfied to think of your wandering about with nothing really behind you—or ahead either; except that I consider your caution and your solid practical sense would teach you to deal with such an undertaking far better than I ever could.

From your practical standpoint, then, I should consider it expedient to concentrate my efforts on engaging a certain limited number of stars, letting the orchestra and the details of the setting be inferior in cost and effects,—as very little could be expected from such a travelling concern.

Though this plan may have succeeded hitherto, yet in the long run I think it could hardly be successful, for your audiences will soon perceive that the strength of my effects lies in the balance of all the parts.

Naturally I am telling you nothing new; for you very well know what it is your performances lack and how much effort it would take to put you on a solid basis.

On these lines I had contemplated founding a theatre in Berlin—absolutely on the Bayreuth plan. I had never even spoken to you of it, but what you tell me now leads me to conclude that you either have not yet arranged for the funds you spoke of, or have failed in your attempt. Consequently I shall drop the matter for the present.

To contemplate accepting Bremen as a means of accumulating funds for your purpose is tantamount to abandoning the whole idea. You would meet there a most commercial spirit and practically be frozen fast to the spot, and though of course the stipend would be considerable, they would simply be paying munificently to keep you in a second-rate theatre! You could never carry out any large ideas there.

If Berlin is impossible, why not try Leipsic again? If there were any way to manage this, I stand ready to help you with all the influence at my command. As to Prague I fully agree with you, yet the people there are so very musical that the race prejudice of the Czechs would not cut much figure. Only—at best—Prague would be a refuge and not a point of departure.

My advice, then, would be to return to Leipsic; but as this place—for the present—seems impossible, I go back naturally to our old Berlin project. That of course would take considerable capital, and for this I know you undertook your present tour. Up to this time, however, you have not been able to accumulate a balance, for your out-lay I can see must be tremendous. Simply the item of your theatre rents is most outrageous. (Bremen, where they took in about twenty thousand Marks, asked you twelve thousand of rent—and you still consider going to these people!)

I firmly believe only America can serve your purpose now, and you should centre all your efforts on that field. As far as I am concerned, remember your own proposition to me on those lines two years ago. I really considered it quite seriously and as I had very advantageous offers I hoped I might yet be able to leave a competency to my son. I have had to abandon this plan, however, on account of the great nervous strain involved. You will not be surprised, then, if I suggest your going in a measure as my represent-ative, in the hope of your making a financial success of what is now impossible to me. If this hope should be fulfilled—even on a small scale—you would know that I should be eagerly following your difficult course and keenly interested in its results.

So let me repeat: where I can, I will stand by you with all my powers.

(By the way, have you heard that Pollini was involved in that London bankruptcy and is being followed up?)

Now for to-day I shall simply add an affectionate fare-well and wish you good luck!

Always your devoted

Rich. Wagner.

January 13, '83.

P. S. Please keep sending me short notices of your undertakings.   R. W.

This letter shows clearly how eagerly the Master clung to his cherished plan of founding a Wagner theatre in Berlin modelled after Bayreuth and under my director-ship. I shall never cease to regret my having doubted the adequacy of the means placed at my disposal for the purpose. For I felt that the cost of an up-to-date model theatre would be tremendous, and that the entire amount must be subscribed beyond a shadow of a peradventure before we began our huge task.

.   .   .   .

Many in our Brussels audiences were Paris music-lovers who had taken this opportunity of running down to hear a performance that at that time was such a novelty. The greatest of the French critics had come, as well as several eminent composers, Massenet, Lalo and others. At the close of our engagement these men united with the dignitaries of Brussels to give an elaborate banquet in our honour, at which toasts were drunk to the success of our enterprise and to the hopes of our soon appearing in the French capital.

Our season here was simply one round of constantly augmenting triumphs. In these later days it will hardly seem credible that an audience would often clamour for the repetition of such scenes, for instance, as Mime's " Sorglose Schmiede." And not only were whole scenes encored and single artists applauded, but the work in its entirety,—our staff of singers,—the orchestra with Anton Seidl at its head,—were more appreciated in Brussels, and we found more genuinely musical audiences here than in any other city of our tour.

I shall tell now of George Unger in that famous rôle of his, " Indisposed, and unable to sing! " He was to be the Loge in our first " Rhinegold " at Brussels. Coming to my office late the night before I found a note saying he was " ill " and would be unable to appear. Fortunately his rôle of Loge was my sole concern, as I had a good substitute for his Siegmund in Adolf Wallnöfer. But I sent off telegrams in at least a dozen different directions to secure a Loge for that occasion. The next day I sent for Unger, who had been seen at supper at two o'clock that morning, apparently in the best of health, so they told me;

and after telling him rather energetically what I thought
of him, I ended by saying that if I were forced to close
the theatre that night on his account, I should hold him
financially responsible for our losses. The good fellow
looked rather sheepish, and assured me as he left that he
would be on hand that night without fail. That evening
after the performance he blandly announced to his colleagues,—as he usually did on such occasions,—" Boys, I
think I never *was* in better voice than I am to-night!"

After our Brussels season we gave a great concert in
Ghent and another in Antwerp, then back into Germany
to Detmold, where Hans Förster, our advance agent, was
waiting for us. He had arranged for concerts at Darmstadt, Mannheim, Carlsruhe and Heidelberg, as well as
Munich, Baden-Baden and Zurich. And now came a critical moment for the Richard Wagner Opera Company.
Förster had not been able to secure suitable theatres for
our " Nibelungen " performances and had concluded we
must confine our energies to this series of concerts.

Heretofore our concerts had been on the off nights, and,
as extra performances, had simply helped out the budget
in the matter of the tremendous cost of transportation.
But such evenings by themselves would by no means cover
our expenses. It would have a bad effect also upon our
chorus and the scene-shifters, who must be abandoned in
Brussels, in some doubt naturally as to their coming pay.
To assure them of my good faith I left my treasurer behind in Brussels, to set up his office in the Grand Hotel
and to satisfy their demands until we sent for them again.

In Darmstadt, then, Förster and I were to arrange our
future plans. But he had been detained in Basle by illness and could only wire that he had closed contracts with
the theatres in Basle and in Strasburg for one performance each of the " Nibelungen " cycle.

It was then the first of February and no prospect of an
operatic performance until late in March! That would

never do! So I sent for my old Leipsic secretary Rosen-
heim and ordered him to arrange for theatres in Aix and
Düsseldorf; sending Heinrich Telle meanwhile to Mainz
and Wiesbaden to make similar arrangements, while I
myself undertook to provide a stage in the Grand-ducal
theatres of Darmstadt and Karlsruhe, and at the Royal
Opera House in Stuttgart.

In Darmstadt I persuaded the directors that after my
performance they could add to their own repertoire by
acquiring the " Nibelungen " rights from me. These excellent people saw my point, and after some preliminary
deliberations asked for an audience with the Grand Duke,
with whose august sanction our contract was closed that
very day. But on two conditions, they told me: First,
that they were to acquire the operas for their repertoire;
and second, that the first two rows of the orchestra were
to be reserved at half price for the officers of the Grand
Duke's army!

These conditions the Grand Duke himself emphasised
the following day. He had been present at our performances in London, and I had asked for an audience to thank
him for the order with which he had decorated me on that
occasion. He furthermore remarked: " Do you know
whom you should thank for that honour? My brother-in-
law, the Prince of Wales. He told me one day I must do
him a favour. He wanted to give you an order, but had
none on hand just then—so he asked me to do this for
him. And, I can assure you, I was very glad of the
opportunity."

After happily adjusting affairs at Darmstadt I left for
Karlsruhe, as our concert there was set for the following
day. In an interview with his Excellency von Putlitz I
mentioned my hopes of giving the " Ring " in Karlsruhe.
" But where, my dear fellow? In the Academy of Music? "
" No, your Excellency; in your own Opera House! " He
was rather taken aback at this, and after a pause re-

marked, " I'm afraid that's hardly possible."   " Then
your Excellency never intends to give these operas here? "
" Not quite that," he answered, " but I'm not yet certain
that they could be adapted to our stage." Here I remarked, " This would be your opportunity for testing
the matter. Let my men undertake the difficulties of the
installation, and if we find your stage room adequate,
your staff would later simply follow in our footsteps."
" But as to the copyright? "   " I shall be charmed to arrange all that with your Excellency." So he went to
his desk and made out the contract, saying, " This is
Friday, and I am not sure when I can have an audience.
But I shall try. I shall see you to-morrow surely, at your
concert, and then possibly I shall have news for you."

Our concert as usual was a huge success. The house
was crowded with a brilliant audience and enthusiasm
ran high. Our two great numbers were the final septette
from the first act of " Tannhäuser " and the " Ride of the
Valkyre," which I had introduced on our concert programmes under a storm of protest. At the close of these
selections, which we naturally gave with a magnificent
finish, the enthusiasm seemed to have no bounds. And
here in Karlsruhe, as in other places, the Grand-ducal
family, which was fully represented, honoured the artists
with bursts of spontaneous applause.

Back in my hotel, I was sitting at supper with Anton
Schott, the well-known tenor from Hanover, who had
taken Vogl's place in our ranks, when a court groom came
up and handed me a note from his Excellency: " 11.30
P. M. Just returned from an audience. His gracious
Majesty sanctions ' Nibelungen ' performance at Royal
Opera House. Don't leave to-night. I expect you to-mor-
row at 8 A. M. to sign contract."

The news that two court theatres had opened their portals to us comforted my poor " Nibelungen tribe " somewhat, and to add to our joy we had word from Aix and

Düsseldorf that performances had been arranged for in both places.

So Anton Seidl, with his orchestra and his artists, made the tour of Mannheim, Heidelberg, Baden-Baden and Freiburg, giving their great Wagner concerts there; while I went direct to Stuttgart after closing my contract with von Putlitz, to see what I could arrange with Feodor von Wehl, or possibly with the all-powerful minister of state, von Gunzert.   The opera, as well as everything else in this principality, was in the hands of the prime minister, who was nicknamed " The King of Würtemberg! " Feodor von Wehl, one of the most distinguished figures in the theatrical world, was a charming, polished, and fascinating creature, but a man of no initiative; von Gunzert, on the other hand, was diametrically his opposite,—their only point of similarity being the cleverness of both. The latter came of a humble family and boasted of his plebeian origin.

Von Wehl was gentle and courtly; von Gunzert, on the other hand, a perfect Tartar! Aggressive, inconsiderate, moody, sarcastic, quick in his judgments, and practical and rapid in his calculations—in short, a man to be handled rather carefully.

After my first interview in Stuttgart, where von Gunzert had not been present, I had gone to Aix with our technical staff, scene-shifters, chorus, etc.   On February 14th we were to open the cycle there with the " Rhinegold."

Arrived the night before, I was about to leave my hotel in the morning when Hans Förster came in, saying, " Director, prepare yourself for very bad news! "

It had been the standing joke of our tour to come to me with this introduction when they were about to announce that the house had been completely sold out.   So I shoved Förster out of the way, saying carelessly, " Yes, yes, I know! Not a single seat sold! " But he held me fast, saying earnestly—" But really I have some frightful news for you—you will be shocked! " Then I noticed that something was wrong and burst out, " Well, tell me quickly! What's happened? " " Richard Wagner is dead! " said he.

The news stunned me so that I reeled into the next room and clutched the bed, saying, " What's that you say? " " Richard Wagner died yesterday in Venice," said Förster. " The news is on the street already! "

This sad news from Venice called forth a sobbing echo throughout the wide world, but I cannot describe the deep effect it had on those of us who had known and loved the Master well. Here this evening was to be " Rhinegold " with the Richard Wagner Opera Company, and there on his bier in Venice lay the great creator of these dramas whose name we bore. Could we, *should* we play? After a hasty consultation with our members, with the directors, and with Seidl, we decided that we were pledged to the performance and must certainly go on with it.

Under the influence of this tragic news, and bearing in mind a quotation from the Master's last letter, I now made an appeal to every theatre in Germany to give a benefit performance and start a fund for Richard Wagner's son. This proposition, which came from a spirit of deepest devotion, was not accepted at Bayreuth, however, and our receipts for the " Rhinegold " that night (some four thousand Marks, which we sent as a first tribute) were declined witl thanks.

After having decided to go on with the performance, Seidl and I made some further arrangements. We planned to close the " Rhinegold " with the " Siegfried funeral march " from " Götterdämmerung."

When I returned to my hotel shortly before the performance the porter handed me a letter. What was this? It was addressed in the well-known hand of the Master for whom I had just been arranging a funeral service—and the certainty came over me that Richard Wagner was *living.* The news of his death had been false!

I hurried back to my rooms, the letter still unopened in my hands, and stronger and stronger grew the glad conviction—I wanted to shout it out to all the world—"Richard Wagner is *not* dead!"

Sending for Seidl and all the company in my office, I reverently opened the letter—and it was as though the Master himself had spoken to me.

My dearest Friend and Associate:

Did you ever get my letter in Amsterdam? I answered all your questions there.

Since then I've done nothing but follow your rapid and capable footsteps, trying helplessly to see how in the world you will ever recuperate after such labours!

In March you go to Prague, Pressburg and Pesth? This I see by the papers.—What next?

Are you really contemplating Venice? I fear that would be an unlucky notion; for of all the Italian (cities) Venice certainly is the least progressive; yet I myself should not advise you to try any of the others. There's only one topic in this town just now—"Revenge for Oberdank!" *

Germans mix well with Slavs, but never with Romans or Latins: Belgium is a good hybrid, half and half Flemish, etc. In Paris you'll see—or you would have seen—some interesting results! Russia, Stockholm, Copenhagen, even Hungary—that will all do!

I should like to have another good talk with you; but surely your head must be so spinning with all the rapid changes you have made, that your recollections are more or less kaleidoscopic.

We had most detailed accounts of Brussels from M.

---

* An Italian patriot condemned to death in Trieste for complicity in a plot against the life of the Austrian Emperor.

Geehrtester Freund und Gönner!

Haben Sie meinen Brief nach
Amsterdam erhalten? Ich beant-
worte darin Ihre Fragen. —

Seitdem ist mir nichts übrig
geblieben, als Ihre rastlosen
Fortschritte zu verfolgen und einiger-
maassen mir vorzustellen, wo
Sie doch endlich einmal anwachsen
wollen. —

Im März wollen Sie nach
Prag, Pressburg u. Pesth? So las
ich in der Zeitung. — Was weiter?
= Hatten Sie wirklich Venedig
im Sinne? Das wäre eine unglück-
liche Idee gewesen: von allen Itali-
enischen ist gewiss Venedig am
meisten gesunk; doch möchte ich
selbst zu irgend einer anderen auch
nicht rathen. Hier herrscht jetzt
nichts als „Revanche für Oberdeutsch."

Germanen und Slawen – das geht,
nur nicht Lateiner u. Romanen:
Belgien ist gut gemischt, ein
Halbvolk, vlämisch u. s. w.
In Paris werden – oder: werden
Sie was Schönes erfahren.
Russland – Stockholm – Kopenhagen
– am Ende auch Ungarn – alles
gut. Gern hätte ich einmal mit
Ihnen geplaudert: gewiss wird es
Ihnen kaum so bunt im Kopfe
sein, dass Sie sich auf nichts
von Ihren Fahrten mehr recht
besinnen.
Von Brüssel hatten wir durch
Ned. Zeitungen sehr genaue Berichte.
Seidl freut mich sehr. Hätten
Sie nur einen Tenor: Vogl war aller-
dings wie auserwählt von Schicksal
für Sie, aber – ich nenne noch alles
Deuten – Heimweh u. Therese – auch
ich habe daran gelitten.

Hier also die Zeugnisse über das
vortreffliche Benehmen Königsbergs.
Da haben Sie Gutes gewirkt. —
Wenn Sie in der zweiten
Hälfte des März wieder Feld
schlagen möchten, wäre mir
das sehr lieb: meine hierundörten
Reserven möchte ich gern etwas
erstarken lassen. —

Jetzt nehmen Sie allen Segen
des Himmels dahin und sagen
meine herzlichsten Grüße,
von denen ich Sie bitte noch
aufeinst weiter zu vertheilen.

Ihr

ergebener

Richard Wagner

Venedig.
Palazzo Vendramin Calergi.
11 Febr. 1883.

Tardieu. I am so delighted with Seidl. But if you only had a tenor! Vogl certainly was created for you and sent you by the gods, but . . . I can imagine what you had to put up with—" Heinrich and Therese! " I've had some experiences in that line myself!

I have the record of your splendid performance in Königsberg. You did well there.

I should be very glad if you could send me more money in the latter half of March. I should like to add a bit to my deposit at home.

And now may all the good blessings from Heaven be with you, to which I add my heartiest greetings and ask you to bestow them further as you see fit.

Yours devotedly,

Venice,   Richard Wagner.

Palazzo Vendramin Calangi,

    February 11, 1883.

He lives—he is not dead—was still my firm conviction! But when they called my attention to the difference in time between the post and the telegraph, it took some moments for me to realise the truth. Finally I read the letter over again, and the closing words sounded like a farewell message from above.

That night, as the final strains of " Rhinegold " faded from our ears, I stepped to the footlights and there, surrounded by my company, said a few brief words expressing our unspeakable sorrow, and then read them the closing paragraph of the Master's last letter. And now Anton Seidl began the funeral march from the " Götterdämmerung," and the whole house rose and stood in reverent silence,—finally to file out quietly and awe-struck, overcome with grief.

Seidl and I had arranged to go to the Master's funeral at Bayreuth. But first came another duty. Reicher-Kindermann, not yet recovered from her late illness, had been left in Brussels and had sent for me on urgent business. So I left on the 15th and hurried to Brussels, to reassure her as to her income during her convalescence. The following morning I was back in Aix and ready to leave with Seidl for Bayreuth.

There we found a gathering of friends of the Master. But as to the ceremony, I must confess I found it most unsuitable. For I felt within my soul that a god had left this earth,—and they gave him a funeral whose pomp befitted a " prominent citizen of Bayreuth "! There was no dignity, no grandeur, no reverent awe in that great final moment when Richard Wagner, who had created a world, was consigned himself to the earth.

That very night Seidl and I left Bayreuth for Düsseldorf, where we were to proceed with our cycle. Meanwhile Paul Geissler, my second conductor, had directed the " Ring " in Seidl's absence.

As I have said, one of my main endeavours was to keep peace in the company; and I make it my boast that from the beginning of September to the end of February my relations with these one hundred and thirty-four members had been of the friendliest, in spite of all the perplexities and cross-purposes of our wandering life. It was not until Düsseldorf that the second misunderstanding arose in the Richard Wagner Opera Company (the first was that with Heinrich Vogl in Bremen). The artist I speak of was not only a magnificent dramatic singer but an LL.D as well, and often displayed his legal lore in matters of contracts and penalties. We had made a rule, for instance, that all the singers in the first act must report at least an hour before the curtain, and those in the later acts must be on hand at the opening of the overture. As one of our members had almost wrecked a performance by non-appearance, we felt this step to be quite necessary.

Since the installation of this rule our Doctor of Laws had been the only one to break it, and we finally found it necessary to collect the penalty from him. This he took exception to, on the score that we had not said, " You are *ordered* to appear at such and such a time," but— " We *beg* you to appear," etc. Had he been ordered, he said, he would certainly have obeyed. But being simply begged, it left him free to come or not as he pleased. In the face of such an argument I naturally had nothing to say, so I smiled and told him the fine would be remitted for that time, but then and there I should *order* him to be on time in future.

This was the man who now came to me at the last moment, when it was impossible to get a substitute, declaring he would only sing his rôle of Gunther on condition that I paid him the salary he claimed for a performance of " The Valkyre " in Berlin, for which he had been billed—but which he had not sung, " Owing to an indisposition! " Called to order on this point, he went on to base his claims for extra pay on the fact that he had sung his contract number of performances for that month, and all future appearances must be paid for in advance. This I had to admit, but according to our contract he was asking twice the stipulated price. That was not to be tolerated for a moment. It would have established a precedent that would have shipwrecked our concern. So I met his demands with a stern refusal. As he still insisted, I suspended him then and there from our pay-rolls, and assured him that he could never again hope for an engagement under my management. I should have dismissed him outright but that I did not care to have a lawsuit on my hands; so I offered to lay his case before the board of our Theatrical Association, letting them decide what course I should take. His name was to be struck off all our programmes, and at the coming concert in Wiesbaden Julius Lieban was to sing his songs—a thing our Doctor had considered utterly impossible.

Shortly after our departure from Düsseldorf he came to

ask where I would send the decision of the court on its arrival. I asked where his family lived. " In Hamburg." " Then I shall send it to Hamburg!" He had not expected this, thinking I would banish him to some pleasant little retreat; so instead of going to Hamburg, he followed us to Wiesbaden and asked if he might apologise for his mistake, which he now thoroughly recognised. I answered, " For the sake of keeping the peace on this tour I shall accept an apology—on condition that you make it fully and freely, and in the presence of our entire membership, soloists, chorus, orchestra and all."

This struck him as decidedly severe; but those were my final terms. Then he tried to make me see how unjust it would be to lay his case before a public board of arbitration—at which I simply told him, he should have considered *that* in Düsseldorf.

In the course of an hour he returned to say that he agreed to my conditions. So that night, in the intermission of our concert, all our members assembled in a side hall placed at my disposal by the management, and the culprit stepped up and publicly acknowledged his fault. This was Dr. Franz Krückl, the former vice-President of the German Theatrical Association and a most capable artist; but I think, had he stayed by the law, he would have made quite as great a name.

From Wiesbaden we went to Mainz, and here had a disagreeable encounter with the publishing firm of B. Schott and Sons—or rather with their manager, Dr. Strecker. We had already had one clash at our second performance of the " Ring " in Berlin, which Dr. Strecker had attended as representative of his firm. He had insisted on certain rights on the strength of an earlier agreement between us.

The " Ring " at that time was considered of so little importance that this firm, which had spent forty thousand Marks for its publication, felt that a single performance in each city could hardly create a demand for their wares, and that all their librettos would be left on their hands. This view I did not share, for it was my firm conviction that the tour of the Richard Wagner Opera Company would be an important factor in the propagation of the cult. And this proved true indeed.

The firm, however, demanded an indemnity of one hundred and fifty Marks for each city where we gave a performance of the " Ring." This I refused, making the counter-proposition that I would pay three hundred Marks for every city, if they would turn over their librettos to me and let me sell them at my own rates. This they gladly accepted, for at that time the custom was that each theatre, large or small, took librettos to the amount of three hundred and twenty-seven Marks: whether in Vienna, Leipsic, Hamburg or Frankfort.

The firm further stipulated that I should take this same contract for the towns I had already visited (twenty-two in number, among them London, Berlin, Dresden, etc.). So I paid my six thousand six hundred Marks; and I frankly confess that both parties were most hugely pleased with their bargain. When I took out my note for the sum, the agent of the firm looked at me with a pitying smile as much as to say, " You'll never see that good money again!" I've often remembered his air of disdain. But his expression was not what you might call fixed—for before many weeks had passed I began to smile myself.

I had not acted on an impulse; for I remembered well that at the time of the production of " Carmen " fully three thousand francs had been paid for librettos in one city during a single season. And here were the four complete books of the greatest musical drama of any age turned over to me by the publisher himself for three hundred and seventy-two Marks—that is, ninety-three Marks for each book!

Their smile meant, of course, " You'll whistle for your money!" and I counted naturally on whistling for a while; but I think they miscalculated the time I should have to wait.

Our next performances took place in Darmstadt and Karlsruhe. Shortly after my departure from Mainz I had closed contracts with the theatres in both these places for the acting rights of the " Ring." Let me mention here that I personally have never made the least profit on these transfers of the rights of Richard Wagner's operas. In every case I turned over the entire amount to the Master, deducting no percentage whatsoever—which is a thing I might easily have done by raising the price.   The whole proceeds simply flowed into the treasury of Bayreuth. On the other hand, however, I did not fail to press my undeniable advantages, as in the case of Schott and Sons, or to defend my rights, which I had won simply by a clear foresight as to the value of the work in question.

On signing the contracts for the transfer of the copyrights to Darmstadt and Karlsruhe, I mentioned the fact that I had the rights for the librettos as well.   When they asked my price, I answered " fifteen hundred Marks." Then, with no further discussion, a clause to that effect was inserted in the contract, and the entire amount was paid.   The same was true in Stuttgart, where I asked two thousand Marks, which von Gunzen paid without a question.

In Karlsruhe our Kindermann returned to the company—cured, as she assured us, but still delicate; though the moment she trod the boards again she seemed to gain in vitality and youthful fire.   So she fascinated and enslaved all those who saw and heard her here.   From the court boxes to the topmost gallery, they all clamoured for her.

At the close of the second act of " Götterdämmerung " von Putlitz came behind the scenes, inviting me to the

anteroom of the Ducal box, where I was received with
gracious cordiality. The Grand Duke said, " We've been
speaking of you to-day. How difficult it must be to carry
out such an enterprise! They tell me you travel with five
freight cars full of scenery, etc.!" I answered, " The
freight cars don't trouble me as much, however, as the
one hundred and thirty-four people I have to manage."
At this his Highness laughed uproariously, and turning to
his wife, he chuckled—" I say, Louisa! What do you
think of that? " The Grand Duchess looked amused and
answered, " I can very well believe it, I'm sure!" Then
his Highness dismissed me with a few words of pleasant
recognition and handed me, as I left, the cross of his
Order of the Lion.

It is my pleasant duty here to mention the cordiality of
Felix Mottl, who showed his interest in our behalf by
speaking warmly of our project to von Putlitz and to the
Grand Duke himself, who settled many of our minor difficulties, as well as some important ones, and who welcomed Anton Seidl in the true spirit of artistic fellow-
ship.

Another incident in connection with our visit here goes
to prove that the Director must not only have perfect
command over his one hundred and thirty-four subor-
dinates, but over himself as well. And also, that this tour
was not as remunerative as some persons have said.

It was the day of our final " Götterdämmerung," when
the advance agent of the transportation firm of Jacob and
Valentine came to collect the money due for their excellent care of our properties—as he did usually at the end of
each cycle. That week, however, the reckoning against us
was fifty thousand Marks, as the good Krause had not
pressed me for his dues for some time. This sum I
ordered my secretary to pay; but to my despair there was
not enough in the treasury so I had to make up the final
one hundred Marks out of my own pocket. My need of

calm self-control may be estimated when I assure the reader that this was absolutely the last hundred-Mark note that I had in the world!

To be sure, we had twenty-eight thousand Marks to our credit in the Grand-ducal treasury, but it was a point of honour with me not to touch this until the close of our engagement.

We left Karlsruhe to give the cycle in Strassburg before Easter. Here I was received in the most courtly manner by General Manteuffel of the department of Alsace-Lorraine; yet at the same time he issued a private order to his officers that he should be highly displeased if they attended the theatre during Holy Week. At this time, too, of course, the national hatred was still intense, and the French element of Strassburg looked with scornful disfavour upon a German opera troupe. Yet in spite of these drawbacks our success was so great that Director Amann of the Strassburg theatre planned to give " The Valkyre " after our departure, and gladly paid one thousand Marks for the score of this opera alone.

After Easter we went to Basle. Here a queer incident took place that might have been a death-blow to the final scene of the first act in " Siegfried." In some unexplained way the anvil which Siegfried's sword is to shatter at the end of that scene, came to pieces of itself in the course of the act. As I noticed this from my box, I hurried behind the scenes, ordered the stage darkened, and called for a clever scene-shifter, who used to play the bear for us. We dressed him again in the bearskin in which he had already appeared and sent him onto the darkened stage, telling him to crawl carefully over to the anvil and arrange it for the final stroke. The audience simply saw a vague shape grovelling about on the stage; it appeared for a moment and then vanished. They hardly noticed the passing incident, and the great final scene was thus carried out successfully.

In Basle I caught a severe cold, yet I left for Stuttgart to arrange for our next " Nibelungen " performance, while my concert staff carried out a programme in Zurich.   Arrived in Stuttgart I was forced to succumb, and when finally the doctor allowed me to see visitors, Adolf von Gross from Bayreuth and his lawyer were announced. They had come for further particulars of our tour, which I was very glad to give them.   I wish to emphasise the fact that Herr von Gross gave our enterprise every assist-ance in his power and always took a lively personal in-terest in our success.

Here in Stuttgart my negotiations with Minister von Gunzert were resumed.   Feodor von Wehl had enthusias-tically subscribed to my proposition and insisted that the " Ring " should be given at the court theatre, first by us and then by their own staff.   It took us not quite half an hour to arrange our part of the contract.   But, as von Wehl said, the whole thing hinged on the Minister's sanction.

While we were discussing some minor details, the mighty one himself strode into the office and we laid our plans before him.   Von Gunzert at once now took the helm; and what von Wehl and I had already arranged, he utterly ignored.   Things had to be explained from the beginning, and each small point obstinately fought out and discussed.   Finally, after a most stormy debate he made a remark which gave me my cue: " I'll tell you what!   You say you're going to give this thing in Karls-ruhe next week?   Save me a seat and I'll run down and hear your show!   If I like it—she goes!   If I don't—she don't!" he said, in his broad peasant dialect.

The naïve self-confidence of this speech was amusing, so I calmly said, " Ah,—then, your Excellency, we may as well decide against it now on the spot!"   Quite taken aback, he asked, " And why *now?* "   " Because you would then be saving yourself the public disgrace of having misjudged so great a work at the first hearing. If you should condemn it now *without* a hearing, your Excellency's ignorance would be your best excuse!"

Quick to catch a point, he looked at me keenly for an instant, and then in his ready way he rapped out, "You're right! Well, come on! We'll make out that contract. But do you know, you've taken the devil of a rise out of me! We're both of us done up with all this talk; let's take a few hours off. You turn up again at six o'clock, and we'll sign that contract."

And so it was decided: but—*but*—our conference began at seven, and by half-past ten things were not yet settled quite to the satisfaction of the Minister, who finally said to von Wehl, " I'll tell you what, Wehl; you go home and go to bed. Director Neumann and I can manage this business alone all right!" and we did, but not until nearly midnight.

When I returned to Stuttgart von Gunzert expressed his astonishment at the enthusiasm of the public. They had stood in line all night for the seats, and when the box office was finally opened special policemen had to be detailed to keep order. On the day of the " Rhinegold," as I was talking things over with von Gunzert, came a royal lackey with a message from the Queen—" Would his Excellency please reserve a seat for one of her ladies-in-waiting? The Minister sent back word that there was not a seat left in the house. But presently the lackey returned, saying, " Her Majesty begs that you will kindly put a chair in the aisle for the lady," to which von Gunzert answered with characteristic curtness, " Tell her Majesty I won't! It's against police regulations!"

Hedwig Reicher-Kindermann sang for us again here, and now I must tell a charming anecdote of Marianne Brandt, who had been singing her rôles during her convalescence in Munich. When Brandt came to my office the morning of the " Götterdämmerung " I confessed to

her my anxieties about Kindermann. " I fear, I fear—she
will go back on us—though she says she is quite well
again! So be ready to help in case you're needed." The
singer, naturally piqued at being considered an under-
study, said she'd rather not substitute again. If she were
announced on the bills, that would be a different matter.
I ignored her remarks, knowing this was the best way to
manage her, and finally, as she left, she said, " By the
way, Herr Director,—if you should need me suddenly to-
night, I am dining with Madame so and so! "

At the very opening of our successful career I had received many invitations to go to Italy. But the Master,
who was then still with us, had earnestly advised my refusing; and the offers had not been sufficiently tempting
for me to insist. Now, however, Signor Avoni had sent me,
in Karlsruhe, invitations from Venice and Bologna which
I finally decided to accept. So we left Stuttgart and said
our good-bye to Germany in Munich, where we gave a
great concert. Here for the first time Marianne Brandt
and Hedwig Reicher-Kindermann were billed together.
They gave the matchless scene between Brunhilda and
Waltraute from the " Götterdämmerung," and won such
applause as I never since have heard upon the concert
stage.

CHAPTER XVIII

ITALY

OUR first cycle was to open in Venice the 14th of April, so at midnight on the 9th, after the close of our final " Götterdämmerung " in Stuttgart, I saw to the shipment of all our technical apparatus for Italy. And here it was that the foresight and experience of my advance agent Krauss began to tell so wonderfully. To avoid delay at the frontier he travelled with the freight himself, and by this means was able to set up our entire paraphernalia in the Teatro Fenice early on the 13th, after tremendous difficulties in transporting the material from the station to the opera house by canal.

On the 14th opened our memorable first production of the " Nibelungen Ring " in Italy. Those Italians are such thorough artists that the greatest innovations are understood and appreciated at their first hearing. How keenly the Master would have enjoyed seeing his beloved Venetians, with whom he had always felt himself so thoroughly at home, glorying in that first scene of the Rhine maidens with an enthusiasm we had never witnessed, even in our own native Germany. And we must consider that this public had never been in any way educated up to this much criticised work, heretofore considered so obscure.

Enthusiasm mounted to a frenzy as the acts progressed. But a great surprise was now in store for us. Just before the appearance of Erda, Kindermann, who was not singing that night, came to beg, " Herr Director, let me do the Erda this evening—please—*please!*" She had sung this rôle in Bayreuth once in 1876, but never since that time. I refused, saying she had quite enough to do with the Brunhilda in all three of the coming performances. But she insisted and plead,—finally saying, "Just for this one night! You must remember this is our first night in Italy! Let me sing Erda just this once—I shan't ask for any pay!"

Still doubtful as to the strain, in view of her coming performances, I finally gave way, and there was just only time to throw the long grey veil over her evening dress and to beg the singer of that night to resign in her favour, for at that moment came Erda's cue!

As she rose from her cleft in the rocks, imagine the surprise of all the artists on the stage—the gods and giants in Walhalla—when those mighty tones rang forth from out the cavern. Even Seidl was nonplussed for an instant, for no one had had the least inkling of it.

At the close of her song the enthusiasm of the audience was not to be restrained—they sprang from their seats and leaned over the rails of the boxes, calling loudly for a repetition of the scene. Once,—yes, even twice,—we encored that scene;—think of it,—the Erda song,—and the frenzied Italians would not be satisfied till Seidl tapped impatiently for the continuance of the performance.

This I should truly call the most remarkable triumph of her remarkable career—for the applause was spontaneously given, not to the world-renowned Reicher-Kindermann, but, as it was supposed, to a simple unknown Rosa Bleiter.

The following morning the Italian papers came out with glowing headlines on the glories of our Bayreuth production, mentioning Rosa Bleiter at great length as the greatest operatic star of the future. Now, however, appeared Rosa Bleiter herself at my office, complaining that Reicher-Kindermann had ruined her reputation by setting a standard she could never live up to. But I soothed her, and said that in future when Kindermann sang that rôle, she would do so under her own name.

After a triumphant night of " The Valkyre " we had a day of intermission, and early that morning Count Arco, attorney for our Embassy at Rome, was ushered in. He had come to Venice to hear this " Nibelungen Ring " and, as agent of the German ambassador, to propose our giving a gala performance in Rome on the occasion of the coming marriage of the Grand Duke of Genoa with a Bavarian Princess. The municipal council of Rome, with Prince Torlonia at their head, had added their appeals to those of the ambassador. In the course of our conversation Count Arco, a man of charming cultivation, mentioned Scaria, whom he had heard as Wotan in Berlin; saying how fitting it would be to invite him to sing this rôle in Rome.

My only objection to all this was the cost of such a step, and the doubt that Roman society would take any interest in our German performances. Count Arco now assured me in the name of the German ambassador that all my expenses would be guaranteed, and asked if he might telegraph at once from my office, making arrangements for a special train and for Scaria's engagement—all of which costs were to be covered by his Excellency. With that he bowed himself out.

Returning again a few hours later he showed me a wire from his Excellency the ambassador: " The city of Rome undertakes to pay for Scaria's engagement. The railroad department of the government grants a rebate of seventy-five per cent. for special trains in all parts of Italy." What an extraordinary concession—and how much that meant in the carrying out of all my plans! The special train from Bologna to Rome, which under ordinary circumstances would have cost me eight thousand four hundred lire, was now arranged for at two thousand one hundred. So I closed the contract with the Teatro Apollo in Rome, and Count Arco returned that same night in great satisfaction.

On April 17th came our first performance of "Siegfried" in Venice. This was less successful than the others, owing to the indisposition of our Siegfried, George Unger, who had one of his periodical attacks of singing off the key. These Italians have such correct and sensitive ears that they made it rather unpleasant at times that night for the singer. But Kindermann's magnificent impersonation of Brunhilda roused them to such a pitch that, before the final act, we hoped they had forgotten their first unfortunate impression. Yet here we were mistaken.

So far, we had been spoiled by our successes; but the next day was to present a very different picture. Notwithstanding the triumphs of Kindermann as Erda and Brunhilda, in spite of their enthusiasm for Seidl and his orchestra,—no matter how keen they were for Anton Schott, Julius Lieban and all the others in their several rôles,—George Unger they could not and would not tolerate, these keen Italians!

Next morning the German consul came to my hotel announcing a deputation of students who declared that if Unger sang the rôle of Siegfried that night in "Götterdämmerung," they would make such a demonstration that the opera could not go on. And each time that this unlucky singer was billed, they threatened to be there and to interrupt his performance. The consul had come to warn me, simply in my own interests, to change the cast. But this I hardly considered expedient, though either Anton Schott or Adolf Wallnöfer could have sung the rôle. I felt sure George Unger could be depended upon for that night; for not only is his rôle less difficult here, but Siegfried is never alone on the stage in "Götterdämmerung," so there would be no call for a demonstration.

The friendly consul tried to make the students accept

my statements, but could not move them from their purpose.

After the gentlemen had left, I sent for Kindermann and the stage manager and made a few precautionary arrangements. In the introduction to the " Götterdämmerung," Siegfried, as is well known, precedes Brunhilda on to the scene, crossing from the cavern in the rocks and traversing the whole stage before Brunhilda follows him with Grane. This first moment would be just their opportunity! So we arranged that Brunhilda, the idol of the populace, should enter at once with Siegfried, shielding him with her presence. In order not to alarm Kindermann I gave some vague explanation of not leaving Unger alone on the stage, and asked her to arrange to enter on the side of the footlights and keep her left arm about Siegfried's shoulder.

The clever artist caught my notion at once and promised to carry it out. But when the manager proposed this change to Unger he said jauntily, " No, you don't! We play that scene as we always do!" But Kindermann finally persuaded him to change; he had not the faintest idea, however, what he had thus saved himself. For it all went as we had foreseen. Scarcely had Brunhilda appeared, when a storm of jubilation broke out all through the house and Unger's entrance was quite unnoticed. Not even the slightest hiss mingled with the acclamations of their favourite. And as Unger was in very good voice that night, he got through his performance quite successfully.

On the evening of the 19th we held a concert in the magnificent hall of the Conservatorio. But that afternoon on the Grand Canal, before the house where Richard Wagner lived and died, the members of the Master's Opera Company arranged a stately tribute to his memory that was worthy indeed of the name they bore. The municipality of Venice had placed at our disposal their great gondolas of state—and in these Anton Seidl and all his orchestra took their places. The artists followed in six smaller gondolas, linked together in well-known Venetian fashion, and all about us darted the slender boats conducting us in state to the Palazzo Vendramin. Here they hovered about,—flower-decked and beauty-laden! All the nobility of Venice was on the Grand Canal, and as many strangers as could find a boat. All deeply impressed, they floated a silent throng, celebrating with us the apotheosis of our hero.

Arrived at the Palazzo Vendramin I joined our group of artists on the balcony, while Anton Seidl below with his orchestra began the first great strains of the funeral march from "Götterdämmerung." Reverently we uncovered our heads as the music floated up from the water, and all about us the crowds mutely followed our example—crowds in boats and on the quays, even on the roofs of the adjacent houses. In utter silence they listened to this mighty masterpiece, that came like a message from the gods,—wafted across the waters in all the matchless glitter of that warm Italian sunshine, and mingling with the scent of gardens and the throb of spring in the air among those verdant islands.

After a suitable pause came the "Tannhäuser" overture, which called forth thunders of applause though the first had been received in fitting silence. With this we closed our pageant, and to the inspiring strains of the "Marcia reale" the whole flotilla wandered slowly homeward down the Grand Canal, or threading in and out among the smaller ones.

That night at the Richard Wagner concert Herr Gross from Bayreuth and the scene painter Joukovski, who had planned the "Parsifal" decorations, were our guests. Among the many memorable evenings of our tour this concert, after our recent stately memorial service, made the most indelible impression on my mind. It was a

mild evening in April, full of the mysterious magic of
Venice; a night of perfume and the shimmer of moonlight
among its gardens. The great casements in the music
hall stood wide, and past and present mingled in indis-
tinguishable harmony as the music stole gently out over
the silent waters. One could imagine no more perfect
setting for the duet between Elsa and Ortrud. Augusta
Kraus as Elsa with her fresh young beauty and her
glorious voice; and Kindermann as Ortrud—singing as
even *she* had never sung before! That was our farewell
to Venice.

The next day we left for Bologna, where all was ready
for us, and on the 21st began our performance of the cycle
at their magnificent Teatro Communale.

After " The Valkyre " here, the day of our intermission
was set for a great concert. This was to be made up of
six numbers as usual, of which Seidl was to conduct three,
and Mancinelli (the celebrated maestro, who lived at that
time in Bologna) had been invited to lead the others.
We looked forward with some trepidation to these rehearsals under a strange conductor. The duet between
Elsa (Klafsky) and Ortrud (Kindermann) was on his
share of the programme, and now we noticed the difference
between the Italian and the German tempi. No Italian
conductor can direct Wagner, any more than a German
can bring out the full possibilities of Italian opera!

At first we merely smiled at the altercations between
the singers and the Italian maestro. Anton Seidl and I,
who sat in the front row, now began to make fun of the
artists, telling them to " be good and mind what the
conductor said—and to keep their eye on the baton!"
But we soon saw that matters were going rather badly,
and at the fourth failure poor Klafsky began to cry, thinking it must be her fault. Finally Mancinelli in despair
gave up and offered to retire, handing his baton to Seidl.
I tried to tell him that our people were so accustomed to

the latter that they were not quick in following any other
leader; which the maestro accepted with true Italian
grace and, being a most excellent musician, understood
perfectly. But he refused point-blank to conduct at the
concert. I pointed out that in this case we should have
to give it up entirely, for he had been billed, and we should
be mobbed if the public were defrauded of his presence.
Every seat had been sold on this understanding. Yet
he persisted, and I persisted too; so finally, the concert
was given up.

The following day came " Siegfried," and the next night
we closed with " Götterdämmerung." It was here in
Bologna that Adolf Wallnöfer undertook to substitute
in the rôle of Siegfried for George Unger (who had
announced an " indisposition " that very morning) and
carried his performance to a successful finish without a
single orchestra rehearsal! To be sure, the young singer
had been drilled in the rôles of Loge, Siegmund and both
the Siegfrieds from the beginning of our tour in view of
just such an emergency, yet it proved his capacity and
left no doubts in our minds that he was a valuable adjunct
to the company.

I have often mentioned the triumphs of Kindermann,
but here in Bologna they reached their highest pitch as
to manner of expression. Flowers in every form and
variety, such as we never see in Germany, were heaped
upon her, and at the close of the "Götterdämmerung " she
had an ovation such as I have never since witnessed.

The President of the Theatrical Society in Bologna, a
certain Count ——, came behind the scenes at our rehearsal for the " Rhinegold," and noticing the escaping
steam (an effect upon which we always rather prided ourselves), called my attention to it in an excited manner and
begged me to dismiss my careless engineer at once. It
was all I could do to calm him and make him understand

that this was part of the performance. But the next
night, at the close of the " Rhinegold," the Count hurried
out from his box to congratulate me on the success of
those *magnificent* clouds of steam, and to assure me that
he had not understood yesterday their great importance—
all this with many bows and a great deal of handshaking.

Before closing this chapter I wish to dwell upon our
thanks for the kind and genial hospitality of the German
consul in Bologna, Herr Kluftinger.

On April 25th, at nine o'clock in the morning, we started
in our special train across the Apennines to Florence;
then on to Rome. The scenery for " Rhinegold," " The
Valkyre " and " Siegfried " had been stowed in the train
at the close of each performance, and that very night we
had packed and shipped the setting for the " Götterdämmerung " and the orchestra instruments. Each man had
his own special work, and thanks to their efficiency and
general interest, things went off most smoothly.

It was a bright spring morning as we left the walls of
Bologna behind us, sped on our way by hosts of new
friends who had come to see us off. Handkerchiefs, flags
and banners waved in the sunlight, and—" Arrivederci "
they shouted in true Italian fashion. Their wish that we
might return was never, alas! fulfilled; yet I must say that
after an interval of over twenty years I look back with
grateful pleasure to those days in Bologna,—that stately
old Italian town, the Nuremberg, one might say, of Italy.
The place too where " Lohengrin " found its first early
recognition on that side the Alps.

We came to Florence this afternoon in time for a delightful stroll along the Arno, and that very night held
our first concert,—with the usual success. The house had
been sold out before our arrival, and at its close we
hurried on to Rome.

Early on the morning of the 27th our special lay along-

side the Porta del Popolo. As we pulled in we saw Count
Arco and a deputation which had come down to receive
us. On our arrival at the theatre the police met us with
the announcement that our scenery must be subjected to a
fireproofing process—a frightful calamity, which however was averted by the kind intervention of Count Arco
and the German ambassador. The commissioners nevertheless went through their forms, and coming on to the
stage gravely held a candle to each piece of scenery till
it began to glow, and then declared themselves perfectly
satisfied!

The interest of the society people of Rome, as the ambassador had predicted, was colossal. Herr von Keudell and
Count Arco had both made it a matter of personal effort
to sell as many boxes as possible. Whenever either of
them appeared at the box office asking for seats and were
told there were no more, they seemed as pleased as though
we had given them a pass, and their glee at our success
was quite touching to behold.

We gave " Rhinegold " on the 28th, and the next night
" The Valkyre." The King and Queen had promised their
presence for that evening, and it had been requested that
at their entrance we should play the National Anthem.
As they entered their box half-way through the first act,
Seidl's feelings may be imagined when he was forced to
stop his orchestra suddenly in one of the most beautiful
passages of " The Valkyre " and break out into the stir-
ring " Marcia reale "—while the audience stood to applaud the King, and he stood bowing to the audience!
After this official greeting the course of " The Valkyre "
was resumed. Queen Margherita, at that time in the
full splendour of her beauty, was so enchanted with
this opera that she became one of the most enthusiastic patronesses and was present at two more performances.

After one day of intermission came " Siegfried " on the

1st of May, and our great concert on the 2d. The night before, the city of Rome had given a brilliant ball in honour of the wedding of the Duke of Genoa and the Bavarian Princess, at which all the court, and naturally all the diplomatic corps, were present. And the following day the city had arranged a great popular pageant with fireworks and all kinds of games. Von Keudell told me the next morning that the Queen, who is famous for her love of music, had beckoned to him at the ball, and when he hurried up had told him how disappointed she was not to be able to hear our concert on account of the popular games. Von Keudell immediately answered, " Your Majesty, it is we who will be disappointed,—for without Queen Margherita and her court the concert surely cannot take place! " The Queen then turned impulsively to her husband, who was standing near, and told him what the ambassador had just said. The King looked at von Keudell gravely for a moment, and then, smiling at his wiife, he said, " Ah, then we shall have to go! " Whereupon he called for the Sindaco, Prince Torlonia, and told him it was her Majesty's desire to attend this Wagner concert, and that he must postpone his games until the following day.

The next morning came Herr von Keudell, bringing me a message from the Queen. Her Majesty signified her gracious intention to be present at the concert if I would consent to omit one number on the programme—the duet between Elsa and Ortrud. Her reason for this request was that she had been present at a concert the year before when this duet had been hissed, and now that the King had consented to be present she did not wish him to be subjected to any such disagreeable experience, as it might prejudice him against the German music.

I answered that on *our* programme that very duet would be the success of the evening, and begged her Majesty to accept my word for it that the number not only would fail to be hissed, but would be most enthusiastically applauded.

I think hardly another diplomat in the world could have arranged this matter satisfactorily, but Herr von Keudell (a friend of Bismarck and a finished statesman as well as a connoisseur of the arts) achieved it perfectly. He himself was bent on having the duet, which had failed so signally the year before, received with honours by a Roman audience; so he hurried to his interview with the Queen and returned presently, beaming with joy. Her Majesty had accepted our word for the results, but had made one further stipulation. "Tell Herr Neumann," she said, "that I wish he would add a few Schubert songs to his programme. It is years since I've heard one, and I long to hear them again." At first I was nonplussed. Schubert songs in a Wagner concert! It could not be done. But rather than send von Keudell again to the Queen I gave in, and we arranged that the numbers should be added at the end of the programme and that Julius Lieban, a delightful ballad singer, should interpret them.

As to the effect of this concert I shall simply say that our "Tannhäuser" overture had to be repeated twice amid thunders of applause, and that the "Lohengrin" duet the Queen had been so fearful of was received with such enthusiasm as I have seldom seen, even in Italy. At its close the Queen leaned forward nodding and smiling at von Keudell, and fairly beaming with satisfaction; then she whispered a few words to her husband, who rose and coming forward, nodded at von Keudell as well—while all this time the applause went on like mad! They were clamouring for an encore, but as the court chamberlain had announced their Majesties' time was limited, we could not grant this wish.

After the Schubert songs her Majesty sent von Keudell to usher us to her box,—Julius Lieban, Anton Seidl, and myself. She expressed her delight to the singer, thanking

him for the songs she knew and loved so well; then turning to Seidl and to me, she thanked us for our programme
and congratulated us on our triumphs, especially the
success of the much-decried duet. Then beaming at Herr
von Keudell, she said, "You may *well* be proud of your
countrymen!" During this talk the King had stood
silently by, his earnest face gentle and thoughtful; and as
we left, he shook hands and said a few graceful words of
recognition. King Humbert was one of the most interesting and sympathetic personalities it has ever been my
fortune to meet. His face was stern and strong, but the
wonderful great dark eyes,—grave or gay as the occasion
demanded, or kindled with the passing mood,—gave token
of his noble nature and his broad humanity.

The next day, at the close of the "Götterdämmerung,"
we were invited to the house of the artist Lenbach. Herr
von Keudell had said he wished to give us a parting
celebration; but as he himself was in mourning it should
take place at the Palazzo Borghese, in whose wonderful
rooms Lenbach had his studio. The artist and the diplomat received us together, while hosts of eminent men of
all ranks crowded the rooms, where the flower of Roman
society lent a glitter to the occasion. But the crown and
centre of that whole assemblage was—as usual—our Hedwig Reicher-Kindermann!

In the course of the evening von Keudell presented me
to an Italian Princess whose name I have now forgotten,
and who insisted we must give our cycle in Naples. I
answered that much as we should wish to, having felt
already the charm of Naples, we were bound by contract
to a routine and must carry out our programme of going
direct to Turin. The Princess was deeply distressed and
spoke of it again to von Keudell, calling me to a second
interview. She would undertake, she said, to pay Turin
an indemnity of forty thousand francs if we consented to
her proposition. After some consultation with von Keu-

dell I concluded that my word was pledged to Turin; the Sindaco had made all preparations for our coming, our performance was to be the nucleus of the wedding festivities for the Prince of Genoa, and much as it grieved me I must give up Naples.

I shall mention a few more interesting details of our stay in Rome. On the day of our " Rhinegold " performance a delegation from the orchestra appeared in my office to give notice that unless they had an immediate increase of thirty per cent. in their salary, they would all resign on the spot. This revolt was all the more unexpected as the most perfect harmony had always existed between us. I asked their deputy to repeat his statement more clearly, and soon saw that the plan had been evolved by some few disgruntled members, of whom there are always several in each organisation. This matter was not to be carelessly handled. So I calmly pulled out my watch, looked carefully at the time, and said, " Gentlemen, you have surprised me somewhat; for I had considered we had treated you rather well so far, and flattered myself that I had done everything possible for your convenience. I shall give you just one hour to consider this matter, and shall expect a written answer at the end of that time as to your decision. In case you hold to your present determination, I shall immediately appoint a receiver, and the Richard Wagner Opera Company will be dissolved."

When the men had left the office, my secretary, pale with terror, stammered out, " What are you going to do now? " I answered quietly, " Nothing! But this evening I want you to be at the box office to see that no one gets wind of the matter." " But the orchestra? " he insisted. " Oh, they'll play, you may be very sure! " I said, with perfect composure. And so they did. Just as I had expected, before the hour was up I had a written notice saying they would consent to play.

As I was about to leave one night for the theatre a card was handed me—" Matteo Salvi," late director of the Royal Opera in Vienna. Why, this man's death had been in all the papers fully a year ago!   "Is the gentleman waiting to see me? " I asked, with a strange feeling that I was having a visitor from the other world. " Yes." " Then show him up in Heaven's name! " In another moment Matteo Salvi himself appeared at the door, hurried to embrace me, and told me how very glad he was to see me again.   The same old Salvi,—enthusiastic and gushing as usual! The obituary notices had not robbed him of any of his sprightliness. My doubts as to his being a shadow vanished at once, and from now on to the end of our stay he and his charming wife were with me constantly.

We finished our engagement in Rome with " The Valkyre " on the 5th of May.   They had begged for a repetition of the first day of the Trilogy, and their enthusiastic reception of it need not be dwelt upon. I shall simply say that on this occasion her gracious Majesty was one of our most eager listeners, and it was her applause that led all the rest,—stimulating them to a perfect frenzy of acclamation.

The following day our special train took us to Turin. We held our cycle at the Teatro Regio, from the 8th till the 12th of May, the 10th being reserved for our great Wagner concert.   It was a wonderful sight, that magnificent theatre festively decorated for these gala performances.

Turin is celebrated for its beautiful women; and I must admit that I never saw a more bewildering array of lovely faces, all in the glory of their festal toilets. When the Grand Duke and his bride entered their splendid box, diamonds gleamed and plumes nodded as all the ladies bent in graceful greeting; while the men behind them stood revealed, their fine dark heads and clear-cut profiles showing for that moment to the best advantage. Like a ripple it ran through the house, that swaying courtesy to the royal guests, and the charm of the whole picture was heightened to-night by the wonderful floral setting. The orchestra space had been filled in and transformed into a garden with gravelled paths, lawns and mossy nooks, set with all the wonderful flowers of an Italian spring! So between the orchestra and audience had arisen as if by enchantment this Garden of Armida, through which the music came with soft bewildering effect.

Later in Vienna and in Prague I have used this same idea with equal satisfaction.

Lieban's success as a ballad singer in Rome and his introduction to the Queen had spurred on Anton Schott, who now begged to be allowed to appear in this Turin concert, saying he would gladly waive all claims to any salary. Just to humour him, I changed the programme and put him on. But unfortunately for the poor singer, court etiquette in Turin was strict,—and far from receiving an ovation, as Lieban had in Rome,—all applause was most severely interdicted. After our first number, the "Tannhäuser" overture, Seidl came to me rather perturbed, saying, "What can the matter be—didn't they like it?" and then went back to his desk, perplexed and disappointed.

Finally came the turn of our jovial Anton Schott. Not a hand stirred. An icy silence after his splendid performance! Furious and chagrined, he came to me later, saying ruefully, "Well, if I'd known that, I'd never have begged you to let me sing just on this very night when they all have to sit there like fishes! And without a cent of extra pay too!"

On the 11th of May came our performance of "Siegfried," and here the managers, by some misunderstanding,

played us a horrid trick.   Our gala concert had been set
for 8.30; consequently they thought " Siegfried " was to
begin at that time too.   Fancy our horror when we saw
this announced the very day of the performance,—too late
to make the change.   We began at 8.30 and did not close
till after two!   To be sure, the audience—in Italy they are
accustomed to such late hours—seemed not' to mind this
as much as we.

On the 12th of May with the " Götterdämmerung " we
ended our engagement in Turin.

It was here that we had to abandon Katharina Klafsky.
This charming artist had risen to be second in rank to
Reicher-Kindermann, and it was with heavy hearts that
we left her in a Turin hospital, dangerously ill with
typhoid fever.   Three months later she accepted an engagement in Bremen which was the opening of her wonderful career, meteor-like in its brilliancy, but only all
too short!

Count Dal Verme, owner of the theatre of that name in
Milan, had invited us to stop there on our way from Turin
to Trieste and give our " Nibelungen " cycle, offering us
the fixed sum of forty thousand francs.

On writing to Trieste I found I could postpone our performances there, and so closed at once with the offer from
Milan.   Immediately their papers published a glowing
account of the important musical event they were so
breathlessly expecting, and as the public of Milan is really
a music-loving one *par excellence,* our coming was the
sole topic of discussion for society.   But suddenly Mme.
Lucca, head of the great publishing firm there, who had
come down to Turin to see our performances, laid her
absolute veto upon this entire arrangement!

At our first appearance in Venice she had introduced
herself as owner of the copyrights for Wagner's works in
Italy, on the strength of an early contract with the Mas-

ter for which she had paid ten thousand francs, and which had long since lapsed. She had then declared that she should forbid our production of the " Nibelungen " in Venice and Bologna—and by law, if necessary! Yet I noticed directly that she seemed keener about money than about the law, and asked her how much she wanted.

Mme. Lucca was a tall stately woman with imposing features and a great deal of manner. She had been charmingly cordial, and it was indeed on the occasion of a dinner she gave in our honour that all this transpired. She assured me in her magnificent way that the matter could be arranged quite amicably if I paid her a certain indemnity for each city. Venice was rated at two thousand francs, Bologna at one thousand two hundred, Rome and Turin at two thousand, and Trieste (which she, in her kindly generous way, added to the map, and called an Italian town) at one thousand francs.

As I did not care to keep my " Nibelungen hordes " idle while I awaited the result of a long and tedious process at law, there was nothing to do but to pay her demands.

When all arrangements had been made, and our contract then signed with Milan, Mme. Lucca surprised me one night in the midst of the second act of the " Götterdämmerung " with the announcement that she should forbid our Milan performances. Nothing I could say or do seemed calculated to move her. She declared she had only given her permission for the first specified cities, thinking we should fail in our undertaking; but now that she realised how tremendously successful we had been, she wished to reserve the rights for herself. She, *personally*, would present the " Ring " in Milan.

I tried to show her the utter absurdity of attempting such a work with only foreign artists; and then to make her see how deeply she was injuring the sacred cause of Art. But clinging to her point, she announced her firm determination to give the " Nibelungen " herself in Milan,

no matter what the cost. So nothing was left but to wire
frantically in all directions, and keep our original contract with Trieste.

Our season in Turin closed most brilliantly with the
" Götterdämmerung " on the 12th.

As our special train pulled into Milan at noon the following day, what was my surprise to see an immense
gathering of people there to greet us ! To my further huge
astonishment the door of our carriage was opened before
we had come to a full stop, and two men hurried in and
guarded both the doors. Presently, when I tried to leave
the train, a group of men stepped up to me and one of
them, pressing a roll of notes into my hand, said to his
companions, " I call you all to witness, gentlemen, that I
have fulfilled our part of this contract. Now, Director
Neumann, fulfill yours." Whereupon the station master
stepped up to me, accompanied by the German consul and
an interpreter, saying, " M. le Comte Dal Verme has
closed his contract by paying M. le Directeur Neumann
the sum of ten thousand francs : and whereas your part of
the agreement was to present the ' Nibelungen Ring ' in
Milan, I am under orders to hold all your properties,
scenery, etc., until this contract is carried out." This
order he now proceeded to obey by uncoupling our freight
cars, and side-tracking all our apparatus.

When this had been done the guards bowed and stepped
aside from all the carriages, leaving us free to depart if
we chose. I felt naturally that I was not exactly off on a
pleasure trip with my company, and that without our
paraphernalia, instruments, etc., our going to Trieste
would be rather a farce. So, as the Count Dal Verme
would not relinquish our property, I thought we had better stay by it.

And now enter the Count Dal Verme himself. He
stepped up to explain that they had sold sixty thousand

francs' worth of seats for our performances,—but if I were to pay him an indemnity of forty thousand francs I might take up my goods and depart. As this was clearly absurd, and yet he was not to be moved, I finally rallied my people about me and said, "I am going to engage rooms at the Hôtel de l'Europe. If you will all meet me there at five o'clock, I shall tell you my further decision." Then turning to the consul, I asked him to come to the hotel, where I wished to show him my Italian contract with Wagner.

Finally I asked the station master to send me up my trunk—which he politely but firmly refused. On my earnest appeal to be allowed at least to take out a clean shirt they assured me, after some conference, that all the effects of the Richard Wagner Opera Company had been confiscated, and that my linen was part of the " theatrical properties "!

I was carrying a small bag which was the treasury of our company, and all the members knew it well by sight. If Count Dal Verme or one of his agents had thought to confiscate this, they would have had what they wanted without further trouble—our money. So now Hedwig Kindermann stepped up to me carelessly and said, quite unconcerned, " O thank you so very much, Herr Director, for holding my bag. I'll take it now, and see you later at the hotel. Good-bye." With that she coolly appropriated our funds and walked off, saving us for the moment from that danger at least. But here we were, stalled in Milan until further orders.

On laying my contract before the German consul and Count Dal Verme it proved that Mme. Lucca had the prior rights, as her agreement was dated 1868 and mine had been drawn up in 1882. An attempt to mollify the firm of Lucca now failed signally, and the Count Dal Verme was forced to admit that he had done the Richard Wagner Opera Company a grievous wrong. We soon came to

terms, however, and compromised on a performance of
" Fidelio " in the Teatro Dal Verme on the 15th of May.
Our cast was as follows:

Hedwig Reicher-Kindermann...........Leonore
Augusta Kraus....................Marcelline
Anton Schott......................Florestan
Dr. Franz Krückl....................Pizarro
Julius Lieban.......................Joaquino

Then, on the following night, we gave a great Wagner
concert. Half the gross receipts for both performances
we turned over to Count Dal Verme, and we paid him an
indemnity of two thousand francs as well.

The ovation which greeted our " Fidelio " in Milan is one
of the most thrilling memories of our tour. We gave the
overture No. 1, and it seemed they could not be satisfied
with one hearing. Marcelline had great applause both
for her aria and for the duet with Joaquino, though
Pizarro's great aria was not well received at all. His
next duet with Rocco, however, the audience greeted with
rapture. And as for Reicher-Kindermann in her wonderful Leonore aria—words fail me to describe it. In the
boxes, in the parquet, all over the house people rose and
cheered: handkerchiefs waved and scarves fluttered—and
when this no longer sufficed, they stamped with their feet
and pounded with the chairs, demanding just one more
encore. This finally lasted so long that I went behind
the scenes and ordered Kindermann to refuse, for she was
not yet quite strong and the strain was far too great. The
prisoners' chorus and the grand finale, as well as the
whole second act, called forth a storm of wild Italian
jubilation. The " Leonore " overture No. 3, which we
played in the intermission, was encored with a spirit that
one rarely sees even in Germany, and I was finally forced
to protest against a second encore as really too much for
the orchestra.

The wonderful keenness and musical sensibility of the Italians was shown again in these Milan audiences. They never hesitated either to praise or to blame; and their ears were so acute that at the least false note of one of the horns, for instance, some one would rise in his seat, and pointing to the unfortunate offender, would hiss loudly.

I think we all left the theatre that night in rather an exalted mood;—Augusta Kraus, Anton Schott, Dr. Krückl, Lieban, and above all Seidl with his orchestra and Reicher-Kindermann,—each came to me in turn to say how fortunate they felt themselves to have taken part in such a glorious performance.

The following night was our great Wagner concert. And again Mme. Lucca appeared at my office, like Banquo's ghost, to announce that she must protest against our playing the "Tannhäuser" overture, which had always been our opening number. This categorical refusal, which the lady issued in her well-known imperious manner, made little or no impression on me, since I had heard it before—so I answered calmly, "The 'Tannhäuser' overture will be played, madame, even if you do call in the police!" Then she triumphantly pointed out the fact that the "Tannhäuser" overture had been hissed a year ago at a concert conducted by the great Faccio himself— and *he* had a magnificent orchestra of fully one hundred men! How much more surely we should fail with our paltry force of sixty. With that she sailed out, still firm in her threats of interference, and leaving me quite as firm in my determined resistance.

That night just as Seidl raised his baton for the opening of the overture, Mme. Lucca stalked majestically into her box. I am not sure whether she recognised the first few bars, but a gentleman who accompanied her soon leaned over and whispered something in her ear, at which she turned suddenly and scowled into my box, which was near!

Although the success of this number had hitherto been most unqualified, I confess I looked forward to its reception here in Milan with some uneasiness. But the audience broke out at its close into rapturous applause, and Seidl had to give his men the signal for an encore. Then Mme. Lucca rose abruptly from her seat and frowningly withdrew to the gloom of the background.

I shall merely add that the audience now clamoured for a second encore, which could not, however, be granted.

Our triumphant success naturally did not modify Mme. Lucca's mood, as she wanted the field to herself for the tour she contemplated next year. Yet in spite of all this we parted the best of friends. " Only," said this remarkable woman, " you are the first man who has ever dared to oppose my will! " Then she asked me if I would come if she sent for me the following year to conduct a tour she had planned, with an Italian orchestra and singers from La Scala. To this I answered that neither I nor any other man could ever carrry out such a project. Mme. Lucca was rather furious at this answer, yet I could see it had made some impression. I afterwards learned that this clever and energetic woman had made the most determined efforts to carry out her plan. She even applied to many of our artists to help her out, Klafsky, Schott, Lieban and others, asking them to learn the rôles in Italian and join her troupe. Yet, as was naturally to be expected, such an enterprise never materialised.

CHAPTER XIX

AUSTRIA

AFTER this concert our special train, which had been held up in this remarkable manner, was released, and we went on to Trieste. During the day the heat was now intense but the evenings were decidedly cool. Kindermann had bought the lightest of summer frocks in Milan, and I was quite anxious as I saw she had no wrap for the trip. But she laughed my uneasiness to scorn. At five o'clock next morning we arrived at Trieste. Although our scenery had passed a fire inspection in Rome the process had to be repeated, more thoroughly this time, and it was tedious and difficult in the extreme.

On the 18th of May, then, we opened our engagement with the "Rhinegold," and here too Kindermann begged to be allowed to sing the Erda, though she was to sing Brunhilda in the whole cycle. Her success was no less than in Venice and she had to encore the great warning to Wotan. Like a voice from a far-off world rang out her mighty tones—deep, mystical, soul-searching, and convincing. "All that is,—must end!"

When at the close of the opera Kindermann came to say good-night I begged her to go directly home and save herself for the coming performances. But she laughingly said she had seen a café where they advertised Munich beer, and had invited the company there to supper. "But not in the garden, whatever you do! And don't stay too late" was my last warning as she bent and kissed my hand—a ceremony she always obstinately insisted on performing. She was always most touchingly responsive,

303

and one of the most grateful and lovable members of our company.

Next day, as I started for the theatre to inspect our scenic arrangements, Kindermann's maid came in with such a tragic face that I knew at once the artist would not be able to sing that night. I went directly to see her, found her in a raging fever, and sent at once for the doctor. Then back to the theatre I flew to arrange with Seidl for substitutes. While we were thus occupied Baron Morpurgo, the director of the theatre, was announced. He greeted me by saying, " Your Kindermann will not be able to sing this evening,—what? " " But how did you know that! " I asked in amaze. " I could have told you that last night! " said he. Then he said he had noticed a group of our artists in the café gardens at supper, and hearing that Mme. Kindermann was among them, had gone out to congratulate her upon her triumph of that evening and to beg them all to join him inside, as the night air of Trieste was considered suicidal. Kindermann thanked him, saying, " Ah, but it is so charming here! We could not leave this spot! " They had all stayed late, but after two o'clock a sudden shower came which sent the artist shivering home in haste. From this and from my face the Baron had guessed the worst.

" The Valkyre " and " Siegfried " took place the 19th and 20th of May, without our Kindermann, but she finally insisted on singing the " Götterdämmerung " the following day. The doctor shook his head gravely, but said it would really do her more harm to cross her ; so finally, and most reluctantly, I consented to let her sing.

But Brunhilda's great farewell in the final act of " Götterdämmerung " was her own last song as well— for they carried her from the stage when it was over and took her to her bed, completely prostrated—yet still brave. For we had to leave her to the gentle care of the hotel-keeper's wife and the excellent doctor, and with firm spirit she assured us she would join us presently in Buda-Pesth.

We left Trieste at eight in the morning on the 22d of May, the Master's birthday. Before leaving I made an early visit to Kindermann, little dreaming it was to be our last meeting—I wonder if she guessed the truth? Twice she called me back as I started for the door and made me promise she could join us in time to appear in "Siegfried," which it seems she had set her heart upon. And so I left.

We came to Buda-Pesth at three A. M. on the 23d, and that very night began our cycle. Here again our technical staff had worked wonders. For just as in Brussels, where the stage at midnight was still set with all the complicated paraphernalia of Boïto's "Mephisto," they had to unload the theatre of all its decorations before we could take possession at 3.30 the next morning, and set up our still more complicated machinery for "Rhinegold." The steam connections fortunately had been made some days before.

Our first cycle ended on the 27th, and on the 28th we repeated "The Valkyre" and added a performance of "Fidelio" on the 29th. Amalia Materna took Kindermann's rôles in Buda-Pesth. The general enthusiasm was so great that the manager of the Royal Hungarian Opera House came at once to close a contract with me for the further rights.

Although our original plan had been to end our tour with the month of May, yet while we were in Venice we had made a contract with Gratz which now must be fulfilled. So late on the 30th we left Buda-Pesth and arrived in Gratz early the next morning. Here our last cycle began on the 1st of June.

I now felt proud and glad that in spite of the endless difficulties and complications of a tour on such a scale, we were to close our venturesome enterprise with perfect mutual satisfaction. My colleagues in the field will all surely understand my feelings as the time approached when I could draw a full breath of relief and say devoutly, " Thank God, that's safely over! " With this thought in my mind I came down to my office one day, when the secretary handed me a note which I had to read several times to make sure I fully understood it.

In Leipsic, when I was engaging our staff, a singer (whose name I shall suppress) had come to me, complaining he was in desperate straits and asking to be enrolled in our company. I had no vacancy for him, but finally consented—after numerous appeals and threats of desperate deeds on his part—to hire him conditionally as under-study for Fafner, the dragon in " Siegfried," a position I created for his benefit. This seemed to satisfy him, but I told him he need not consider himself bound, and in case anything better turned up he must surely accept it. As nothing had so far offered, he was still with us, and when our original Fafner left one day this under-study took up that important rôle

His note then was a curt announcement that if I did not at once pay him an extra three hundred francs over and above his salary, he, the undersigned, refused to appear. Unfortunately he knew that we had no one now to take his place, and forgetting his late necessities and recognising only the fact that he had me by the throat, he took this first occasion of proving his deep gratitude.

So after three careful readings of the missive, to make sure I had not mistaken the artist's meaning, I calmly handed the matter over to my attorney. After hearing the case the lawyer said with a grin, " Just hand me three hundred francs, Herr Director, and give me your blessing and no questions asked—I'll return them when I get ready! "

The performance took place in due order, Fafner being represented with no further demur from the artist,—and the next morning the lawyer walked into my office and

laid the three hundred francs on my desk. I looked so
amazed that he laughed as he answered, " That was one
of the pleasantest and simplest things I ever undertook;
and I'm only too glad to have been able to contribute to
the smooth and successful ' finale' of your tour!" Then
he said he had merely sent for the gentleman and told
him the three hundred francs had been deposited with
him on call—*after* the performance! The artist had then
signified his perfect readiness to sing, and had done so.
But on calling that morning, the lawyer had told him that
if he drew the three hundred francs we should be forced
to bring suit against him for " unjust claims and unwarrantable pressure "—and our case was good enough to
hound him off the stage. So he saw the point and withdrew with chastened spirit.

The most remarkable part of this episode was that I
could not make the lawyer accept the slightest fee for his
services!

At the close of the performance that night, they handed
me a telegram saying, " Reicher-Kindermann died this
morning. Funeral to-morrow on account of heat." What
a shock! I could hardly credit my senses. None of us
had expected this, and all mourned her loss unspeakably.

After a hurried consultation with Seidl, and a wire to
delay the burial till I came, I started for Trieste; getting
there just in time to conduct the funeral services. Heart-
broken I stood by the side of her bier and paid a last inadequate tribute to this flower of our German stage. Her
loss to the operatic world was hardly to be estimated.
She was beyond question the greatest dramatic soprano
of her day and generation, as the late Schröder-Devrient
had been in hers. Her Brunhilda, Erda, Fricka, Ortrud—
her Leonore, Eglantine, and last but not least her Carmen,—have never been approached by any other artist
within my realm of observation. Those of us who have

heard her duet with Telramund and her wild appeal to the
gods,—her Leonore aria, or the third act of Carmen,—her
annunciation to Siegmund and Sieglinda,—her farewell
to Wotan, or the awakening in " Siegfried,"—her triumphant landing with Gunther, or the wild " Ho-jo-to-ho!" of
her " Valkyre" cry, and to crown all her last rapturous
song of farewell and greeting in " Götterdämmerung,—
will never forget these moments till the end of their
existence.

She was a personality of such magnetic force and an
artist of such exalted ability that her equal would be hard
indeed to find. And this marvellous diva, after a career
of only twenty-nine brief but brilliant years, must go the
way of all flesh; regretted by all as a genial companion
and a peerless singer.

The day after the funeral, where her two sisters and I
had been the only mourners, I was back again in Gratz,
plunged deep in the affairs of the Richard Wagner Opera
Company, which was to close its great tour here on the
1st of September, 1882.

CHAPTER XX

RUSSIA

A NEW era had dawned. Each town where we had given the "Nibelungen" now eagerly clamoured for the rights of presentation—and our great mission was fulfilled. My call to the management of the Bremen theatre now absorbed all my capacities,—for here, too, I meant to further the Master's cause.

Meanwhile Max Stägemann, who had succeeded us in the Leipsic theatre, seemed to think his audiences had tired of Wagner; so he gave them the "Helianthus" of Goldschmidt instead. But popular criticism soon forced him to open up negotiations for the "Nibelungen" rights; yet, as he was unwilling to accept my terms, the matter then came to nothing.

To justify himself before his impatient audiences, he now threw the blame on me,—publishing articles in the Leipsic *Gazette* accusing me of sacrificing the interests of the Wagner estate to satisfy my own personal spite and greed, and declaring I made a good thing of my contracts. This stab I answered with a brief statement of the facts. Setting aside all the returns from our foreign tour, I asked him to compare his record with mine, and offered to show the books of the Bremen Opera House in order to prove which one of us had contributed most to the treasury at Bayreuth. Stägemann was silenced, and I had the pleasure of receiving the following telegram from Berlin:

Have just read your controvery with Stägemann. Am all on your side.

Hans von Bülow.

309

This pleased me especially, as von Bülow was a firm partisan of Stägemann and had worked for his election in Leipsic. When Bülow came later to Bremen with the Meiningen orchestra I called to thank him personally, and to clear up an old misunderstanding between us. In his quaint and charming way he answered, " But, my dear fellow, *of course!* I was furious at that attack. I told Stägemann so at the time, and he himself acknowledged it was unjust."

The misunderstanding between us had been as follows: While I was managing the Leipsic theatre, Bülow had come down at my invitation to conduct Beethoven's Ninth Symphony—for no one could excel him in this.   Later at a benefit concert for the orchestra pension fund he was asked to repeat this; and in his generous way he offered to do it free of charge, stipulating, however, that we should hold a few preliminary rehearsals under his first violin and his first 'cellist, whom he would send down for this purpose.

Directly I heard this news I knew it must be broken gently to the Gewandhaus orchestra.   But Förster had already mentioned it to one of the men, and now there was nothing to be done.   They were furious, of course, at the suggestion of " *leading-strings* " from Meiningen and declared positively they would never play for von Bülow. All my efforts and my usual powers of persuasion were in vain, and nothing was left but to write von Bülow that we had decided not to give the Ninth Symphony after all.   The latter, however, never suspecting the true cause, felt there had been some intrigue against him, and the matter was not cleared up till three years later.

The Master's fears that I should find no musical atmosphere in Bremen were fortunately quite unfounded.   In my first year I added " Tristan " and the " Ring " to their repertoire, and our two great concerts dedicated to

Richard Wagner were an enormous success. To be sure, Bremen, as the Master had felt, was a narrow field indeed after the wide sphere of activities I had become accustomed to.

I had long been negotiating with Dr. Franz Schmeykal and Dr. Waldert of the two great theatres in Prague as to the establishment of a permanent German opera there. And now, through the energetic efforts of Alexander Richter, this was at last to be accomplished. Remembering the words of Richard Wagner, that I should find a most thoroughly musical public here, I finally decided to devote my energies to the cause of German art in the capital of Bohemia. Here I assumed the directorship of a celebrated institution rich in stately tradition, but neglected and fallen to decay for lack of the proper impulse. To reorganise this great concern, and to supply this necessary impulse, was henceforth to be my task.

No more far-reaching plans now for me; though I had constant invitations for tours in various directions,—particularly from America. Wagner himself had been most anxious for me to occupy this latter field, yet at that time I had not been able to see my way clear.

Later, when I was occupied with the affairs of Bremen, the two Gye brothers asked me to bring the Richard Wagner Opera Company to London again, this time to Covent Garden, but it was then out of the question. Finally Sir Augustus Harris, that most distinguished of English managers, opened up negotiations, which likewise came to nothing. I had invitations as well from Copenhagen, Stockholm and Christiania, but refused them all; knowing that the difficulties would be great and the returns too small. From Italy, too, I had quite urgent calls, but always gave the same answer. On our former tour our paraphernalia had been in stock, and everything had gone like clockwork. To get this gigantic and complicated apparatus together again would have been a most difficult matter, and no single one of these calls would have justified such an outlay. As for Paris, they had recently renewed their offers, but my Wagner contracts for France had in the meantime expired.

So the Richard Wagner Opera Company undertook no further expeditions until finally a call from St. Petersburg in 1899 seemed to warrant our setting out again.

The agent of the Royal Opera House in St. Petersburg had come twice to Prague to see me with reference to this proposition, and finally the contract was drawn up to our mutual satisfaction. I was to furnish the artists, conductors, managers, inspector, prompter, mechanics and engineers, as well as scenery, costumes, properties and the scores, while the Royal Opera was to furnish the building, lights, scene-shifters and general staff,—a full orchestra, and finally a complete male chorus trained in German for the " Götterdämmerung." The proceeds were to be divided: three-quarters for the Richard Wagner Opera Company, and the rest for the treasury of the Czar.

We were to give four full performances of the cycle, for which the dates were set in advance, and two great Wagner concerts; beginning our engagement on the 11th of March, 1889 (according to the Greek calendar).

Our conductor was to be Dr. Karl Muck from my German theatre in Prague, and for the mechanical and scenic effects I was fortunate enough to get Karl Lautenschläger from the Royal Opera in Munich.

I had sent the conductor on ahead for careful preparatory rehearsals, and Dr. Muck acquitted himself magnificently of his task. I can safely say that, as far as orchestra was concerned, our " Nibelungen " performances in St. Petersburg compared most favourably with Bayreuth itself. Aside from Muck's understanding of his subject and his ability, he gave himself up to the work with such genuine eagerness and such an unselfish devotion to his art that he deserved the highest possible praise, and called forth the admiration and the appreciation of all.

On my arrival in Petersburg my first care was the inspection of our chorus for " Götterdämmerung," which, together with the orchestra, was to be furnished by the Royal Opera House. Muck and I had previously agreed that this chorus should be supplemented from our own company at Prague. But these Russians had done their part so well that we decided no auxiliaries were needed. Their first rehearsal was a revelation. Such marvellous baritones, such majestic figures, and such diction! I have never—no, not even in Bayreuth—heard the German text more perfectly enunciated than in this magnificent Russian chorus.

Heinrich Vogl, though still an incomparable Loge, was no longer the matchless " Siegfried " of the old days of London, Berlin and Munich, yet he was very well received. But his wife, long used to triumphs and spoiled by adulation, was now so severely criticised in " The Valkyre " that I feared for the success of our enterprise, and sent for Therese Malten from Dresden, and Marie Rochelle from Prague, to carry out her rôles.

Let me mention here a story in connection with our orchestra. I had brought with me Professor Beer of Prague as our horn soloist, for the technical difficulties of the " Götterdämmerung " were almost insurmountable, and even these magnificent Russian musicians were hardly capable of playing it on such short notice. On the day of our first production of this opera Dr. Muck came to me in despair, saying that Professor Beer, upon whom we were so utterly dependent, had a raging toothache and a swollen face, so he could not possibly play. This was a tragedy indeed!

I sent for Beer, and the moment he came we realised that the performance was impossible for that night.

" What shall we do, Herr Director? " he asked anxiously.
" There's nothing for it, my dear Professor, but to postpone the opera." " What, just on *my* account? " " Certainly. We can't give ' Götterdämmerung ' without the
horn solo! " " No, I can't stand that! You must never
do that, sir—I'll see how it goes—perhaps I can blow, after
all! The doctor may be able to give me something for it!
I'll blow if I possibly can! " And the plucky fellow really
did blow that night,—and marvellously well too! He
saved our performance in the most splendid shape.

At the close of our second cycle, which was attended by
all the court, and on several nights by the Czar himself,
Moscow, jealous as usual of St. Petersburg, asked us to
come and play an engagement there. On the 21st of
March I had a note from Count Voronzov-Dashkov inviting me to call. The messenger added that the Count
would be at home that evening and that the business was
important. His Excellency greeted me eagerly as I
entered and said the Czar had commissioned him to arrange for our giving the " Ring " in Moscow. Naturally
I was delighted at the prospect, and we then discussed the
dates and terms. My one stipulation was that the royal
orchestra should go with us to Moscow. At this the
Count gravely shook his head. " The Czar's orchestra?
I fear it can't be done! " " If the Czar wishes his subjects
in Moscow to hear the ' Ring,' it must be done! " I answered. " But do you think this orchestra is any better
than the one they have there? " " Not that," said I, " but
consider all the rehearsals they've had. Six full weeks
before we came! "
At this his Excellency looked thoughtful. " Yet still I
fear it can't be done," he said. " You see, it's never been
done before! " Here my answer seemed to irritate him a
bit, for I coolly remarked, " We all have to do things for
the first time occasionally—there's nothing so alarming

in that! The Richard Wagner Opera Company never came to Petersburg before!" "That's another matter," he said rather stiffly. "This question must be considered a while. I shall lay it before his Majesty and see. Then I shall let you know." "May I express an opinion, your Excellency?" "Oh, pray do!" "I'm convinced that the Czar will say yes!" "Oho!" he laughed. "That's all you know about it! You don't know the Czar!" And here my audience was at an end.

That very night I had a card from the Count, asking me to call again. He received me most genially, saying, "Do you know, you're the deuce of a fellow! Can you guess now what the Czar said?" "He said yes,—of course!" "Oh, no, no, no! It hasn't come to that *yet!* The Czar simply asked me to find out, in case he did give his consent, what the expense would be. You see, there are one hundred and six men in the orchestra." "The costs," I said quietly, "will be covered by the Richard Wagner Opera Company. The railroads naturally will give us a rebate, as we are a very large company. I shall give the musicians ten Rubles per capita for each day of their stay in Moscow. Whether they continue to draw their salary from the Czar or not, is none of my affair!"

The Count looked thunderstruck at this, but expressed his approval of the plan. Then, as I left, he said cordially, "I shall see the Czar directly—and really now I think he *will* say yes!"

Our performances at the Marientheater in Petersburg began on the 11th of March (by our calendar) and closed the 2d of April. We gave four cycles of the "Nibelungen Ring" and two great Wagner concerts, one for the benefit of the orchestra. At the close of our third cycle the Czar's management asked if I could possibly arrange for a fifth; but I concluded not to do this, thinking it wiser to close with crowded houses in Petersburg and then go on to Moscow. Our final "Götterdämmerung" was naturally somewhat in the nature of an ovation. The singers were called out again and again, and the city presented me with a laurel wreath of silver in commemoration of our tour. I then made a little speech, particularly thanking the Czar and all his household for their friendly interest, and expressing my gratitude then to the managers of the Opera House, to the general public, to the press, and last but not least to their wonderful orchestra so ably led by our friend Dr. Karl Muck.

This little tribute, so simply expressed but so earnestly felt, roused the wildest enthusiasm in the house and they cheered us to the echo.

I must not forget here to add the gratitude due to our friends at court. Their interest in the success of our production was most delightful. Among these were the Austrian ambassador and his wife (who as Mme. von Schleinitz had been so deeply interested in our Berlin performers), Baron von Aehrenthal, General von Schweinitz (our ambassador to Russia), General Werder and many others.

We now prepared for our Moscow trip, starting the 4th of April. After the Czar's consent the director had appointed an advance agent to make all preparations for our arrival. This man was not in the least sanguine as to our success, and dolefully predicted that we should not take in two hundred Rubles in our whole Moscow season—for the town, he said, was centuries behind the world in all artistic matters. I could not agree with him, however, so we waited the outcome with some impatience. What a surprise for the doubters when the message came from Moscow, "Advance sales forty-one thousand one hundred and forty-three Rubles." The maximum capacity of the house was only forty-three thousand Rubles, so the cycle promised rather well, so far.

At six P. M. on the 4th of April we started in our special train with all our company, plus the royal orchestra,

and landed in Moscow next morning at ten. Here we
gave the " Ring " on the 6th, 7th, 9th and 10th of April,
putting in a concert on the 8th, and on the 11th we closed
our season with a repetition of " The Valkyre." Though
the audiences here were not as keenly enthusiastic as those
in Petersburg, our houses were full, and our friends were
many. Count Leo Tolstoi attended an entire performance
of the " Ring "; though to be sure he only came to criticise,
as he had once before in the case of Beethoven's " Kreutzer
Sonata." He found the Bayreuth music *shocking!* so he
said.

On April 12th we closed our business with the management, and I was invited by the directors to present their
cheque at the Royal Treasury of Moscow. I admit I
have never seen anything to equal that institution in all
my life. Great arched vaults crowded to the keystone
with currency, and packages of notes from the smallest
denomination up to the highest, which is only one hundred
Rubles! As the cashier paid me over my amount, which I
had considered rather important that morning, it seemed
to dwindle and shrink, and what a trifling sum it now
appeared after all.

I must add here that, there being no copyright law in
Russia, the directors of the Opera would not accept a
percentage—so the extra royalties I then of my own free
will turned over to the Bayreuth treasury. This amounted
to fifteen thousand Marks.

Having sent the orchestra back to Petersburg and the
members of our company to their respective homes, I left
Moscow the evening of the 13th, glad to have closed this
tour without the smallest cloud on the horizon.

Before I left Petersburg they had asked me to return,
but I answered I feared such a fortunate undertaking
could never be repeated. I should be charmed to make

another attempt,—but only after the lapse of several years.

These apprehensions proved only too true, for Pollini of Hamburg tried it the next year with lamentable lack of success. Performances were announced and dates fixed, but it all fell through for lack of subscribers. After a second attempt on his part the following year—also unsuccessful—they telegraphed for me, asking if I would come and put it through. Unfortunately, however, I had to decline.

Another manager eventually tried to carry out this plan, but after the failure of so clever and experienced a man as Pollini, nothing was to be expected but a complete shipwreck. So this last attempt fell through again, leaving an unfortunate impression of the Royal Petersburg Opera among all our German impresarios.

This trip to Russia was my last great undertaking in the service of Richard Wagner and his art. I have renounced my soaring plans, and have bent all my energies, for this quarter of a century, to the building up of our national opera here in this charming town of Prague. The annual musical festival which we have instituted here was inaugurated to carry out the original designs of the great Master of Bayreuth.

It has been my sole ambition, since those early days of my first activities in Leipsic, to realise as far as possible the wonderful ideals of that great artistic Radical— Richard Wagner.

INDEX

INDEX

321

328 INDEX

27, 44, 60, 64-6, 70, 77-9, 86, 90, 93, 111

"Tannhäuser," 3, 9-11, 18, 28, 66, 67, 126-7, 196, 252, 285, 291, 295; exclusive rights of, 129; first act of, 265; in Paris, 131; rights for Paris, 125
Tausig Concert, 4
"Telramund," rôle of, 5, 11, 12, 197, 308
Theatrical Association Board, 271
TOLSTOI, Count, 317
TORLONIA, Prince, 282, 290
Trieste, 296-8, 303, 305, 310
"Trilogy." See "Nibelungen Ring"
"Tristan und Isolde," 4, 28, 29, 101, 104-6, 111, 139, 206-7, 248; at Weimar, 215; cast of, 206; rights for, 227, 235
TRUCHET (NUITTER), CH., 213, 214
Turin, 292, 294-6, 298; Grand Duke of, 294

UNGER, GEORGE, 26-9, 31-2, 44-5, 75-6, 96, 242, 244, 262, 283; as "Siegfried," 22; affairs of, 85, 87; contract with, 77, 79
United States. See America
Unter den Linden, 151
Utrecht, 259

"Valkyre," the, 19, 21, 39, 53, 54, 57, 60, 61, 62, 69, 70, 78, 81, 91, 110, 112, 117, 119, 128, 136, 143, 146-9, 153, 163, 172, 188, 223, 241, 242, 243, 249, 257, 259, 265, 271, 276, 282, 286, 288, 289, 294, 304, 305, 313, 317; horse for, 130; technical apparatus for, 35
Venice, 184, 222, 267, 280, 282, 284-6, 296, 297, 303, 305
VERDI'S "Aïda," 18
VICTORIA, Princess, 152
Victoria Theatre, 93, 109, 111, 112, 117, 133, 135, 159, 178, 236, 254; orchestra, 136
Vienna, 30, 112, 169, 224, 241,

273, 295; compared with Leipsic, 88; contract, 39; papers, 246; royal opera of, 3-9, 12, 15, 30, 33, 36, 65, 86, 294; theatre, 127; Hofburg, 15
VOGL, HEINRICH, 101, 112, 142-3, 149, 155-7, 160, 162, 167, 169, 196, 201-2, 206, 208, 223, 243, 244, 251, 252, 255, 265, 269, 270; as "Loge," 21
VOGL, THERESE, 101, 112, 142-143, 144, 196, 241, 242, 247, 255, 269
VOLTZ, agent, 126, 235, 237
VORONZOV - DASHKOV, Count, 314

WAGNER, RICHARD, his personal appearance, 4; began career, 4; call to Munich, 6; financial straits, 6; as an actor, 9-14; his innovations, 14; methods, 21; description of, 56, 57; dramatic unity, 97; speech to Berlin audience, 153-9; birthday poetry, 164, 165; reception of NEU-MANN'S speech, 169; children, 188; concessions to NEUMANN, 193; health, 221; his quatrain, 226; reception episode, 231; trouble with MARIANNA BRANDT, 233; talks with NEUMANN, 231-4; "Parsifal" agreement, 236; death reported, 267; funeral, 270; letters to FORSTER, 25, 26, 28-31, 38, 39, 41, 45, 46, 72, 88, 91, 96, 112, 161, 165, 172, 180, 221, 222; letters to GORRES, 211, 213; letters to NEUMANN, 56, 62, 72, 74, 76-80, 82, 85-91, 94, 96, 98, 99, 101, 103-5, 109, 110, 113, 123, 125-7, 131, 132, 138, 140, 154, 155, 159, 166, 171, 180, 182, 187, 191, 193, 194, 209, 210, 214, 227, 235, 237, 245-6, 249, 250, 268; letters to SEIDL, 103, 161, 162; letters to SUCHER, 26, 27, 111; quoted, 8, 23, 114, 146, 170, 184
Wagner Concert, 242

"The best single help to the study of Parsifal with which I am acquainted . . . for its purpose, the book has no adequate fellow."—H. E. KREHBIEL in the Introduction.

KUFFERATH'S WAGNER'S
PARSIFAL

Translated by LOUISE N. HENERMANN.

XVIII + 300 pp., 12mo, $1.50, *net* (by mail, $1.61).

This remarkably comprehensive book contains an Introduction by H. E. KREHBIEL; eight full-page illustrations in halftone of the scenery at the Metropolitan Opera House; The Motifs in Musical Notation; Chapters on The Legend, History and Poetry; The Perceval of Chrétien de Troies; The Parzival of Wolfram Von Eschenbach; The Drama (Wagner's); The Genesis of Parsifal; The Bayreuth Performance; The Score.

MR. KREHBIEL further says in his Introduction :

"The production of "Parsifal" in New York was the most notable occurrence compassed by the annals of the lyric stage in America. " Parsifal " stands apart, not only from all other operas, but also from the lyric dramas sprung from the same creative mind. It is not easy to find the properest frame of mind in which to approach it. . . . If any work of dramatic art invites study and is likely to repay it, it is "Parsifal." It was necessary that a scholar should gather into a compendium the most important things discovered by the investigation of specialists, which throw light on Wagner's work, add to its charm, and present it lucidly, entertainingly and convincingly to the many. This M. Kufferath has done. His book stands quite alone in the field of Wagneriana. . . . Kufferath makes many a pretty walk into by-paths which Wolzogen never knew . . . more voluminous, more delightful than the one on the score, and equally valuable, are the chapters devoted to the vicissitudes of the Grail legend before Wagner seized upon it as dramatic material; the story of how the work grew in Wagner's mind; the account of its first performance; the exposition of the philosophy of pity and its relation to Wagner's personal character and religious speculations; and, finally, the exposition of the drama itself. . . . Kufferath's German origin lent him seriousness of purpose, sympathy with Wolfram Eschenbach's poem, and the capacity for patient research; his French breeding and literary training, deftness of touch and skill in narrative; his musical learning, capacity to understand and facility to expound Wagner's music, and love for Wagner's art, fired him with an enthusiasm which illumines nearly every page."

HENRY HOLT AND COMPANY,

PUBLISHERS   NEW YORK.

DRAMATISTS OF TO-DAY

Rostand, Hauptmann, Sudermann, Pinero, Shaw, Phillips, Maeterlinck

By Prof. EDWARD EVERETT HALE, Jr., of Union College. With gilt top, $1.50 net. (By mail, $1.60.)

An informal discussion of their principal plays and of the performances of some of them. A few of those considered are *Man and Superman, Candida, Cyrano de Bergerac, L'Aiglon, The Sunken Bell, Magda, Ulysses, Letty, Iris,* and *Pelleas and Melisande.* The volume opens with a paper "On Standards of Criticism," and concludes with "Our Idea of Tragedy," and an appendix of all the plays of each author, with dates of their first performance or publication.

Bookman : "He writes in a pleasant, free-and-easy way. . . . He accepts things chiefly at their face value, but he describes them so accurately and agreeably that he recalls vividly to mind the plays we have seen and the pleasure we have found in them."

New York Evening Post : "It is not often nowadays that a theatrical book can be met with so free from gush and mere eulogy, or so weighted by common sense . . . an excellent chronological appendix and full index . . . uncommonly useful for reference."

Dial : "Noteworthy example of literary criticism in one of the most interesting of literary fields. . . . Well worth reading a second time."

The GERMAN DRAMA of the NINETEENTH CENTURY

By GEORG WITKOWSKI. Translated by Prof. L. B. HORNING. 12mo. Probable price, $1.25 net.

This brief but brilliant monograph after a great success on the continent is to be published simultaneously in America and England.

The book is divided into five headings, representing chronologically the distinct periods which marked German dramatic literature during the nineteenth century :

(1) The German drama at the end of the eighteenth century ; (2) The German drama from 1800–1830 ; (3) The German drama from 1830–1885 ; (4) The German drama from 1885–1900 ; (5) The product of the century.

Kleist, Grillparzer, Hebbel, Ludwig, Wildenbruch, Sudermann, Hauptmann, and minor dramatists receive attention.

HENRY HOLT AND COMPANY

PUBLISHERS   NEW YORK

Recent Poetry of Distinction

HERO AND LEANDER

By Martin Schütze of the University of Chicago. Probable price, $1.25 *net*.

A poetic drama of unusual merit. While several authors have tried this theme, probably no one before has brought these ill-starred lovers so close to our sympathies. Professor Schütze has imagined new and striking episodes, and minor characters who lend added life and body to the original slender legend.

RAHAB

A Poetic Drama in Three Acts. By Richard Burton, author of "Literary Likings," "Forces in Fiction," "Life of Whittier," etc. 119 pp. 12mo. $1.25 *net*. By mail, $1.31.

A drama of the fall of Jericho, and especially of the part which the enchantress, Rahab, played.

". . . A poetic drama of high quality. . . . Simply and fluently written, with many felicities of phrase. . . . Plenty of dramatic action."—*New York Times Review.*

"Handled with great ingenuity and often with strong dramatic effect . . . much poetic beauty in the lines . . . and the action is well sustained."—*Chicago Record-Herald.*

THE PRINCESS OF HANOVER

A Play. By Margaret L. Woods, author of "A Village Tragedy." $1.50 *net*. By mail, $1.57.

Thomas Hardy calls this play "the book I have read with the most interest and pleasure during the year." The London *Times* says: "It reminds us at every turn of some of the best Elizabethan dramatists."

APOLLO AND THE SEAMAN AND OTHER POEMS

By Herbert Trench. 12mo. Probable price, $1.50 *net*.

The author is already very favorably known by his *Deirdre Wedded and Other Poems.*

"Full of magnificent things."—William Archer.

"Unique as 'The Ancient Mariner.'"—C. K. Chesterton in the *Daily News.*

"Deep with thought; deep with significance."—George Meredith.

"Here at length is an Englishman singing from the heights which Goethe reached."—Frank Harris in *Vanity Fair.*

Arthur Colton's HARPS HUNG UP IN BABYLON

Some forty poems, many of which first appeared in *The Atlantic, Century, Scribner's*, etc. $1.25 *net*. By mail, $1.30.

"His opening lyric is as lovely a bit of melody as one will find in recent poetry. Mr. Colton's work . . . has a touch of its own and a charm of personality."—Miss Jessie B. Rittenhouse in *Putnam's Monthly.*

"He has grace, scholarship—his adaptations of Horace are excellent—and unfailing optimism."—*The Spectator* (London).

HENRY HOLT AND COMPANY Publishers New York